The Rebel Sell

Joseph Heath is an associate professor of Philosophy at the University of Toronto. He is the author of two books: *The Efficient Society* and *Communicative Action and Rational Choice*. Heath lives in Toronto.

Andrew Potter is a research fellow at the Centre de recherche en éthique de l'Université de Montréal (CREUM). His work has appeared in the *National Post* and he is a member of the editorial board of *This Magazine*. He lives in Montreal.

The Rebel Sell

How the counterculture became consumer culture

Joseph Heath
and
Andrew Potter

CAPSTONE

First published 2005
This edition published 2006
Capstone Publishing Limited (a Wiley company), Th Atrium, Southern Gate Chichester, West
Sussex, PO19 8SQ, England Phone (+44) 1243 779777

Email (for orders and customer service enquires): cs-books@wiley.co.uk
Visit our Home Page on www.wiley.co.uk or www.wiley.com

Published by arrangement with Harper Collins Publishers Ltd, Toronto, Ontario, Canada

Other Wiley Editorial Offi ces
John Wiley & Sons, Inc. 111 River Street, Hoboken, NJ 07030, USA
Jossey-Bass, 989 Market Street, San Francisco, CA 94103–1741, USA
Wiley-VCH Verlag GmbH, Pappellaee 3, D-69469 Weinheim, Germany
John Wiley & Sons Australia, Ltd, 33 Park Road, Milton, Queensland, 4064, Australia
John Wiley & Sons (Asia) Pte Ltd, 2 Clementi Loop #02–01, Jin Xing Distripark, Singapor
129809
John Wiley & Sons Canada Ltd, 22 Worcester Road, Etobicoke, Ontario, Canada, M9W 1L1

British Library Cataloguing in Publication Data
A catalogue record for this book is available from the British Library

ISBN-10: 1-84112-655-1
ISBN-13: 978-1-84112-655-5

Typeset in Adobe Caslon Pro by Sparks, Oxford – www.sparks.co.uk

for my parents – AP

for Astrid – JH

Contents

Acknowledgments

Special thanks are owed to Julie Crysler, the former editor of *THIS Magazine*, along with Chris Bucci at HarperCollins Canada and Marion Manneker at HarperCollins in the United States. Thanks to Kevin Olson, June Clark, Sean Silcoff and Suzanne Board for helpful comments on the manuscript, and to Vida Panitch for invaluable assistance with preparation of the final copy. Sarmishta Subramanian helped get the whole project going. We would also like to acknowledge the Social Science and Humanities Research Council of Canada for financial assistance.

Our greatest intellectual debt is to Thomas Frank, who is to be credited with having first thematised the 'countercultural idea' and who demonstrated the role that it played in promoting 'hip' or 'rebel' consumerism. Frank's most important insights are so profound that most of his readers have simply failed to grasp their import. This book aims in part to correct that deficit.

A note on the collaboration: Although this book was written jointly, we have chosen not to use the authorial 'we' beyond the introduction. Apart from the fact that the 'we' sounds pompous in many instances, we also both have a tendency to illustrate our arguments with little anecdotes and recollections, in which the use of 'we' would be inappropriate. Rather than referring to ourselves in the third person, we have chosen to adopt the more conversational 'I', but without bothering to identify which one of us is telling the story. Our assumption is that the reader will not particularly care which one of us had purple hair and a nose ring in 1988, which one had a father in the military, which one grew up in Saskatoon or in Ottawa, or which one of us sang *Free to Be You and Me* in his primary school choir. Either way, it doesn't really affect the argument of the book.

Introduction

September 2003 marked a turning point in the development of Western civilisation. It was the month that *Adbusters* magazine started accepting orders for the Black Spot Sneaker, its own signature brand of 'subversive' running shoes. After that day, no rational person could possibly believe that there is any tension between 'mainstream' and 'alternative' culture. After that day, it became obvious to everyone that cultural rebellion, of the type epitomised by *Adbusters* magazine, is not a threat to the system – it *is* the system.

Founded in 1989, *Adbusters* is the flagship publication of the culture-jamming movement. They are perhaps best known for having started 'Buy Nothing Day', which has since spread to over 55 countries. In the *Adbusters* worldview, society has become so thoroughly permeated with propaganda and lies, largely as a consequence of advertising, that the culture as a whole has become an enormous system of ideology – all designed to reproduce faith in 'the system'. The goal of the culture jammers is quite literally to 'jam' the culture, by subverting the messages used to reproduce this faith and blocking the channels through which it is propagated. This in turn is thought to have radical political consequences. In 1999, *Adbusters* editor Kalle Lasn argued that culture jamming 'will become to our era what civil rights was to the '60s, what feminism was to the '70s, what environmental activism was to the '80s.'

Five years later, he's using the *Adbusters* brand to flog his own trademark line of trainers. What happened? Did *Adbusters* sell out?

Absolutely not. It is essential that we all see and understand this. *Adbusters* did not sell out, because there was nothing to sell out in the first place. *Adbusters* never had a revolutionary doctrine. What they had was simply a warmed-over version of the countercultural thinking that has dominated leftist politics since the 1960s. And this type of countercultural politics, far from being a revolutionary doctrine, has been one of the primary forces driving consumer capitalism for the past forty years.

In other words, what we see on display in *Adbusters* magazine is, and always has been, the true spirit of capitalism. The episode with the trainers just serves to prove the point.

Lasn describes the sneaker project as 'a ground-breaking marketing scheme to uncool Nike. If it succeeds, it will set a precedent that will revolutionise capitalism.' Yet how exactly is it supposed to revolutionise capitalism? Reebok, Adidas, Puma, Vans and a half-dozen other companies have been trying to 'uncool' Nike for decades. That's called marketplace competition. It is the *essence* of capitalism.

In fact, it didn't take long for other 'alternative' retailers to begin emulating the *Adbusters* business model. Within a year, the venerable *Mother Jones* magazine started selling their own Mojo No Sweat Sneaker. (Their business partner, No Sweat Apparel, is perhaps best known as the purveyor of the increasingly popular 'No Logo Tees and Tanks'.) The *Mother Jones* marketing pitch was a straightforward inducement to competitive consumption: 'Be the first on your block to walk the walk on fair trade', they urged their readers. Thus began the unseemly spectacle of duelling 'alternative' footwear.

Lasn defends the sneaker project against critics, pointing out that his shoes will not be manufactured in 'sweatshops'. This is nice. But 'fair trade' and 'ethical marketing' are hardly revolutionary ideas, and they certainly represent no threat to the capitalist system. If consumers are willing to pay more for shoes made by happy workers – or for eggs laid by happy chickens – then there is money to be made in bringing these goods to market. It's a business model that has already been successfully exploited to great effect by The Body Shop and Starbucks, among others.

★

Culture jammers are not the first to try to break the system through consumer revolt. Countercultural rebels have been playing the same game for over forty years, and it obviously doesn't work. With the hippies, nothing symbolised their rejection of the 'consumerism' of

American society more than love beads, Birkenstocks and the VW Beetle. Yet during the '80s, the same generation that had 'tuned in, turned on and dropped out' presided over the most significant resurgence of conspicuous consumption in American history. The hippies became yuppies. And nothing symbolised the yuppie worldview more than the four-wheel drive – the vehicle that one commentator aptly described as 'a gated community on wheels'. So how does one get from a VW Beetle to a Ford Explorer? It turns out to be not so difficult.

The crucial point is that (contrary to rumour) the hippies did not sell out. Hippie ideology and yuppie ideology are one and the same. There simply never was any tension between the countercultural ideas that informed the '60s rebellion and the ideological requirements of the capitalist system. While there is no doubt that a *cultural* conflict developed between the members of the counterculture and the defenders of the establishment, there never was any tension between the *values* of the counterculture and the functional requirements of the capitalist economic system. The counterculture was, from its very inception, intensely entrepreneurial. It reflected, as does *Adbusters*, the most authentic spirit of capitalism.

Hippies bought VW Beetles for one primary reason – to show that they rejected mass society. The big automakers had been the target of withering social criticism for well over a decade, accused of promoting 'planned obsolescence' in their vehicles. They were chastised above all for changing their models and designs so that consumers would be forced to buy a new car every few years in order to keep up with the Joneses. The tail fin was held up by John Kenneth Galbraith and others as an object of special scorn – as both embodiment and symbol of the wastefulness of American consumer culture. Against this backdrop, Volkswagen entered the US consumer market with a very simple pitch: Wanna show people that you're not just a cog in the machine? Buy our car!

When the boomers started having children, the old VW obviously was no longer sufficient. Yet there was no question of buying a wood-panelled estate car, the kind that their parents used to drive. They may have had kids, but they were still rebels at heart. And no vehicle appealed to this desire for rebel chic more perfectly than the four-wheel drive. Off-road capability was the major selling point – even the Grateful Dead sang its praises. 'The system' tells you that you have to drive in a straight line, down some 'road' that The Man has built for you. The rebel can't be tied down like that; he yearns for freedom. He needs to be able to veer off at any time and start following his *own* road.

What a perfect vehicle! To anyone who passes by, it says, 'I'm not one of those losers with kids, living in the suburbs. My life is an adventure.' It tells them that you're not a square, not a cog in the machine.

If the boomers were obsessed with cars, Generation Xers seem to have had a special preoccupation with shoes. Shoes were an essential element of the punk aesthetic from the beginning, from army boots and trainers to Doc Martens and Blundstones. And instead of the big three automakers to play the villain, there were the shoe companies: first and foremost, Nike. For antiglobalisation demonstrators, Nike came to symbolise everything that was wrong with the emerging capitalist world order.

Yet this animus toward Nike did create occasional moments of embarrassment. During the famous anti-globalisation riots of Seattle 1999, the central Niketown was trashed by protestors, but videotape recorded at the scene showed several protestors kicking in the front window *wearing Nike shoes*. It occurred to many people that if you think Nike is the root of all evil, you really shouldn't be wearing their shoes. Yet if thousands of young people refuse to wear Nike, that creates an obvious market for 'alternative' footwear. Vans and Airwalk were both able to leverage some of the rebel chic associated with skateboarding into millions of dollars of sneaker sales. It's the same story all over again, and *Adbusters* is just trying to get a piece of the action.

*

The question is why would anyone think that selling trainers could be subversive? To understand the answer, it is useful to take a closer look at the first film in the *Matrix* trilogy. Lots has been written about the 'philosophy of the Matrix', most of it wrong. To understand the first film, one must look very carefully at the scene in which Neo sees the white rabbit. He hands a book to his friend, and on the spine of that book we can see the title: *Simulacra and Simulation* by Jean Baudrillard.

Many commentators on the film saw the core idea of *The Matrix* – that the world we live in might be an elaborate illusion, that our brains are simply being fed sensory input by machines, input that tricks us into thinking that we live and interact with a world of physical objects – as simply an updated version of René Descartes' sceptical 'How do you know that you're not dreaming?' thought experiment. This is a misinterpretation. *The Matrix* is not intended as a representation of an epistemological dilemma. It is a metaphor for a political idea, one that traces its origins back to the '60s. It is an idea that found its highest expression in the work of Guy Debord, unofficial leader of the Situationist International, and his later disciple Jean Baudrillard.

Debord was a radical Marxist, author of *The Society of the Spectacle* and one of the prime movers behind the Paris 1968 uprising. His thesis was simple. The world that we live in is not real. Consumer capitalism has taken every authentic human experience, transformed it into a commodity and then sold it back to us through advertising and the mass media. Thus every part of human life has been drawn into 'the spectacle', which itself is nothing but a system of symbols and representations, governed by its own internal logic. 'The spectacle is *capital* to such a degree of accumulation that it becomes an image', Debord wrote. Thus we live in a world of total ideology, in which we are completely alienated from our essential nature. The spectacle is a dream that has become necessary, 'the nightmare of imprisoned modern society, which ultimately expresses nothing more than its desire to sleep.'

In such a world, the old-fashioned concern for social justice and the abolition of class-based society becomes outmoded. In the society of the spectacle, the new revolutionary must seek two things: 'consciousness of desire and the desire for consciousness'. In other words, we must try to discover our own sources of pleasure, independent of the needs that are imposed upon us by the system, and we must try to wake up from the nightmare of 'the spectacle'. Like Neo, we must choose the red pill.

In other words, when it comes to rebellion and political activism, there is no point trying to change little details in the system. What does it matter who is rich and who is poor? Or who has the right to vote and who doesn't? Or who has access to jobs and opportunities? These are all just ephemera, illusions. If commodities are just images, who cares if some people have more of them, others less? What we need to do is recognise that the entire culture, the entire society, is a waking dream – one we must reject in its entirety.

Of course, this idea is hardly original. It is one of the oldest themes in Western civilisation. In *The Republic*, Plato compared life on earth to a cave, in which prisoners are shackled to the floor, seeing only shadows flickering across the wall from the light of a fire. When one prisoner escapes and makes his way to the surface, he discovers that the world he had been living in was nothing but a web of illusions. He returns to the cave bearing the news, yet finds that his former companions are still embroiled in petty disputes and bickering. He finds it difficult to take these 'politics' seriously.

Centuries later, early Christians would appeal to this story as a way of explaining away the execution of Jesus by the Romans. Prior to this event, it had been assumed that the arrival of the Messiah would herald the creation of the kingdom of God here on earth. The death of Jesus obviously put an end to these expectations. Some of his followers therefore chose to reinterpret these events as a sign that the real kingdom of God would be not on this earth, but in the afterlife. They claimed that Jesus had been resurrected in order to convey this news – like Plato's prisoner returning to the cave.

Thus the idea that the world we live in is a veil of illusion is not new. What does change, however, is the popular understanding of what it takes to throw off this illusion. For Plato, there was no question that breaking free would require decades of disciplined study and philosophical reflection. Christians thought that it would be even harder – that death was the only way to gain access to the 'real' world beyond. For Debord and the Situationists, on the other hand, the veil of illusion could be pierced much more easily. All that it takes is some slight cognitive dissonance, a sign that something's not right in the world around us. This can be provoked by a work of art, an act of protest or even an article of clothing. In Debord's view, 'disturbances with the lowliest and most ephemeral of origins have eventually disrupted the order of the world.'

This is the origin of the idea of culture jamming. Traditional political activism is useless. It's like trying to reform political institutions inside the Matrix. What's the point? What we really need to do is wake people up, unplug them, free them from the grip of the spectacle. And the way to do that is by producing cognitive dissonance, through symbolic acts of resistance to suggest that something is not right in the world.

Like the Black Spot Sneaker.

Since the entire culture is nothing but a system of ideology, the only way to liberate oneself and others is to resist the culture in its entirety. This is where the idea of counterculture comes from. The inhabitants of Zion, in *The Matrix*, are a concrete embodiment of how countercultural rebels since the '60s have conceived of themselves. They are the ones who have been awakened, the ones who are free from the tyranny of the machines. And the enemy, in this view, is those who refuse to be awakened, those who insist on conforming to the culture. The enemy, in other words, is *mainstream society*.

Morpheus sums up the countercultural analysis perfectly when describing the Matrix: 'The Matrix is a system, Neo. That system is our enemy. But when you're inside, you look around, what do you see? Businessmen, teachers, lawyers, carpenters. The very minds of the people we are trying to save. But until we do, these people are still a part of that system and that makes them our enemy. You have to understand, most of these people are not ready to be unplugged. And many of them are so inured, so hopelessly dependent on the system, that they will fight to protect it.'

★

In the '60s, the baby boomers declared their implacable opposition to 'the system'. They renounced materialism and greed, rejected the discipline and uniformity of the repressive '50s, and set out to build a new world based on individual freedom. What ever happened to this project? Forty years later, 'the system' does not appear to have changed very much. If anything, consumer capitalism has emerged from decades of countercultural rebellion much stronger than it was before. If Debord thought that the world was saturated with advertising and media in the early '60s, what would he have made of the 21st century?

In this book, we argue that decades of countercultural rebellion have failed to change anything because the theory of society on which the countercultural idea rests is false. We do not live in the Matrix, nor do we live in the spectacle. The world that we live in is in fact much more prosaic. It consists of billions of human beings, each pursuing some more or less plausible conception of the good, trying to cooperate with one another, and doing so with varying degrees of success. There is no single, overarching system that integrates it all. The culture cannot be jammed because there *is* no such thing as 'the culture' or 'the system'. There is only a hodgepodge of social institutions, most tentatively thrown together, which distribute the benefits and burdens of social cooperation in ways that sometimes we recognise to be just, but that are usually manifestly inequitable. In a world of this type, countercultural rebellion is not just unhelpful, it is positively counterproductive. Not only does it distract energy and effort away from the sort of initiatives that lead to concrete improvements in people's lives, but it encourages wholesale contempt for such incremental changes.

According to the countercultural theory, 'the system' achieves order only through the repression of the individual. Pleasure is inherently anarchic, unruly, wild. To keep the workers under control, the system must instil manufactured needs and mass-produced desires, which can in turn be satisfied within the framework of the technocratic order. Order is achieved, but at the expense of promoting widespread unhappiness, alienation and neurosis. The solution must therefore lie in reclaiming our capacity for spontaneous pleasure

– through polymorphous perversity, or performance art, or modern primitivism, or mind-expanding drugs, or whatever else turns your crank. In the countercultural analysis, simply having fun comes to be seen as the ultimate subversive act. Hedonism is transformed into a revolutionary doctrine.

Is it any wonder then that this sort of countercultural rebellion has reinvigorated consumer capitalism? It's time for a reality check. Having fun is not subversive, and it doesn't undermine any system. In fact, widespread hedonism makes it more difficult to organise social movements, and much more difficult to persuade anyone to make a sacrifice in the name of social justice. In our view, what the progressive left needs to do is disentangle the concern over questions of social justice from the countercultural critique – and to jettison the latter, while continuing to pursue the former.

From the standpoint of social justice, the big gains that have been achieved in our society over the past half-century have all come from measured reform within the system. Both the anti-racism and the feminist movements have achieved tangible gains in the welfare of disadvantaged groups, while the social safety net provided by the welfare state has vastly improved the condition of all citizens. But these gains have not been achieved by 'unplugging' people from the web of illusions that governs their lives. They have been achieved through the laborious process of democratic political action – through people making arguments, conducting studies, assembling coalitions and legislating change. We would like to see more of this.

Less fun perhaps, but potentially much more useful.

Part I

The birth of counterculture

Early on the morning of April 8, 1994, the electrician arrived to start work on a new security system being installed at an upscale home overlooking Lake Washington, just north of Seattle. In the greenhouse, he found the owner of the cottage, Kurt Cobain, lying dead on the floor in a pool of blood. Cobain had taken a lethal overdose of heroin, but, for good measure, had decided to finish the job by blowing off the left side of his head with a Remington 20-gauge shotgun.

When the news of Cobain's death spread, very few were surprised. This was the man, after all, who had recorded a song called 'I Hate Myself and Want to Die'. As frontman of Nirvana, arguably the most important band of the 1990s, his every move was followed by the media. His previous suicide attempts were a matter of public record. The note lying beside his body didn't leave much room for interpretation: 'Better to burn out than fade away', he wrote. Nevertheless, his death generated a small cottage industry of conspiracy theories. Who killed Kurt Cobain?

In one sense, the answer is obvious. Kurt Cobain killed Kurt Cobain. Yet he was also a victim. He was the victim of a false idea – the idea of counterculture. While he thought of himself as a punk rocker, a man in the business of making 'alternative' music, his records sold in the millions. Thanks in large part to Cobain, the music that used to be called 'hardcore' was rebranded and sold to the masses as 'grunge'. But rather than serving as a source of pride to him, this popularity was a constant embarrassment. It fed the nagging doubts in the back of his mind, which suggested that he had 'sold out' the scene, gone 'mainstream'.

After Nirvana's breakthrough album, *Nevermind*, began to outsell Michael Jackson, the band made a concerted effort to lose fans. Their follow-up album, *In Utero*, was obviously intended to be difficult, inaccessible music. But the effort failed. The album went on to reach number one in the Billboard charts.

Cobain was never able to reconcile his commitment to alternative music with the popular success of Nirvana. In the end, his suicide was a way out of the impasse. Better to stop it now, before the last scrap of integrity is gone, and avoid the total sell-out. That way he could hold fast to his conviction that 'punk rock is freedom'. What he failed to consider was the possibility that it was all an illusion; that there is no alternative, no mainstream, no relationship between music and freedom, and no such thing as selling out. There are just people who make music, and people who listen to music. And if you make great music, people will want to listen to it.

So where did the idea of 'alternative' come from? The idea that you had to be unpopular in order to be authentic?

Cobain was a graduate of what he called the 'Punk Rock 101' school of life. Much of the punk ethos was based on a rejection of what the hippies had stood for. If they listened to the Lovin' Spoonful, we punks would listen to Grievous Bodily Harm. They had the Rolling Stones, we had the Violent Femmes, the Circle Jerks and Dead On Arrival. If they had long hair, we would have Mohicans. If they wore sandals, we would wear army boots. If they were into *satyagraha*, we were into direct action. We were the 'un-hippies'.

Why this animus toward hippies? It wasn't because they were too radical. It was because they were not radical enough. They had sold out. They were, as Cobain put it, the 'hippiecrits'. *The Big Chill* told you everything you needed to know. The hippies had become yuppies. 'The only way I would wear a tie-dyed T-shirt', Cobain liked to say, 'would be if it were soaked in the blood of Jerry Garcia'.

By the beginning of the '80s, rock and roll had been transformed into a bloated, pale imitation of its former self. It had become arena rock. *Rolling Stone* magazine had become a complacent corporate sales rag, dedicated to flogging crappy albums. Given his attitude, one can only imagine Cobain's embarrassment when he was asked to appear on the cover of *Rolling Stone*. His compromise: to do the shoot in a T-shirt that read 'Corporate rock magazines still suck'. Cobain persuaded himself that, in so doing, he was not selling out, he was simply going undercover: 'We can pose as the enemy to infiltrate the mechanics of the system to start its rot from the inside. Sabotage the empire by pretending to play their game, compromise just enough to call their bluff. And the hairy, sweaty, macho, sexist dickheads will soon drown in a pool of razorblades and semen, stemmed from the uprising of their children, the armed and deprogrammed crusade, littering the floors of Wall Street with revolutionary debris.'[1]

One can see here quite clearly that, while Cobain and the rest of us punks may have rejected most of the ideas that came out of the hippie counterculture, there is one element of the movement that we swallowed hook, line and sinker. This was the idea of counterculture itself. In other words, we saw ourselves as doing exactly the same thing that the hippies saw themselves doing. The difference, we assumed, is that, unlike them, *we* would never sell out. We would do it right.

Some myths die hard. One can see the same cycle repeating itself in hip hop. The countercultural idea here takes the form of a romantic view of ghetto life and gang culture. Successful rappers must fight hard to retain their street cred, to 'keep it real'. They'll pack guns, do time, even get shot up, just to prove that they're not just 'studio gangstas'. So instead of just dead punks and hippies, we now also have a steadily growing pantheon of dead rappers. People talk about the 'assassination' of Tupac Shakur, as though he actually posed a threat to the system. Eminem claims his arrest for possession of a concealed weapon was 'all political', designed to get him off the streets. It's the same thing all over again.

This wouldn't be so important if it were confined to the world of music. Unfortunately, the idea of counterculture has become so deeply embedded in our understanding of society that it influences every aspect of social and political life. Most importantly, it has become the conceptual template for all contemporary leftist politics. Counterculture has almost completely replaced socialism as the basis of radical political thought. So if counterculture is a myth, then it is one that has misled an enormous number of people, with untold political consequences.

★

The idea that artists must take an oppositional stance toward mainstream society is hardly new. It has its origins in 18th-century Romanticism, a movement that went on to dominate the artistic imagination throughout the 19th century. It found its highest expression – and most enduring commercial success – in Giacomo Puccini's *La Bohème*, a celebration of alternative 'bohemian' lifestyles in Paris. In those days, 'real' artists had to die of consumption (tuberculosis, that is), not heroin overdoses or drive-bys. But you get the idea.

The key to understanding early Romanticism is to appreciate the impact that the discovery of the New World, and in particular the Pacific Islands, had upon European consciousness. Before these encounters, Europeans simply assumed that humans had lived, throughout all of history, in hierarchically organised class societies. Kingship, aristocracy and class domination were simply a part of the natural order. St. Thomas Aquinas summed up the received wisdom when he wrote, back in the 13th century:

> *Everything that happens in nature is good, because nature always does what is best. The standard form of government in nature is the rule of one. If we consider the parts of the body, we see that there is one part that moves all the rest, namely the heart. If we look at the parts of the soul, we find that there is one faculty that rules the rest – reason. The same is true of bees, who have but one queen, and of the universe as a whole, which has only one God, who has created and governs all things. This is not without reason, since a plurality is always derived from a unity. Since the products of art imitate the works of nature, and since a work of art is the more perfect, the more closely it resembles the works of nature, the best government for a people is necessarily the government of one.*[2]

Five hundred years later, Jean-Jacques Rousseau could agree with the first line of this passage – that everything in nature is good – but disagree with all the rest. Thanks to the discovery of the New World, thinkers like Rousseau knew that there were people who lived without social hierarchy, without landed aristocracy or monarchy, and sometimes even without settlements or cities. It didn't take long to infer that this was in fact the 'natural' condition of mankind, and that the major world civilisations, with their elaborate social hierarchies and systems of privilege, represented a terrible distortion of the natural order.

Thus Rousseau concluded that all of society was a giant fraud, a system of exploitation imposed upon the weak by the strong. The emergence of civilisation, he argued, 'gave new fetters to the weak and new forces to the rich, irretrievably destroyed natural liberty, established forever the law of property and of inequality, changed straightforward usurpation into an irrevocable right, and for the profit of a few ambitious men henceforth subjected the entire human race to labour, servility and misery.'[3]

As far as sweeping indictments of society go, this one is right up there. After reading it, Voltaire was moved to write to Rousseau: 'I have received your new book against the human race, and thank you for it. Never has such cleverness been used to show that we are all stupid. One longs, upon reading your book, to walk on all fours. But as I have lost that habit for more than sixty years, I feel unhappily the impossibility of resuming it. Nor can I go off in search of the savages of Canada, because the illnesses to which I am condemned render a European doctor necessary to me.'[4]

Yet despite the broad scope of his claim, Rousseau's intention was not actually to condemn 'the human race' or to recommend a return to savagery. As his work on the social contract made clear, he was not opposed to social order itself, or to the rule of law. He was opposed to the specifically hierarchical form that this order had taken on in his own society. It was the perversion of the natural order into class domination that angered him.

In other words, despite the sweeping nature of his indictment, Rousseau's critique was directed against a specific class enemy – the aristocracy. Furthermore, he regarded the general population – the masses – as a natural ally in the struggle. The social upheavals that his thought inspired, up to and including the French Revolution, were not anarchic uprisings against society at large. They were aimed quite specifically at the ruling classes. (Which is why, by the end of the

18th century, almost the entire French aristocracy was either dead or in hiding.)

Even 19th-century anarchists were not really anarchists in the modern sense of the term. They were not opposed to social order, nor were they individualists. In many cases, they did not even want to smash the state. They simply opposed the coercive imposition of social order and the militarism of the early modern European nation state. Mikhail Bakunin's 'Revolutionary Catechism', one of the founding documents of political anarchism, calls for nothing more radical than voluntary federalism as the principle of national organisation, along with universal suffrage of both sexes. Bakunin, the famed anarchist, was actually one of the first to call for the creation of a 'United States of Europe'.[5]

So while society may have been roundly condemned as a rigged game, no one was in doubt about who had rigged it against whom. The goal of radical political activists and thinkers in the 18th and 19th centuries was not to eliminate the game, but to level the playing field. As a result, radical politics throughout the early modern period had an overwhelmingly populist character. The goal was to turn the people against their rulers.

But in the second half of the 20th century, radical politics took a significant turn away from this pattern of thought. Instead of treating the masses as an ally, the people began to be regarded, to an ever-increasing degree, as an object of suspicion. Before long, the people – that is, 'mainstream' society – came to be seen as the problem, not the solution. Whereas the great philosophers of the Enlightenment had railed against 'obedience', as a slavish disposition that promoted tyranny, radicals began to view 'conformity' as a far greater vice. The story of this remarkable reversal provides the key to understanding the origins of the myth of counterculture.

With the so-called bourgeois revolutions of the 18th century, there was a gradual elimination of aristocratic privilege in Europe and, above all, in the United States. But rather than abolishing class domination altogether, the effect of these revolutions was primarily to replace one ruling class with another. Instead of being peasants, ruled by an aristocracy that had control of all the land, the masses were gradually transformed into workers, ruled by capitalists who controlled the factories and machines. As the nascent market economy began producing wealth on an unparalleled scale, money quickly became more important than either land or lineage as the basis for privilege.

There could be no mistake about the hierarchical nature of this emerging society. In the 19th century, capitalism seemed to be clearly in the process of dividing society into two antagonistic classes. The division between rich and poor was as stark as it is in many underdeveloped countries today. Most people had to work for a living. This meant a life of dangerous toil under unbearable conditions in the factory, combined with grinding poverty at home. Then there were those who lived off the work of others, enjoying fabulous returns on their invested capital. There was not much in between.

Yet while it seemed obvious to contemporary observers that the masses had traded one form of exploitation for another, there was one key difference between the form of class domination that emerged out of the bourgeois revolutions and the aristocratic hierarchy that preceded it. Unlike the peasants, who were literally coerced into staying on the land and working for its lord, the working classes were formally free to do whatever they wanted. They were no longer tied to the land; they were free to move as they liked, to live where they liked and to take any job that was available or that appealed to them. Thus the class domination that existed in capitalist societies appeared to have an entirely voluntary character. When workers were injured at the factory or in the mine, the owner could evade responsibility by saying, 'Nobody forced them to take the job. They knew the risks when they signed up.'

There was no shortage of critics lining up to condemn the exploitation and suffering caused by early capitalism. But these critics were forced to confront a fundamental problem. If conditions were so terrible, why did the working classes tolerate them? Revolutionary socialists began arguing that workers should simply seize control of the factories where they worked. Yet the working classes were surprisingly reluctant to do so. This required some explanation. After all, since it seemed to be clearly in the *interest* of the working classes to take control of the means of production, what was stopping them?

This is where Karl Marx stepped in, with his famous critique of 'ideology'. The problem, Marx argued, was that the working class was the victim of an illusion, which he referred to as 'commodity fetishism'. Rather than perceiving the economy as a set of essentially social relationships between individuals, the market gave it the appearance of a system of natural laws. Prices and wages moved up and down, seemingly at random. Losing your job seemed to be a matter of bad luck, like getting caught in a rainstorm. The ups and downs of the market were determined by forces completely outside anyone's control. So if wages dropped or the price of bread went up, there appeared to be no one to blame.

In Marx's view, this objectification of social relationships had gone so far that workers had become alienated from their own activity. They saw their own labour as merely a means to the attainment of other ends. Capitalism had created a nation of clock-watchers. Marx argued that the working classes were unwilling to engage in revolutionary politics because they were completely caught up in this nexus of false ideas. Commodity fetishism and alienated labour provided the ideology of capitalism. All of this was wrapped up in a bow by traditional Christian religious doctrine, which promised workers paradise in the afterlife, on the condition that they behaved themselves here and now. Thus, religion was the 'opiate' that kept the imposed suffering from becoming unendurable.

Given this diagnosis of the problem, the role of the Marxian social critic was not necessarily to get directly involved in the organisation of the working class. Communists and socialists were often greeted with suspicion on the factory floor. The workers needed to be 'radicalised' before they could be organised – through the cultivation of class consciousness. This meant freeing them from the grip of bourgeois ideology. The mindset of the workers needed to be changed, *so that they could come to see where their own interests lay*. Only when freed from the mental cage in which they were imprisoned could they begin to saw away at the bars of the real cage that society had constructed around them.

The working class, unfortunately, turned out to be a terrible disappointment. Rather than agitating for the revolutionary overthrow of capitalism, workers tended to focus more on incremental gains, such as higher wages and medical benefits. From the Marxist perspective, this sort of 'reformism' didn't address any of the fundamental issues; the workers were just redecorating the cage in which they were imprisoned. But once they came to see their situation more clearly, they would inevitably rise up.

Yet as the 20th century wore on, this diagnosis of the problem became increasingly unpersuasive. For example, the initial reluctance to give workers the vote was based upon the assumption, universally shared among the ruling classes in Europe and America, that if you let the people vote, the first thing they would vote for would be the dispossession of the propertied classes. In other words, they would use the vote to seize the property of the wealthy. Yet this is not what happened. Workers voted for reform, not revolution.

After the Russian Revolution, it became increasingly difficult to dismiss this peculiarly altruistic behaviour on the part of workers as the effect of 'commodity fetishism'. How could the workers possibly believe that capitalism was natural and unalterable when the development of the Soviet Union showed quite clearly that it was optional? The Russians had proved that workers, if they wanted, could get rid of the capitalist system and replace it with one of their choosing. Furthermore, until the '60s it was still very much unclear which economic system would prove to be more efficient. The early history of the Soviet Union convinced many people that communism might produce more wealth than capitalism. So what could explain the passivity of the European and American working classes?

Capitalism had proved to be a much tougher nut to crack than many on the left had suspected. In order to avoid the conclusion that workers might actually *like* capitalism, Marxist theorists began to retool the theory of ideology. In the '20s, for instance, Antonio Gramsci began arguing that capitalism created false consciousness in the working classes not by inspiring particular false beliefs about the operations of the economy, but by establishing a complete cultural 'hegemony', which in turn reinforced the system. He suggested, in effect, that the entire culture – books, music, painting – reflected a form of bourgeois ideology, and so needed to be discarded before the working class could achieve emancipation. He argued therefore for the 'necessity of creating a new culture'.[6]

Initially this argument fell upon deaf ears. Marx's claim that the state was merely the 'executive committee of the bourgeoisie' already smacked of paranoia. The idea that the bourgeoisie could be controlling the entire culture seemed even more far-fetched. How could the whole culture be nothing but a scam? It seemed hard to believe that a fraud could be perpetrated on such a scale.

It got a whole lot easier to believe, however, after the rise of Nazi Germany.

*

It is impossible to understand the way history unfolded in the 20th century without grasping the massive impact that the Nazi regime – and, more importantly, the Holocaust – had upon political thinking in the West. What happened in Germany reminded everyone that when politics goes wrong, it has the potential to produce much more than just bad government. It can create a living nightmare.

This is something that the ancient Greeks and Romans knew quite well. They believed that absolute power provoked a special sort of madness in the tyrant. Plato argued in *The Republic* that tyranny reveals a part of the soul that is usually only awakened in sleep, when the rest of the soul – the reasonable, gentle and ruling part – is slumbering … Then the beastly and savage part, full of food and drink, casts off sleep and seeks to find a way to gratify itself. You know that there is nothing it will not dare to do at such a time, free of all control by shame or reason. It does not shrink from trying to have sex with a mother, as it supposes, or with anyone else at all, whether man, god or beast. It will commit any foul murder, and there is no food it refuses to eat. In a word, it omits no act of folly or shamelessness.[7]

Yet what Europeans saw in the Nazi regime was far more chilling than these ancient forms of tyranny. Whereas the madness in antiquity was confined to the ruler himself, and perhaps his inner circle, in Germany the entire country seemed to have gone mad. Nazism had all the appearances of mass psychosis. How else to describe a society in which bureaucrats in the concentration camps kept meticulous files, recording such details as the number of ounces of gold extracted from the dental fillings of the inmates who were being systematically exterminated?

People have always known that mobs can be dangerous. When swept away in a riot, otherwise law-abiding citizens may begin to loot and steal. Mild-mannered people may cry out for blood and vengeance when they are caught up in a crowd calling for the same. Human sentiment is highly contagious. Being in a crowd full of people who are laughing makes everything seem more funny. Being in a crowd full of angry people has a parallel effect. As a result, individuals often behave a bit 'crazy' – or at least contrary to their own considered judgments – when they find themselves in a crowd.

Furthermore, it is extremely difficult to go against the judgment or sentiment of the group. Crowd psychology imposes conformity. One need only look at the tyranny imposed by the audience of a typical TV talk show. Only certain ideas, expressed in a certain way, meet with the approval of the mob. All participants fall under intense psychological pressure to fall into line. As Charles Mackay wrote in his 19th century bestseller *Extraordinary Popular Delusions and the Madness of Crowds*: 'Men, it has been well said, think in herds; it will be seen that they go mad in herds, while they only recover their senses slowly, and one by one.'[8]

In the second half of the 19th century, Europeans had been fascinated by these forms of mass behaviour. Books such as Mackay's and Gustave Le Bon's *The Crowd* were enormously popular. Yet for all this, it was also generally thought that group 'madness' was transitory. Popular delusions took the form of 'fads' and 'enthusiasms'. An emotion passes through the crowd but then fades away as quickly as it came. People may act intemperately but, not long after, they begin to regret their actions.[9]

What Nazi Germany appeared to exhibit was crowd psychology; not only on an unprecedented scale, but also sustained over an extraordinarily long time. According to one prominent interpretation, the Nazis were able to achieve this – something unparalleled in human history – because for the first time they had at their disposal the instruments of mass media. Broadcast radio, in particular, had allowed Nazi propaganda to reach millions of homes.

Nazi Germany, in other words, marked the dawn of what came to be known as 'the mass society'. The power structure in ancient tyrannies usually involved only the elites. The majority of the population was simply encouraged to mind its own business and obey the leaders. The modern totalitarian state, by contrast, mobilised the masses. The people themselves were swept up in the enthusiasm, becoming a tyrannical force in their own right. This was made possible by the invention of broadcast media, which, when combined with modern propaganda techniques, allowed the state to cultivate and reproduce the kind of fanaticism and conformity that we see in small groups but on the scale of an entire society. Thus mass society was born: the bastard child of broadcast media and groupthink.

In order to see how the media can facilitate the mass contagion of sentiment, one need only turn on the television or listen to some talk radio. The classic sitcom has a laugh track, and talk shows have a studio audience, precisely because hearing other people laugh itself provokes laughter. The effect works in the same way regardless of whether people are in the same room or the laughter is simply being broadcast through the media. Similarly, talk-radio stations employ a well-known formula for cultivating anger or outrage. The pattern of exchange between the host and the callers is especially effective at generating and sustaining the shared emotional response.

Nazism, of course, presented a rather extreme variant of the genre. But in the Soviet Union, Stalin demonstrated quite clearly how propaganda techniques could be used in the service of a different ideology. In *1984*, George Orwell sketched out a somewhat gentler version of this totalitarian nightmare – suggesting that a society might use more psychological control, and much less overt violence, in order to indoctrinate the masses. Many others thought that totalitarianism would insinuate itself into daily life in even more subtle ways.

These concerns were dramatically amplified in the United States by the anticommunist hysteria of the 1950s. In 1951, after the defection of twenty-one American POWs to the North Korean side, journalist Edward Hunter coined the phrase 'brainwashing' to describe the processes of mind control and 're-education' supposedly imposed by communist regimes.[10] The concept proved extremely popular, and was extended back 'retroactively' to describe the techniques used by the Nazis in Germany. Thus William Sargant, in his 1957 classic *Battle for the Mind*, argued that Hitler had used 'organised excitement and mass hypnotism' to rally the masses.[11]

It was not long before the US military and the CIA got interested. CIA director Allen Dulles took a particular interest in the subject, commissioning a special report on Chinese and Soviet brainwashing techniques. The CIA also began to conduct experiments – using both Korean POWs and unsuspecting volunteers – in order to perfect brainwashing techniques of their own. Since it was common knowledge that this sort of research was being conducted, it was not long before critics of American society began to suspect that these techniques were being used against the domestic population as well as the enemy. Vance Packard's 1957 attack on the advertising industry, *The Hidden Persuaders*, was rooted in precisely this culture of paranoia. Packard's assertion that consumers were being exposed to 'subliminal advertising' fed into popular fear of mind control.[12] People were so disturbed by the suggestion, it took more than three decades for the myth to be finally debunked.

Thus the net effect of anticommunist hysteria was to make people in the victorious Allied nations even more anxious about the possibility of creeping totalitarianism. It is easy for us to look back and claim that these concerns were overwrought. There was certainly no long-term erosion of basic liberties in these nations. But at the time, it was very far from obvious that this would be the outcome. In particular, the fear of propaganda, and of the psychological manipulation that it was thought to make possible, was easily translated into a fear of advertising and the mass media. Even setting aside television, the incorporation of visual elements, such as drawing, photography, logos and design, into print advertising appeared to be intended, just as Hitler's propaganda had been, to bypass the reader's rational faculties and appeal to him or her directly on an emotional level. The potential for manipulation and control seemed ominous.

Many people therefore saw a continuum between modern capitalism and fascism. (After all, Nazism was the 'demon child' of European culture and society. It was hardly outrageous to suggest that the same forces that had led to the emergence of fascism in Germany and Italy might also be exercising more subtle effects in England, France and the United States.) Many people came to see Western democracies as simply more subtle variants of the basic fascist state apparatus.

The outline of this critique was already in place well before the war. In 1932, Aldous Huxley published *Brave New World*, which sketched out a dystopian society in which perfect happiness had been achieved through total manipulation. Set in 632 AF (After Ford), Huxley imagined a world in which genetic manipulation ensures that the working classes are perfectly satisfied with the menial tasks to which they are consigned. The idle upper classes are fed a steady diet of soma, a drug that dulls their senses, creates a diffuse sense of well-being and prevents them from asking too many questions. Individuality is suppressed both literally and figuratively: everyone in the society is a clone.

In the post-war era, it seemed to many people on the left that an explanation for the lack of revolutionary agitation on the part of the working classes was to be found in manipulation of this type. Unlike religion, which promised paradise after death, advertising promised paradise right around the next corner: through purchase of a new car, a suburban home or a labour-saving appliance. Consumer goods had become the new opiate of the people – real-life 'soma'. To Marxists, it seemed that advertising was not just promotion for specific goods, it was propaganda for the capitalist system. It created what came to be known as 'consumerism' – a kind of conformist groupthink transmitted through the mass media. Consumerism produced a simulacrum of happiness, but only by enslaving individuality and the imagination, making it impossible for the working classes to see how much more there could be to life, or to imagine a better world.

The emergence of advertising in the 1950s thus gave a new lease on life to the Gramscian theory of 'hegemony'. Prior to the war, the claim that culture was entirely orchestrated and planned by the bourgeoisie had the whiff of a conspiracy theory. How exactly does the bourgeoisie accomplish all this? But now the answer seemed clear: by bombarding the working classes with advertising, brainwashing them into thinking that cheap consumer goods could make them happy. Suddenly, the idea that the whole culture might be a system of ideology began to seem more plausible. After all, the Germans had been completely brainwashed by the Nazis. Why not us? And if we *were* the victims of total brainwashing, how would we know?

In the early 1960s, Yale psychology professor Stanley Milgram conducted a series of experiments that, in many people's minds, confirmed the worst fears about the relationship between fascism and modern democracy. As the name of his project suggested, Milgram was interested in 'Obedience and Individual Responsibility'. His goal was to determine just how pliable the average citizen might be in the face of a regime of power and authority. He set up a fairly simple experiment: two people came to his lab, ostensibly to take part in a study on memory and learning. One of them was designated the 'learner', the other the 'teacher'. The learner was put in a room and strapped into a chair, where an electrode was attached to his wrist. Meanwhile, the teacher was seated before a large machine called Shock Generator, Type ZLB. On the front of the machine was a series of switches designated, from left to right, 'Slight Shock', 'Moderate Shock', 'Strong Shock', all the way to 'Danger: Severe Shock', and two final switches, simply but ominously labelled 'XXX'. The learner was then told that he would be asked to memorise lists of word pairs and that every time he made a mistake, the teacher would deliver a short, sharp shock of increasing intensity.[13]

The experimental design was in fact an elaborate setup. The true subject was the 'teacher', and the point of the experiment was not to test the effect of punishment on memory, but rather to see how far the average person would go in a situation in which he or she was asked to inflict pain on an innocent and protesting victim. The learner was a plant, and the shocks were faked.

The results were rather extraordinary. Despite the fact that the learner often gave clear evidence that he was in pain (screams of agony, complaints about his heart), the teacher continued to ask questions and administer shocks, often in the face of complete unresponsiveness on the part of the learner (who was actually an actor). Even Milgram himself was astonished: more than half of the residents of New Haven, Connecticut, appeared willing to electroshock a fellow citizen into unconsciousness, even to death, simply because a man in a white lab coat instructed them to do so.

When the results of the experiment were made public, many people were outraged, in part because there were (and still are) legitimate questions as to how ethical the experiment was. But beyond that, Milgram delivered a 'severe shock' to our standard assumptions about human nature and the character of evil. He drew the following conclusion from his tests: 'Ordinary people, simply doing their jobs, and without any particular hostility on their part, can become agents in a terrible destructive process. Moreover, even when the destructive effects of their work become patently clear, and they are asked to carry out actions incompatible with fundamental standards of morality, relatively few people have the resources needed to resist authority.'

This is very much the same conclusion drawn by Hannah Arendt in her 1963 book *Eichmann in Jerusalem*, which contains a series of extraordinary observations about the mindset of Adolf Eichmann, the Nazi bureaucrat responsible for implementation of the 'final solution'. While covering the trial of Eichmann for *The New Yorker*, Arendt came to the conclusion that the prosecution's attempt to portray Eichmann as a sadistic monster was fundamentally mistaken. Eichmann was simply a boring, meticulous bureaucrat who sat at his desk, pushing paper, carrying out his orders. He was, in other words, a conformist. Milgram had conceived of his experiment as a way of testing Arendt's thesis about what she called the 'banality of evil'.[14]

At the time, Arendt herself was subjected to considerable scorn for daring to suggest that a Nazi like Eichmann was anything but evil incarnate. Milgram's experiments did an enormous amount to silence this criticism, and to make the 'banality of evil' a part of the received understanding of human nature in our culture. Milgram also lent considerable plausibility to the parallels that many people were drawing between fascism and the 'mass society' of the United States. Conformity quickly became the new cardinal sin in our society.

Mass society is indelibly associated, in the popular imagination, with the United States of the 1950s. It is a world of perfect families, white picket fences, shiny new Buicks and teenagers 'going steady', yet it is also a world of complete conformity, where happiness is achieved at the expense of individuality, creativity and freedom. It is a world in which, as the Dead Kennedys put it, the comfort you have demanded is now mandatory.

The movie *Pleasantville* dramatises this critique of mass society through a rather quaint cinematic affectation. In the film, two teenagers from the present are magically transported into the world of a 1950s television show. On the surface, everything is perfect: the sun always shines, the home team never loses and there is no poverty, crime or corruption. Everything is pleasant, all of the time. Yet this happiness is achieved at the expense of total uniformity. Inhabitants of the town are blissfully unaware of the existence of a world beyond their city limits. The books in the library are all blank. Everyone eats meatloaf for dinner, every night. Nothing ever changes; the entire world is in stasis.

The film depicts the compromise at the heart of Pleasantville by filming the entire '50s world in black and white. Yet as the teenagers from the present inevitably 'contaminate' the peace and harmony of Pleasantville, by introducing new ideas and new forms of behaviour to the inhabitants, bursts of colour begin to show up in that world: a red rose, a green car, a brightly coloured painting. One by one the inhabitants of Pleasantville themselves begin to change into full colour, as they free themselves from their mental shackles. They become liberated from an existence that is, quite literally, dull and grey.

Here we can see the idea of counterculture in its fully developed form. What people need to be liberated from is not a specific class that oppresses them or a system of exploitation that imposes poverty upon them. People have become trapped in a gilded cage, and have been taught to love their own enslavement. 'Society' controls them by limiting the imagination and suppressing their deepest needs. What they need to escape from is conformity. And to do so, they must reject the culture in its entirety. They must form a counterculture – one based on freedom and individuality.

According to Theodore Roszak (whose 1969 book *The Making of a Counter Culture* introduced the term 'counterculture' into general usage), society as a whole has become a system of complete manipulation, a 'technocracy'. The discipline of the machine and the factory floor has been extended to encompass every dimension of human life. In such a society, 'politics, education, leisure, entertainment, culture as a whole, the unconscious drives, and even … protest against the technocracy itself: all these become the subjects of purely technical scrutiny and of purely technical manipulation.'[15] Under such circumstances, nothing short of a total rejection of the entire culture and society will suffice. In Roszak's view, traditional leftist parties – not to mention communists and trade unionists – have become the stooges of technocracy: 'This brand of politics finishes with merely redesigning the turrets and towers of the technocratic citadel. It is the foundations of the edifice that must be sought.'[16]

It is important to see what a profound reorientation of radical politics this critique represents. Traditional leftist concerns, such as poverty, living standards and access to medical care, come to be seen as 'superficial', in that they aim only at institutional reform. The counterculture, by contrast, is interested in what Roszak calls 'the psychic liberation of the oppressed'.[17] Thus the hipster, cooling his heels in a jazz club, comes to be seen as a more profound critic of modern society than the civil rights activist working to enlist voters, or the feminist politician campaigning for a constitutional amendment.

Stepping back for a moment, it should be obvious that there is something strange about this form of countercultural critique. After all, the traditional objection to capitalism – certainly Marx's primary objection – was that it exploited the working classes, creating poverty and suffering. In other words, the problem with capitalism was that it deprived workers of material goods. 'The immiseration of the proletariat' was what Marx called it.

In this context, it is somewhat odd to turn around and say that the workers have sold out and that the abundance of consumer goods is merely an opiate that pacifies them, preventing them from seeing where their true interests lie. It's like saying that when you give a child something to eat, it doesn't really feed him, it merely 'placates' him so that he forgets that he is hungry. It was precisely the failure of the capitalist system to provide the workers with goods that gave them the reason to overthrow the system in the first place. Thus the critique of consumerism comes perilously close to criticising capitalism for satisfying the workers *too much*. They're so stuffed, they can't be bothered to go out and overthrow the system anymore. But this poses the question: why would they want to?

Roszak in fact criticises the students in the Paris 1968 uprising for having tried to form an alliance with French workers. The workers, he claims, are an unreliable ally, since they have a vested interest in the system of industrial production. 'The touchstone of the matter would be', he argues, 'how ready are the workers to disband whole sectors of the industrial apparatus where this proves necessary to achieve ends other than efficiency, productivity and high consumption? How willing are they to set aside technocratic priorities in favour of a new simplicity of life, a decelerating social pace, a vital leisure?'[18]

One can see here how the traditional interests of the working class have been downgraded to the status of a 'technocratic priority'. Yet Roszak is in danger of simply taking the class interests of intellectuals and students – freeing the imagination, finding a 'new simplicity of life' – and imposing them upon the rest of the population (on the grounds that anyone who disagrees is a victim of the technocracy). The problem with assuming that everyone is the victim of a total ideology is that it becomes impossible to state what would count as evidence for or against this thesis.

In the end, workers didn't seem all that interested in having their imaginations freed. Rather than flocking to art galleries and poetry recitals when given the chance, they continued to show an unhealthy interest in sports, broadcast television and malt beverages. This naturally fed the nagging suspicion that the public at large might actually *like* capitalism, that they might genuinely *want* consumer goods. It suggested that the failure of capitalism to satisfy the 'deeper needs' of the people might not be a problem, simply because *the people have no deeper needs*. Perhaps the students had simply mistaken their own class interests for the general interest – assuming that 'good for me' is the same as 'good for society'. (They would certainly not have been the first to do so!)

The sneaking suspicion that the public might be genuinely satisfied by capitalism is reinforced by the observation that countercultural rebellion didn't seem to do anything. Unlike *Pleasantville*, where the transformation of society is instantaneous, radical and highly visible, in the real world 'freeing the imagination' doesn't seem to galvanise the proletariat, much less cure injustice, eliminate poverty or stop war. Furthermore, the ideological system that sustains capitalism did not seem to be too troubled by acts of countercultural rebellion. The sort of conformist mass culture caricatured in *Pleasantville* is supposed to be very rigid – such that the slightest display of individuality represents a mortal threat. Nonconformity must be stamped out, we were told, or it would destabilise the entire system.

So the first-generation hippies did everything they could to violate the dress code of 1950s society: men grew their hair long and wore beards, refused to wear suits and ties; women adopted miniskirts, threw away their bras, stopped wearing makeup – and so on. But it wasn't long before these items and clothing styles started showing up in advertisements and on mannequins in shop windows. Soon department stores were selling peace medallions and love beads. In other words, 'the system' seemed to regard the hippies less as a threat to the established order than as a marketing opportunity. Punk rock was received in exactly the same way. Designer safety pins were on sale in fancy London shops long before the Sex Pistols even broke up.

How to explain this? The countercultural rebels believed that what they were doing was genuinely radical, that it represented a profound challenge to society. Their rebellion was felt to be an especially potent threat to capitalism, which relied upon an army of docile, pacified workers, willing to submit themselves to the soul-destroying discipline of the machine. And yet 'the system' seemed to take this form of rebellion in its stride. This lack of discernible impact presented a serious threat to the countercultural idea. After all, according to the countercultural rebels, the problem with traditional leftist politics was that it was superficial. It aimed at 'merely' institutional change. Countercultural rebels, on the other hand, were supposedly attacking oppression at a deeper level. Yet despite the radicalism of their interventions, it was difficult to see any concrete effects.

At this point the countercultural idea might have been in serious trouble had it not been for a singular stroke of genius: the theory of 'co-optation'. According to this idea, the 'repression' imposed by the system turns out to be more subtle than, say, the Spanish Inquisition. At first, the system tries merely to *assimilate* resistance by appropriating its symbols, evacuating their 'revolutionary' content and then selling them back to the masses as commodities. It thereby seeks to neutralise the counterculture by piling on substitute gratifications so high that people ignore the revolutionary kernel of these new ideas. It is only when this initial attempt at co-optation has failed that overt repression must be employed, and 'the violence inherent in the system' is revealed.

With this theory of co-optation in place, the counterculture itself becomes a 'total ideology', a completely closed system of thought, immune to falsification, in which every apparent exception simply confirms the rule. For generations now, countercultural rebels have been pumping out 'subversive' music, 'subversive' art, 'subversive' literature, 'subversive' clothing, while universities have been packed full of professors disseminating 'subversive' ideas to their students. So much subversion, and yet the system seems to tolerate it quite well. Does this suggest that the system is perhaps not so repressive after all? 'On the contrary', says the countercultural rebel. 'It shows that the system is even more repressive than we thought – look at how skilfully it co-opts all of this subversion!'

Back in 1965, Herbert Marcuse coined a term to describe this peculiar sort of repression. He called it 'repressive tolerance'.[19] It's an idea that makes about as much sense now as it did then.

Notes

1   Kurt Cobain, *Journals* (New York: Penguin Putnam, 2002), 168.

2   St. Thomas Aquinas, *On the Governance of Rulers*, trans. Gerald B. Phelan (Toronto: St. Michael's College, 1935), 39.

3   Jean-Jacques Rousseau, 'Discourse on Inequality,' *The First and Second Discourses*, ed. Roger D. Masters, trans. Judith R. Masters (New York: St. Martin's Press, 1964), 160.

4   Voltaire, *Voltaire's Correspondence*, ed. Theodore Besterman (Geneva: Institut et Musée Voltaire, 1957), 230.

5   Mikhail Bakunin, *Bakunin on Anarchism*, ed. and trans. Sam Dolgoff (Montreal: Black Rose Books, 1980), 104.

6   Antonio Gramsci, *Selections from the Prison Notebooks*, ed. and trans. Quintin Hoare and Geoffrey Nowell Smith (New York: International Publishers, 1971), 276.

7   *The Republic*: Plato, *Republic*, trans. G. M. A. Grube rev. C. D. C. Reeve (Cambridge: Hackett, 1992), 242.

8   Charles Mackay, *Extraordinary Popular Delusions and the Madness of Crowds* (1841; New York: Harmony, 1980).

9   Gustave Le Bon, *The Crowd: A Study of the Popular Mind* (London: T. Fisher Unwin, 1926).

10 Edward Hunter, *Brainwashing in Red China* (New York: Van-guard, 1962).

11 William Sargant, *Battle for the Mind: A Physiology of Conversion and Brain-Washing* (London: Pan Books, 1957), 142.

12 Vance Packard's 1957 attack: Vance Packard, *The Hidden Persuaders* (New York: Pocket Books, 1957). The subliminal scare was resurrected in 1973 by Brian Wilson Key in *Subliminal Seduction: Ad Media's Manipulation of a Not So Innocent America* (New York: New American Library, 1973). It is Key who is responsible for the idea that one can find hidden images in the ice cubes of liquor ads.

13 Stanley Milgram, *Obedience* (videorecording), ed. Christopher C. Johnson (New Haven: Yale University, 1965).

14 Hannah Arendt, *Eichmann in Jerusalem: A Report on the Banality of Evil* (New York: HarperPerennial, 1977).

15 Theodore Roszak, *The Making of a Counter Culture: Reflections on the Technocratic Society and Its Youthful Opposition* (Berkeley: University of California Press, 1996), 6. All citations used by kind permission of the University of California Press.

16 *Ibid.*, 55.

17 *Ibid.*, 65.

18 *Ibid.*, 68.

19 Herbert Marcuse, 'Repressive Tolerance,' *A Critique of Pure Tolerance*, ed. Robert Paul Wolff (Boston: Beacon, 1969).

Freud goes to California

If you asked the fishes to describe what it's like to live at the bottom of the sea, they would probably neglect to mention that it's extremely *wet*. Sometimes the most important features of our environment escape our attention simply because they are so ubiquitous. Our mental environment is much the same. Some theories are so universal, so taken-for-granted, that we fail to notice that they are even theories.

The work of Sigmund Freud has become, for us, like water to the fishes. It is barely regarded as a theory – something that could prove to be right or wrong. It has become the lens through which we perceive all of reality. This is especially obvious in the United States. Just tune in to any daytime TV talk show. The vocabulary of popular psychology (what critics call 'psychobabble') – 'self-esteem', 'denial', 'closure', 'dependency', 'inner child' and so on – can all be traced back, in one way or another, to the work of Freud. His influence can be found not only in how we talk about ourselves, but also in who we think we are. To take just one example, most people assume that they have something called a 'subconscious' mind. When they have a strange dream or mix up their words or find themselves acting inexplicably, they blame it all on their subconscious. If you tell them that this is all a theory, and that there may be no such thing, they react with a mixture of incredulity and scorn. *Obviously* we have a subconscious. Anyone who denies it must just be in denial.

But if your subconscious mind is truly subconscious, how do you know it's there? If you were directly aware of it, it would no longer be subconscious. So *obviously* it's just a theory. As a matter of fact, before 1900, when Freud published *The Interpretation of Dreams*, people didn't generally think of themselves as walking around with both a conscious and an unconscious mind. The fact that we do now is part of Freud's legacy.

The idea of counterculture would probably never have taken hold had it not been for Freud. The Marxian critique of mass society, all by itself, never had that much influence, especially not in the United States. But when combined with Freud's theory of repression, it became wildly popular. At first, Marx and Freud might seem like odd bedfellows. Unlike Marxism, which is fundamentally optimistic and utopian, Freud's view of society is extremely bleak. According to Freud, civilisation is essentially the antithesis of freedom. Culture is built upon the subjugation of human instincts. The progress of civilisation, therefore, is achieved through a steady increase in the repression of our fundamental instinctual nature and a corresponding decrease in our ability to experience happiness.

Freud himself never doubted that, when forced to choose between civilisation and freedom, it would be unreasonable to choose anything other than civilisation. His basic ambition was simply to draw attention to the tragic character of this choice. In the 1960s, on the other hand, many people began to draw the opposite conclusion. Given a choice between freedom and civilisation, they considered freedom to be the more desirable of the two. The lesson they learned from Freud was that in order to escape from the repression of our instinctual nature, it would be necessary to reject our culture in its entirety. It would be necessary to form a counterculture.

In many ways, the countercultural idea follows almost immediately from Freud's psychological theory. Given the way that Freud analyses the constitution of the human mind, it is very difficult to avoid the conclusion that culture as a whole is a system of repression. And if the problem with society – the reason that we are all so unhappy – is society itself, then the only way to emancipate ourselves is to reject all of culture, all of society. We must 'drop out' of the whole system.

But how does Freud's analysis lend itself to this extraordinary conclusion? It actually follows from elements of Freud's theory we are all quite familiar with, and that are widely accepted in our society. The centrepiece of it all is his theory of repression. Whenever we describe uptight people as 'repressed' or 'anal', whenever we claim that those who are being unrealistic are 'in denial', whenever we suggest that difficult people have a lot of 'pent-up anger' or 'issues', we are implicitly relying upon this theory.

Freud argued that the mind is divided into three components: the id, the ego and the superego. The id, or unconscious, is the site of our instinctual drives and impulses. (In pop psychology it is often called the 'inner child'.) The id is governed by the pleasure principle – it has no sense of reality and no self-restraint. It is simply an unco-ordinated bundle of wild and uncontrolled desires. It is like a small child lying down in the aisle of a toy store screaming, 'I want, I want, I want'. Furthermore, the id respects no values and is subject to no moral constraint. While some of our most basic impulses are altruistic and loving, others are almost unspeakably cruel and violent. This is revealed in the fact that we have not only the inclination to hurt others, but the capacity to take *pleasure* in doing so.

Freud also thought that, at the level of the id, boys want to have sex with their mothers and kill their fathers, girls vice versa. But that's a whole other story.

In *Civilisation and Its Discontents*, Freud described our basic instincts in the following way:

> *Men are not gentle creatures who want to be loved, and who at the most can defend themselves if they are attacked; they are, on the contrary, creatures among whose instinctual endowments is to be reckoned a powerful share of aggressiveness. As a result, their neighbour is for them not only a potential helper or sexual object, but also someone who tempts them to satisfy their aggressiveness on him, to exploit his capacity for work without compensation, to use him sexually without his consent, to seize his possessions, to humiliate him, to cause him pain, to torture and to kill him. Homo homini lupus. Who, in the face of all his experience of life and of history, will have the courage to dispute this assertion?*[1]

The task of imposing some sort of order and restraint upon the id falls to the ego, or the self – our conscious mind. It must persuade the id to be more realistic in its demands, to accept deferred instead of immediate gratification, work instead of play, security over spontaneity. Unfortunately, we are not, in Freud's view, terribly rational creatures. The ego, acting alone, simply does not have the strength or the resources needed to keep the id under control. When our feelings are aroused – feelings of love, anger, jealousy or hatred – we are usually not able to 'talk ourselves out of it' at will. As a result, human society is impossible based entirely upon our native psychological resources. We are simply too volatile and uncooperative. We are not like the bees, who react immediately to certain chemical triggers and perform the actions most needed by the hive. One need only look at chimpanzees, who murder and rape one another for pleasure (despite what you may have seen on the Discovery Channel), to see how humans are 'wired up' biologically.

Thus, social order among humans is initially achieved in much the same way that it is in a wolf pack or in a tribe of chimpanzees. In order to function cooperatively, our ancestors required an 'alpha male', who would institute a dominance hierarchy by beating the 'primal horde' into submission. This alpha male provides the template of the father figure. The appearance of the father gives the ego a new ally in the battle for control of the id. Fear of the punitive, threatening father, when internalised by the child, creates a new psychic structure – the superego. Like the id, the superego is unconscious. Yet it can serve as an ally of the ego in controlling the id. The superego censors our desires and associates feelings of shame and guilt with the satisfaction of our most basic instincts.

It is the interaction of the superego and the id that gives rise to the idea of an 'anal' personality type. As any parent can tell you, children initially take great pleasure from defecation and will do it whenever and wherever they please. The id is deeply scatological and gets enormous pleasure from all bodily functions. Yet in order to function in society, one must learn to control these impulses. This occurs initially through toilet training – when the adult imposes a system of rules upon the child, limiting his opportunities for instinctual gratification. The child's superego develops through an internalisation of the punitive responses of the adult. He begins to associate shame and guilt with certain bodily functions, which in turn gives him the self-control necessary to control his urge to eliminate.

The 'anal' personality disorder can arise when a child is too harshly treated during the process of toilet training. As a result, instead of developing a superego that censors only anal gratification, the child's superego develops a censorious attitude toward all bodily functions. Thus the child develops into an adult who is too 'uptight' or anxious to enjoy any form of bodily pleasure (most importantly, sexual pleasure).

The really key idea in Freud's theory is that, with the development of the superego, none of the underlying instinctual conflicts are ever decisively resolved. Our most primitive desires do not go away; they are simply *repressed*. Freud compares the mind to an old city like Rome, where the ancient districts are never torn down and replaced but are simply surrounded by new subdivisions. From the outside the city may look quite modern, but the centre will still be archaic.[2]

The mind of an adult thus preserves all of the primitive desires of the child intact. It simply learns to control them. There are two primary strategies that are available for this purpose. Instincts can be either repressed or sublimated. Repression means that the superego simply denies the id the opportunity to satisfy some particular desire. The person chooses to 'keep it all bottled up inside'. This creates frustration, anxiety and unhappiness. The alternative is to find a socially acceptable outlet for these urges, a substitute gratification. We can, in Freud's term, learn to 'sublimate' our desires. Instead of killing Dad, we can beat him in an arm-wrestle. Instead of having sex with Mum, we can marry a girl who looks strangely familiar. Instead of murdering people, we can play Grand Theft Auto, and so on.

In Freud's view, the human mind in society is like a pressure cooker after the lid has been clamped on. The steam doesn't go away; it simply builds up (like the frustration that we experience living in society). Sublimation is the safety valve that allows us to blow off some excess steam once in a while. If the heat is not set too high, an equilibrium may be reached and the lid may hold. If not, the whole thing will blow. Neuroses arise when a person is struggling to keep things together and so finds eccentric ways of sublimating desires. As

Freud put it, 'a person becomes neurotic because he cannot tolerate the amount of frustration which society imposes upon him in the service of its cultural ideals.'[3]

Few would doubt that individuals sometimes suffer from neuroses. But if an individual can become neurotic, could not an entire society become so as well? This is the radical question that Freud poses in *Civilisation and Its Discontents*. If our civilisation is, as he puts it, 'founded on the suppression of our instincts', is it possible that the growth of civilisation is a process that makes everyone increasingly neurotic?[4]

Freud's instinct theory is now generally regarded as having been discredited. And certainly, when asked, most people vehemently deny that they want to have sex with either their mother or their father. Yet even those who reject Freud's specific instinct theory generally accept his 'pressure-cooker' model of the mind. According to this theory, the desires that we must renounce in order to make ourselves acceptable in society do not go away; they are simply pushed down below the surface, beneath the threshold of our conscious mind. There they lurk about, waiting to resurface whenever they are given the opportunity.

Part of the evidence for this thesis is that whenever people become disinhibited – like when they are drunk or very angry – they begin to act in an antisocial manner. This suggests that socialisation does not fundamentally transform human nature; it simply gives us the ability to control our fundamental impulses.

Consider, for example, the case of swearing. The first thing to notice is that, when you are angry, swearing *feels good*. Yet the words often have no relationship to the situation. They are simply a set of terms or phrases dealing with taboo subjects: sex, defecation, incest or blasphemy. So why swear? The Freudian theory holds that when a person becomes sufficiently frustrated, the superego is no longer able to exercise effective control. The anger 'boils over', giving the id momentary license to do as it pleases. Thus the person unleashes a stream of invective and derives pleasure from the expression of these – normally repressed – instinctual drives.

The point is that even though Freud's theory seems rather exotic, it is not all that implausible. For another example of the Freudian theory at work, consider his analysis of humour. In Freud's view, humour is all about evading the censorship of the superego. By misdirecting our conscious mind, then springing the punch line upon us, a joke allows the id to slip one past the superego – so that we experience a sudden burst of pleasure associated with a taboo thought before the conscious mind is able to catch up with it and close down the reaction.

Consider, for example, the world's funniest joke (according to LaughLab.co.uk, which tested over 40,000 jokes, and received upward of 2 million responses):

> *A couple of New Jersey hunters are out in the woods when one of them falls to the ground. He doesn't seem to be breathing, his eyes are rolled back in his head. The other guy whips out his cell phone and calls the emergency services. He gasps to the operator: 'My friend is dead! What can I do?' The operator, in a calm soothing voice, says: Just take it easy. I can help. First, let's make sure he's dead.' There is a silence, then a shot is heard. The guy's voice comes back on the line. He says: 'OK, now what?'*

Why is this funny? According to the Freudian analysis, the reason that we find it entertaining is that we derive instinctual gratification from the act of violence described. But the thought of one hunter shooting his own friend as a source of pleasure to us is forbidden. The joke allows us to experience this pleasure by misdirecting our conscious mind so that the thought is able to momentarily evade censorship.

We initially interpret the phrase 'make sure he's dead' in the sense that is appropriate in the context ('check his pulse'), so it takes us a moment to put together the story after we hear the punch line. When the shot rings out and the hunter says, 'OK, now what?' we have to go back to the phrase 'make sure he's dead' and infer that the hunter has interpreted it in the alternate sense ('make it so that he is dead'). This split second of confusion, while our conscious mind retraces its steps, provides a window of opportunity to experience the pleasure that the id takes from the brutality of the event described (not to mention from the stupidity of the hunter).

Thus, comedy, in Freud's view, is all about sneaking things past the superego. This is why we enjoy laughter. It is also why timing is so important to comedy. It explains why humour often shares with swearing a focus on taboo subjects, or else draws our attention to sources of frustration in daily life (so-called observational humour). Freud's theory, whatever its ultimate merits, is therefore not devoid of explanatory value. Has anyone got a better theory of humour?

If we accept Freud's theory of humour, however, we are effectively granting that his theory of repression also has something to it. We often observe that children can be incredibly cruel. Yet if Freud is right, adults are, at bottom, no different. Socialisation does not stamp out cruelty, it just teaches us to control ourselves. If the underlying impulses were not still there, looking for an opportunity to get out, why would so many people find the thought of a hunter shooting his friend so entertaining?

What makes this theory of repression so troubling, at the level of our analysis of society, is that it treats individual self-control as no different in essence from external coercive control. Both represent limitations on our freedom. Either we are subject to the tyranny of the 'primal father' or we internalise it and become subject to a punitive, censorious superego. Either way, our opportunities for achieving happiness are seriously curtailed. All of the rules and regulations that we are forced to obey in order to get along in society are like an ill-fitting suit that constrains our vital movements.

Of course, the idea that civilisation involves a loss of freedom is as old as the hills. Social-contract thinkers such as Thomas Hobbes and Jean-Jacques Rousseau, for example, regarded entry into society as a sort of compromise, in which we give up some of our freedom in return for other goods, such as security. The peculiar twist that Freud gave to the idea comes from his suggestion that none of these ancient longings are ever lost; they are simply repressed. And as this repression builds, unhappiness and frustration also build.

Thus, Freud claims that 'primitive man was better off in knowing no restrictions of instinct.'[5] The only problem was that, due to the lack of social organisation, life was extremely short. Primitive man therefore entered into society in order to get a guarantee of greater security and a longer life. Yet the 'contract' is, in Freud's view, a Faustian bargain. We are able to achieve greater security in society, but at the expense of giving up not just our freedom, but our *capacity to experience happiness*. So while we may strive to improve society in various ways, we must also recognise that 'there are difficulties attaching to the nature of civilisation which will not yield to any attempt at reform.'[6]

The repressive nature of our society is often overlooked because there appears to have been a gradual decrease in the punitiveness of our social institutions. When we compare modern prisons, for example, with 18th century prisons, it is difficult to avoid the conclusion that our society is less repressive. It is certainly much less violent now than it was three centuries ago. In most hunter-gatherer societies, the number one cause of death is murder. In Europe today, it no longer even registers in the top ten. People are far more likely to kill themselves than they are to be killed by others.

Public violence, in the form of torture and execution, was a staple of European life right through to the middle of the 19th century. Imagine watching someone being burned alive. Or consider what it means to be 'drawn and quartered'. Yet not two hundred years ago, parents used to bring their children to observe such spectacles. The guillotine, when first introduced during the French Revolution, was a symbol of enlightenment and progress. Previously, the executioner would often have to chop away four or five times in order to sever a convict's neck. The guillotine was quite humane by comparison.

Over the years, this sort of overt violence has been systematically purged from our institutions: prison guards are no longer allowed to torture inmates; judges cannot impose corporal punishment; teachers are not permitted to beat their students; political leaders (at least in Europe) are not expected to continually wage war. Furthermore, with the growth of democracy and the decline of tyranny, the role of brute force and violence in public affairs seems to have been seriously diminished.

We often take this decline in overt violence to be the hallmark of civilisation. Muslim countries that follow sharia law, and so cut off the hands of thieves or stone adulterers to death, are routinely denounced as 'barbaric'. Yet from a Freudian perspective, even though civilisation does involve a decrease in overt violence, this does not mean that our society has become less repressive. The violence has not gone away; it has simply become internalised. In a sense, early legal codes had to be extremely violent simply because people were so psychologically uninhibited. Unless they were quite literally terrified of the consequences of certain actions, they could not be kept under control. Modern man, on the other hand, is so guilt-ridden and repressed that public disembowelments are no longer necessary to maintain order; the threat of spending the night in jail is enough to deter most crime.

Thus, the history of civilisation is essentially the history of the gradual internalisation of the repressive apparatus of society. As the social world becomes increasingly complex and increasingly well ordered, it requires increasingly strict self-control on the part of individuals, along with increasingly greater renunciation of our fundamental instinctual desires. This is why we have become a society of wimps and complainers; it is because we are genuinely unhappy. The fact that our external conditions of life have improved immeasurably is irrelevant. Unhappiness is produced by internal, not external, conditions. Because the substitute gratifications that are available simply fail to satisfy our primitive erotic and destructive instincts, modern society demands a greater level of renunciation and repression from the individual than ever before. In the movie *Fight Club*, when Tyler Durden says, 'We're designed to be hunters and we're in a society of shopping. There's nothing to kill anymore, there's nothing to fight, nothing to overcome, nothing to explore. In that social emasculation this everyman is created',[7] we all just nod our heads in agreement. The Freudian analysis has become so commonplace that it no longer even registers with us as a theory.

★

One can see the development of increased self-control and inhibition very clearly in the evolution of table manners. Eating is one of the most basic forms of physical pleasure. As such, it becomes a natural target for social control. Instead of descending upon their meal 'like animals', civilised men and women are expected to eat delicately, to exercise restraint. They are supposed to act, in other words, as though they are not hungry.

Sociologist Norbert Elias has used the history and development of manners as part of an extraordinary study of 'the civilising process'. Little handbooks and guides on how to behave politely have been published in Europe for centuries. By tracking the evolution of rules in these guides, one can see clearly how expectations have been ramped up over the years, and how the need for self-control has increased. Consider, for example, the following bits of advice, offered up during the 13th century: [8]

- Those who like mustard and salt should avoid the filthy habit of putting their fingers into them.
- It is unseemly to blow your nose into the tablecloth.
- Do not spit on or over the table.
- It is bad manners to keep your helmet on when serving the ladies.

There were no rules governing the use of cutlery, because people ate primarily with their hands, with some assistance from knives.

Things were not much different in the 15th century:

- Before you sit down, make sure that your seat has not been fouled.
- Do not touch yourself under your clothes with your bare hands.
- Do not offer anyone a piece of food you have bitten into.

Overall, these instructions give us a pretty good sense of what meals were like at the time. After all, if a particular type of behaviour was not relatively common, there would be no reason to explicitly prohibit it in a book of this type. Yet by the time the 17th century rolled around, these sorts of rules were no longer even mentioned. It was simply taken for granted that people would not blow their noses on the tablecloth or wear armour to dinner. And when issues like slobbering came up, it was usually as an example of what children sometimes do but which no adult would consider.

One can see a similar evolution in the rules governing bodily functions. For example, in the 16th century, people needed to be specifically instructed to use toilets: 'Let no one, whoever he may be, before, at, or after meals, early or late, foul the staircases, corridors or closets with urine or other filth, but go to suitable, prescribed places for such relief.' The rule was obviously not always respected, as an 18th century handbook included the instruction, 'If you pass a person who is relieving himself you should act as if you had not seen him, and so it is impolite to greet him.'

Social norms governing flatulence might serve as a metaphor for the repression that society imposes upon the individual. In the 15th century, when the issue first came up, the primary concern was noise: 'If it can be purged without a noise that is best. But it is better that it be emitted with a noise than that it be held back … If it is possible to withdraw, it should be done alone. But if not, in accordance with the ancient proverb, let a cough hide the sound.' By the 18th century, people no longer subscribed to the view that it is better to let it out than to keep it in: 'It is very impolite to emit wind from your body when in company, either from above or from below, even if it is done without noise; and it is shameful and indecent to do it in a way that can be heard by others.'

One by one, all primary bodily functions were eliminated from polite company. The last one to go was spitting. The older tradition held that spitting on the ground or the floor was permissible, so long as one 'put one's foot on the sputum'. Eventually this was outlawed; people were instructed to spit into their handkerchiefs. By the mid-19th century, even this was frowned upon. According to an 1859 guide, 'spitting is at all times a disgusting habit. I need say nothing more than that – never indulge in it.' Yet even in the early 20th century, many upper-class homes had a spittoon in the foyer, where people could discharge some spit upon coming in from the street.

One can see here how the civilising process seems aimed at denying our bodily nature. In many cases, the norms of politeness become completely antagonistic to the possibility of enjoying oneself or of satisfying one's desires. We tend not to notice this, simply because we are so well socialised that we no longer experience the rules as an imposition. Most children in our society have, by the age of ten, acquired more control over their behaviour, and have internalised more rules, than a full-grown adult would have done five centuries ago. This is the price that we pay for civilisation.

Looking through these old guides to good manners, it is difficult to avoid the impression that we are all incredibly repressed. In our day, advice columnists regularly counsel a woman to eat before going on a dinner date, so that she will be able to nibble delicately on her food at the restaurant and not look like a pig. It's not hard to see how chronic dieting, vegetarianism and bulimia can develop as neurotic extensions of the same structure of psychic repression – as women become increasingly alienated from their own bodily desires and begin to fetishise control for the pure sake of control. Is it such a leap, then, to imagine that our entire society might suffer from a similar type of neurosis?

Again, it was the experience of Nazism that made these sorts of bleak assessments of civilisation seem persuasive. One of the most remarkable things about Nazism is just how *mad* it all was. The fixation on exterminating Jews was so extreme, so obsessive, that it was allowed to compromise the German war effort in numerous ways. Furthermore, the anti-Semitic propaganda drew heavily upon images of pestilence, disease and filth in order to promote the objective of making the country '*Judenrein*'. This, combined with the rather self-evidently anal character of German culture, made it easy to characterise Nazism as a kind of obsessional neurosis.

Many '60s radicals began their careers providing psychoanalytic critiques of fascism. Wilhelm Reich's *The Mass Psychology of Fascism* is perhaps the classic work of this genre. Members of the early Frankfurt School, most prominently Theodor Adorno, spent considerable energy working out a theory of the 'authoritarian personality' disorder, in an attempt to explain the psychological roots of fascism. And, of course, the experience of European fascism provides the background to all of Herbert Marcuse's work, most importantly *Eros and Civilisation*. By the end of the decade, this psychoanalytic interpretation of fascism had become commonplace – Pink Floyd's *The Wall* went on to provide what is perhaps the definitive popularisation. (The 'wall' in question, for those who hadn't noticed, refers to the superego.)

What is noteworthy about all of these Freudian readings of fascism is that they do not treat the movement as an aberration or as a lapse into barbarism. A country like Russia never enjoyed much of a democratic tradition and had always had a slightly ambiguous relationship with the rest of Europe, so it was easy to dismiss Stalin as simply a thug, and communist authoritarianism as a type of primitivism. But Germany was widely regarded as the most culturally sophisticated nation in Europe, not to mention the most rational in temperament. (It was, after all, the nation that gave us both Immanuel Kant and Johann Sebastian Bach.) Thus, many critics refused to treat Nazism as a deviation from the path of the European Enlightenment. In their view, Nazism represented the *natural evolution* of modern society. It may have been crazy, but it was no accident. The particular type of craziness on display among the Nazis was the expression of an inherent contradiction in the nature of civilisation.

In the aftermath of World War II, Nazism was therefore widely regarded as the tragic culmination of Western civilisation. The launch of the nuclear arms race between the United States and the Soviet Union, which followed closely on the war's heels, did nothing but reinforce that impression. The Cold War was understood as a form of sublimated aggression, caused by the level of instinctual renunciation imposed upon us by mass society. Thus, Marcuse claimed that 'concentration camps, mass exterminations, world wars, and atom bombs are no "relapse into barbarism," but the unrepressed implementation of the achievements of modern science, technology and domination."[9]

What is striking about this phrase is the continuity that Marcuse sees between fascist Germany and contemporary Western society. For him, concentration camps and nuclear weapons are simply two different manifestations of precisely the same underlying psychological phenomenon. Humans are innately aggressive. We have a death instinct, a desire to kill. Society forces us to repress this instinct. When this control is successful, the instinct will be effectively sublimated and the superego will retain control of the individual. We can thus see the development of the classic military-industrial complex as a form of substitute gratification. When it fails, we get dictatorship, war and genocide.

So when hippies denounced Western governments as 'fascist pig states', they meant it quite literally. While the comparison between totalitarian states and capitalist democracies might seem like a bit of a stretch, from the Freudian perspective it is easy to see how the two could be points on a continuum. All the institutions of 'freedom' are, according to this analysis, actually just forms of substitute gratification. Most importantly, the material wealth produced by the capitalist economy is regarded as a substitute. The wealth of our society is made possible only through mass production, which requires that workers submit to the tyranny of the assembly line. Mechanical production requires mechanisation of the human body, which in turn requires massive repression of our sexual desires. Thus capitalism requires a 'de-eroticisation' of work, and an army of workers who are alienated from their fundamental sexual nature. As Antonio Gramsci wrote, 'the new type of man demanded by the rationalisation of production and work cannot be developed until the sexual instinct has been suitably regulated and until it too has been rationalised.' The best way to regulate the sexual impulse is through 'repressive sublimation', transforming it into a voracious appetite for substitute gratifications, such as consumer goods.[10]

This explains why, when our society does permit sexual liberation, the essential tie-in to consumer goods must be maintained.

Theodore Roszak argued, in this vein, that *Playboy* magazine was nothing but a treacherous parody of 'freedom, joy, and fulfilment'.[11] By promoting conspicuous consumption, it had become 'an indispensable form of social control under the technocracy.' 'Under the Nazis, however', Roszak said, 'youth camps and party courtesans were used for the same integrative purpose – as were the concentration camps, where the kinkier members of the elite were rewarded by being allowed free exercise of their tastes.'[12] Note the extraordinary moral equivalency here: in Roszak's view, a pool party at Hugh Hefner's mansion and the 'joy division' at Ravensbrück are just variations on the same system of repressive control.

One can see quite clearly the power that the countercultural analysis still exerts in the exceptionally positive (and uncritical) response to the movie *American Beauty*.[13] The film is, in essence, a completely uncompromising recitation of '60s countercultural ideology. It's the hippies versus the fascists, still slugging it out three decades after Woodstock. Yet despite the occasional reviewer who happened to notice just how tired the central ideas were, the film went on to take the world by storm, winning Oscars for Best Picture, Best Director and Best Screenplay, along with Best Actor in a Leading Role for Kevin Spacey (not to mention Best Foreign Film at festivals throughout the world).

The characters in *American Beauty* are essentially divided into two groups. There are the countercultural rebels: the narrator, Lester Burnham; his daughter, Jane; and the neighbour kid, Ricky Fitts. You can tell that they are the good guys because they all smoke dope, behave in nonconformist ways (and are thus ostracised by the community) and have a deep appreciation of the 'beauty' that surrounds them. The fascists are also easy to identify: there is Lester's wife, Carolyn; Ricky's father, Colonel Frank Fitts; and the 'King of Real Estate', Buddy Kane. You can tell they're fascists because they are all neurotic, sexually repressed, obsessed with what others think of them, and they like to play with handguns. Just to drive the point home, Colonel Fitts is shown beating his son while screaming about his need for structure and discipline. (And in case anyone still doesn't get it, he also collects Nazi memorabilia.)

The movie opens with a shot of Lester masturbating in the shower, an event that, his voice-over explains, will be the high point of his day. The scene cuts directly to his wife, who is pruning shrubs in their impeccably manicured suburban yard. Lester draws our attention to the way her gardening clogs match the handle on her pruning shears – not by accident. Okay, we get the point. There may be a connection between Lester's repressed sexuality and his suburban lifestyle. Fifteen years in the telemarketing industry have left him incapable of experiencing pleasure. He has accepted the compromise at the heart of our civilisation. Both his wife and daughter think he's a gigantic loser. He admits that they're right, that he has lost something. He hadn't always felt so 'sedated'.

The turning point comes when his boss forces him to write up a job description in order to facilitate an impending downsizing. Lester begins to awaken. He asks Carolyn whether she doesn't find this demand 'kinda fascist'. His wife – the cautious and subdued conformist – agrees, yet cautions him against rocking the boat. Lester ignores her advice and writes up a job description that says he spends most of his day masking his contempt for the assholes in charge and retiring to the men's room to jerk off while fantasising about a life that less closely resembles Hell.

His liberation becomes more complete, however, when he meets the neighbour kid Ricky Fitts, who is also, it turns out, a sophisticated dope dealer. Fitts soon offers him some of his best marijuana, called G-143. (It is, he claims, genetically engineered by the United States Government. Note the classic '60s paranoia – why would the American Government want to genetically engineer marijuana?) Fitts assures him that it's all he ever smokes.

At this point, Lester stages a complete juvenile regression. He becomes the walking, talking id. He blurts out all the things that we are constantly thinking but never have the courage to say. (When his new fitness coach asks him whether he wants to increase his strength or develop his flexibility, he tells him that he wants to look good

naked. When his teenaged daughter's best friend catches him looking at her strangely and asks him what he wants, he looks her in the
eye and says he wants her.) He quits his job, buys a 1970 Firebird and
starts flipping burgers at Mr Smiley's in an attempt to rediscover his
youth. His wife's questions about how he intends to make mortgage
payments are dismissed as just more evidence of her alienated existence. Lester strives to free her from this compulsive conformity. At
one point, it appears that he may succeed, as she begins to welcome
his sexual advances. Yet the moment is lost when she stops him to
prevent beer being spilled on the sofa. He tells her not to worry about
the 'couch'. Agitated, she points out that it is not just a 'couch' but a
$4000 sofa upholstered in Italian silk. Lester yells back even louder,
'It's just a couch!'

The link between consumerism and sexual renunciation is one
of the most constant themes of the movie. Like Lester masturbating
in the shower, Carolyn is incapable of true sexual gratification as long
as she insists on conforming to society's expectations. She begins an
affair with Kane, the 'King of Real Estate' (whose mantra – In order
to be successful, one must project an image of success at all times
– she repeats to herself again and again to stave off what appears to
be an impending nervous breakdown). The affair is driven primarily
by her desire for professional advancement, and their sex is portrayed
in a comical and unflattering light (she sticks her legs in the air and
screams out, 'Fuck me, your Majesty').

All of the fascists make some effort to bring Lester back into
line. Yet when this fails, 'the violence inherent in the system' naturally
begins to reveal itself. Handguns start to appear in the possession of
all three members of the axis. Both Carolyn and Colonel Fitts are
struggling to retain control of their deepest instinctual desires, and
are being driven half mad by the effort that is required. The sight of
Lester's liberation is intolerable to them; it threatens them with a loss
of control. The question therefore becomes not whether one of them
will kill Lester, but rather which one of them will do it.

From the opening minutes of the movie, a great deal is made
of Colonel Fitt's homophobia. He terrorises his wife, beats his son
and hates fags. He also has a crew cut. 'I wonder where all that rage

comes from?' we ask ourselves. 'Why is he such a control freak?' Of course, anyone who doesn't know the answer would have to have been living on a different planet for the past thirty years. It's because he's a repressed homosexual! Thus, in one of the most hackneyed cinematic 'climaxes' in recent memory, Colonel Fitts makes advances on Lester, thinking that he is gay. When Lester disappoints him, the Colonel has no choice but to come back and shoot him. Lester dies, however, with a beatific smile on his face. Even though he has been murdered, what matters is that he has died happily, having succeeded in liberating his 'inner child'.

One of the interesting things about this movie, as opposed to more compromising fare like *Pleasantville*, is that it hangs on to the essential bleakness of the original Freudian vision. In the view of the world articulated by *American Beauty*, it is simply not possible to be a well-adjusted adult in our society. At the age of thirty, one faces a stark choice. One can maintain one's adolescent rebelliousness (smoking pot, hanging out, ignoring all responsibility, not to mention all moral constraint) and remain free. The alternative is to 'sell out', to play by the rules, and thereby to become a neurotic, superficial conformist, incapable of experiencing true pleasure. There is no middle road.

Pleasantville at least accepts that the hippie critique of mass society may not have been entirely correct. The two kids from the present inject the staid '50s suburb with a new vibrancy and colour. Yet in order to 'change colour' themselves, they must both learn a few lessons in 'old-fashioned' virtue. Jennifer must learn to stop being a 'slut' and to appreciate great literature. She changes colour by spending evenings at home reading D. H. Lawrence. David must learn to stop being a wimp and to stand up for himself as a man. He changes colour after punching a group of rednecks who were tormenting his mother. The message is clear: while the freedom achieved through the sexual revolution is important, our society may have become too permissive. There were important virtues to be found in the older social structures. D. H. Lawrence was not just a repressed pornographer who is obsolete now that we have access to the real thing. And David learns that love does not conquer all – sometimes it is necessary to fight for what we believe in. Thus *Pleasantville* is at least open to the idea that the counterculture may not have been right about every-thing. *American Beauty*, by contrast, is completely unreconstructed countercultural ideology. It buys the whole critique, hook, line and sinker. And so, it would appear, did audiences throughout the world.

It should be clear by now just how modest the Marxian critique of society was when compared with the countercultural critique. Fun-damentally, what bothered Marx about capitalism was simply that the people who did all the work were desperately poor while the wealthy sat around and contributed nothing. He was concerned, in other words, about exploitation. This exploitation was produced, he thought, by the prevailing set of economic institutions, in particu-lar by the system of private property. It could therefore be corrected simply by eliminating, or rather reforming, these specific institutions. So the communist movement had fairly clear political objectives – to abolish private property and establish common ownership of the means of production.

The countercultural critique, on the other hand, is so vast and all-encompassing that it is difficult to imagine what could possibly count as 'fixing things'. What limits our freedom, according to this view, is not some specific set of institutions, but rather the existence of institutions in general. This is why the entire culture must be rejected. The '60s icon Abbie Hoffman contemptuously dismissed 'political revolution' on the grounds that politics merely 'breeds organisers'. Cultural revolution, on the other hand, 'creates outlaws'.[14] This cer-tainly makes cultural revolution sound more exciting. But we must keep in mind that the goal of all this is not to provide entertainment for intellectuals, it is to effect some kind of an improvement in society. Being an outlaw is in many ways parasitic upon the existence of an organised society. What if everyone became an outlaw? What does a society with no institutions, no rules and no regulations look like?

Countercultural theorists have traditionally been quite evasive when it comes to answering this question. The standard dodge was to say that there is 'no blueprint for a free society', or that because freeing ourselves from the culture requires completely transforming our consciousness, we are unable to predict what the future society will look like. Michel Foucault was the master of such evasions. Another option was simply to romanticise rebellion and resistance for their own sakes. Resistance to mainstream society was often seen as therapeutic for the individual, and promoted on those grounds. The goal of improving conditions in society at large, or of promoting social justice, receded from view. In this way, the concern for social justice became redirected and absorbed into an increasingly narcissistic preoccupation with personal spiritual growth and well-being.

Yet there were some countercultural theorists who managed to keep their eye on the ball and who made an honest effort to explain what an emancipated society would look like. Marcuse is the most important of these. He realised that the core obstacle to the development of a coherent countercultural project lay in Freud's instinct theory. As long as the id was divided between positive and negative instincts (love and death, eros and thanatos), then there would be no way to avoid Freud's pessimistic conclusion. There would be no avoiding the repression that one finds in civilisation, simply because the only way out would be a return to violent barbarism. Genuine emancipation would be possible only if one could find a way to give eros the upper hand in the battle for control of the id.

Naturally, anyone influenced by a particular type of vague Christian spiritualism could easily be led to believe that the powers of love were great enough to conquer all. Certainly, if love could rule the id and drive out our aggressive and destructive urges, then there would be no reason for superego repression, and thus no reason for social control of any form. We would be free to 'let love rule'. Yet Marcuse was wise enough to realise that Christians had been working the 'love your neighbour' angle for two thousand years without much success at creating a utopian society. And, as people soon learned, you can't even organise a commune, much less an entire society, based upon the assumption that people will behave like saints.

What Marcuse proposed instead was an influential hybrid of Marx and Freud. He argued that the level of instinctual renunciation required throughout the history of civilisation is due not to the inherent strength of the destructive impulses of the id, and thus the requirement that they be kept under control, so much as to the burdens placed upon us by the prevailing conditions of material scarcity. In other words, it is the 'curse of Adam' – the requirement that man must provide for himself by the sweat of his own brow – that makes our society so repressive. With increased automation and factory production, however, we are at the point of lifting this curse. Under 'post scarcity' conditions, machines will do all of the work and people will be left free to laugh, play, love and create.

Thus Marcuse succeeded in hooking the critique of counter-culture into the same type of political analysis that had motivated traditional Marxism. Marx himself, after all, believed that capitalism would lay the groundwork for a future communist society by eliminating scarcity, leaving the worker free 'to hunt in the morning, fish in the afternoon, rear cattle in the evening, criticise after dinner.'[15] In Marcuse's vision, not only would this eliminate class conflict, it would also eliminate the repressive superego. Work would become like artistic production, unleashing the creativity of each individual. Society would no longer have to compel individuals to conform to the 'one-dimensional' model of human life, and all of the rules and regulations that dominate our daily life would melt away.

In the Marxian analysis, what prevents the emergence of this utopia is the class interests of the capitalists. Although capitalism was initially a force for innovation and change, eventually the class relations become 'fetters' on the development of productive technology. After all, once the factories are fully automated, what grounds could there be for keeping them in private hands? What does the capitalist contribute? He isn't even producing any jobs. So why not nationalise the factories and let the people enjoy the benefits they produce?

In this way, the Freudian critique of society was wedded to the Marxian analysis of class. Marx was concerned primarily with the exploitation of the working class; Freud was concerned with repression in the entire population. Out of the synthesis of the two, a new concept was born: oppression. An oppressed group is like a class, in that it exists in an asymmetric power relationship with other groups in society. But it is unlike a class in that the power relationship is exercised not through an anonymous institutional mechanism (such as the system of property rights), but rather through a form of psychological domination. Members of oppressed groups are repressed, in other words, by virtue of their membership in a dominated group. Who are the oppressed? Primarily women, blacks and homosexuals.

The 'politics of oppression' bears some resemblance to the 'politics of exploitation'. The difference, however, is that it considers the roots of the injustice to be psychological, not social. Thus, the first imperative is not to change specific institutions, but rather to transform the consciousness of the oppressed. (Hence the enormous popularity of 'consciousness-raising' groups in the early feminist movement.) Politics begins to resemble a twelve-step programme. The old-fashioned concern with wealth and poverty is now characterised as 'superficial'. Roszak, for example, argues that with the development of the counterculture, 'revolution will be primarily therapeutic in character and not merely institutional.'[16] What an extraordinary phrase: *merely* institutional!

This sort of talk was widespread. Charles Reich, in *The Greening of America*, writes, 'The revolution must be cultural. For culture controls the economic and political machine, not vice versa. The machinery turns out what it pleases and forces people to buy. But if the culture changes, the machine has no choice but to comply.'[17] No one found it exceptionable at all when the Beatles, in 'Revolution', claimed that instead of changing the 'constitution', or any other such 'institution', it would be better to 'free your mind instead'.

One can see here an implicit picture of how society works, with a relationship of hierarchical dependence between social institutions, the culture and, finally, individual psychology. The latter two are thought to determine the first. So if you want to change the economy, you need to change the culture, and if you want to change the culture, fundamentally you have to change people's consciousness. This led to two fateful conclusions. First, it suggested that cultural politics was more fundamental than the traditional politics of distributive justice. Any act of nonconformity was thought to have important political consequences, even if it appeared to have nothing to do with anything that would be considered 'political' or 'economic' in the traditional sense of the term. Second, and even more unhelpful, was the suggestion that changing one's own consciousness was more important than changing the culture (much less the political or economic system). Nowadays, this preoccupation with individual consciousness usually takes the form of self-help. But in the '60s, the primary consequence was a massive diversion of utopian energies into the drug culture. It seems hard to believe now, but many people at the time actually thought that widespread use of marijuana and LSD would solve all of society's problems: that it could affect geopolitics, eliminate war, cure poverty and create a world of 'peace, love and understanding'. Many of Timothy Leary's experiments were aimed at 'expanding consciousness' by undoing the effects of socialisation, scrambling the 'imprints' that individuals received when they were young. Yet it wasn't just self-styled gurus like Leary who bought into these ideas. Even a critical observer like Roszak was tempted by the following argument: 'The "psychedelic revolution" then comes down to the simple syllogism: change the prevailing mode of consciousness and you change the world; the use of dope *ex opera operato* changes the prevailing mode of consciousness; therefore, universalise the use of dope and you change the world.'[18]

The idea that taking drugs might be revolutionary was of course reinforced by the existence of punitive drug laws. Countercultural revolutionaries saw an obvious logic to it all. Alcohol, which dulls and subdues the senses, is perfectly legal. It's like soma, used to placate the working classes. As long as daddy gets his scotch after work, he can tolerate another day in his suburban hell. But marijuana and LSD, rather than dulling the senses, help to free the mind. Thus they cannot be tolerated by 'the system'. These drugs encourage nonconformity, and therefore pose too great a threat to the established order. That's why The Man sends round the fuzz to bust your stash. Or, later, it's why Ronald Reagan felt the need to declare a 'war on drugs'.

And, of course, when repression fails there is always co-optation. Thus, pharmaceutical companies get in on the act, selling sanitised versions of the same drugs but without the subversive, mind-expanding properties. So you get poppers and bennies, and soon you're in the Valley of the Dolls, another 'treacherous parody of freedom and fulfilment'. (To this day, people continue to describe the transformation of the United States into a 'Prozac nation' as though it were a perversion or co-optation of the counterculture, as opposed to merely the logical extension of it.)

Underlying the countercultural analysis of the drug laws there was, of course, a preposterous interpretation of the effects of all these substances, alcohol included. The idea that marijuana liberates the mind is something that only someone who is stoned could believe. Anyone who isn't knows that marijuana users are about the most boring people on earth to talk to. Furthermore, the idea that alcohol is somehow less subversive than narcotics or psychedelics reveals a woeful ignorance of the history of alcohol. The claims that were made about LSD in the '60s are almost identical to the ones made for absinthe in the second half of the 19th century. It is precisely because of its disruptive, antisocial effects that major efforts were made to ban alcohol in the United States during Prohibition. It's also why pubs were once forced to close in the afternoon – to prevent workers from getting loaded up during their afternoon break. Yet during this time, no progressive group was foolish enough to think that alcohol represented a positive force in society, or that it was good for people. Communists and anarchists didn't go around encouraging alcoholism among workers. They could see that creating a more just society would require more, not less, cooperative effort on the part of the broader public. And alcohol certainly didn't encourage that. The hippies, unfortunately, had to learn this the hard way.

The countercultural movement has, from the beginning, been beset by chronic anxiety. The idea that all politics is based on culture, and that all social injustice is based upon repressive conformity, implies that any act that violates conventional social norms is politically radical. Of course, this is an extremely attractive thought. After all, the traditional work of political organising is extremely demanding and tedious. Politics, in a democracy, necessarily requires bringing enormous numbers of people on board. This creates a lot of unappealing work – licking envelopes, writing letters, lobbying politicians, and the like. Assembling such vast coalitions also requires interminable compromise and debate. Cultural politics, by contrast, is significantly more fun. Doing guerrilla theatre, playing in a band, making avant-garde art, taking drugs and having lots of wild sex certainly beat union organisation as a way to spend the weekend. What the countercultural rebels managed to convince themselves of is that all of these fun activities were in fact more subversive than traditional left-wing politics because they attacked the sources of oppression and injustice at a 'deeper' level. Of course, this conviction is based entirely upon a theory. And since it is so obviously in the *interest* of the rebels to believe in this theory, anyone with a moderately critical turn of mind will naturally find it suspicious.

The countercultural rebels have therefore invested tremendous energy over the years trying to persuade themselves that their acts of cultural resistance have important political implications. It is not an accident that Lester, in *American Beauty*, must be killed. This is intended to reaffirm the conviction that his behaviour is such a profound threat to the established order that it must be suppressed at any cost. The death of the rebel protagonist is in fact a staple of '60s cinema. From *Bonnie and Clyde* to *Easy Rider*, the dissidents ultimately have to be put down. In *Easy Rider*, for example, the two cocaine-smuggling hippies (Peter Fonda and Dennis Hopper) are ultimately killed by southern rednecks as they drive through Louisiana. The implied parallel between the hippie counterculture and the civil rights movement is intentional. After all, whom do southern rednecks like to go around killing? Easy rider, freedom rider – same difference. It's all about freedom. And the kind of freedom represented by the two bikers – the drugs, the long hair, the choppers on an open road – is intolerable to the status quo. It's only a matter of time before 'the violence inherent in the system' is revealed. Once again, southern rednecks act as the agents of control.

The attempt to draw the same parallels in *Pleasantville* is notable more for its desperation. The transformation of the community begins when Jennifer, the 'slut' from the future, starts having sex with some of the guys in the high school. Soon all the kids are doing it. The newfound sexual freedom spreads like a virus. (Jennifer, who remains mysteriously black and white, complains that the other kids only have to spend an hour in the back seat of a car and 'all of a sudden they're in Technicolor'.) No one gets pregnant, and no one catches any diseases. Yet the good townsfolk still find it intolerable. The mere thought that others might be enjoying themselves, experiencing pleasure, escaping from the dull, drab conformity, is intolerable. So the Chamber of Commerce holds a meeting to put a stop to it all (organised under a gigantic banner with not-so-subtle fascist insignia). Soon local businesses are hanging 'no colours' signs in the windows, and rednecks are roaming the streets, harassing 'colours' and burning books.

Through the magic of cinema, a bunch of white teenagers having sex becomes equivalent to both the civil rights movement and the struggle against fascism. What's more, the kids don't even have to do anything unpleasant or make any sacrifices in order to achieve this effect. Having fun is the ultimate subversive act. This is an incredibly consistent theme in the popular culture – from the final dance sequence in *Footloose* to the infamous rave scene in *The Matrix Reloaded* – and yet it is so obviously wishful thinking. The Beastie Boys called everyone's bluff a long time ago, when they recorded a 'protest' song with the anthemic title 'You Gotta Fight for Your Right (to Party)'. In the end, this is what most countercultural rebellion comes down to.

Notes

1   Sigmund Freud, *Civilization and Its Discontents*, trans. Joan Riviere, rev. James Strachey (London: Hogarth, 1975), 58.
2   *Ibid.*, 16.
3   *Ibid.*, 34.
4   *Ibid.*, 42.
5   *Ibid.*, 62.
6   *Ibid.*, 62.

7   Internet Movie Database, http://www.imdb.com/title/ tt0137523/.

8   Norbert Elias, *The Civilizing Process*, trans. Edmund Jephcott (Oxford: Blackwell Publishers, 1994), 110–13.

9   Herbert Marcuse, *Eros and Civilization: A Philosophical Inquiry into Freud* (Boston: Beacon, 1966), 4.

10 Antonio Gramsci, *Selections from the Prison Notebooks*, ed. and trans. Quintin Hoare and Geoffrey Nowell Smith (New York: International Publishers, 1971), 297.

11 Roszak, *Making of a Counter Culture*, 15.

12 *Ibid.*, 18–19.

13 All references to *American Beauty* are from Alan Ball and Sam Mendes, *American Beauty: The Shooting Script* (New York: Newmarket, 1999).

14 Abbie Hoffman, 'Foreplay', in *The Portable '60's Reader*, ed. Ann Charter (New York: Penguin, 2003), 259.

15 Karl Marx, 'The German Ideology,' in *The Marx–Engels Reader*, ed. Robert C. Tucker (New York: Norton, 1975), 160.

16 Roszak, *Making of a Counter Culture*, 97.

17 Charles Reich, *The Greening of America*, (New York: Bantam, 1978), 329.

18 Roszak, *Making of a Counter Culture*, 168.

Being normal

The idea of a counterculture is ultimately based on a mistake. At best, countercultural rebellion is pseudo-rebellion: a set of dramatic gestures that are devoid of any progressive political or economic consequences and that detract from the urgent task of building a more just society. In other words, it is rebellion that provides entertainment for the rebels, and nothing much else. At worst, countercultural rebellion actively promotes unhappiness, by undermining or discrediting social norms and institutions that actually serve a valuable function. In particular, the idea of counterculture has produced a level of contempt for democratic politics that has consistently handicapped the progressive left (not least, by refusing to acknowledge the distinction between compromising and 'selling out').

In order to see where it all went wrong, one need look no further than the controversy that erupted over an enormously popular little dating manual called *The Rules*. Published in 1996 by Ellen Fein and Sherrie Schneider, the book was noted primarily for the retrograde character of much of the advice it offered. Women were instructed to play hard to get, to insist that the man pay for dinner, to avoid casual sex and to never, ever tell a man what to do. Feminists responded with outrage. 'I fought in the trenches for years so that my daughter wouldn't have to grow up in the same repressive, sexist culture that I had to deal with', they said. 'And this is how she repays me? By *voluntarily* adopting the same backward rules that we fought so desperately to overcome?'

Yet with all the furore that accompanied this episode, the central lesson was missed. What the popularity of *The Rules* shows is that *bad rules are better than no rules*. Feminists were quite right to fight tooth and nail against the old rules that used to govern relations between the sexes. Those rules were based upon the assumption that the man would go on to become the breadwinner, the woman a housewife. As a result, these rules actively contributed to the reproduction of that pattern. But instead of trying to replace these rules with better ones – ones that would have put men and women on an equal footing – too many early feminists bought into the myth of counterculture. They assumed that the very existence of rules was a symptom of the oppression of women. In order for men and women to be equal, therefore, they concluded that it would be necessary to *abolish* the rules, not reform them. 'Free love' was proposed as a substitute for 'going steady'. Love was like a beautiful flower, they claimed, which should be left free to unfold in its own natural way, without the artificial constraints of social convention.

Thus the sexual revolution had the effect of destroying all of the traditional social norms that had governed relations between the sexes, without replacing them with any new ones. What it left was a complete void. As a result, my generation, which came of age in the late '70s, was forced to invent for itself some way of dealing with all the tricky problems of adolescence. The result was not liberation, it was hell. The absence of settled rules meant that no one knew what to expect from anyone else. For a bunch of adolescents, this was deeply anxiety-provoking. We never knew where we stood with one another, or what we were supposed to do next. Anything that resembled 'dating' was deeply uncool and therefore out of the question. So you couldn't ask a girl out. You could try to bump into her at a party, maybe hang out, get wasted and then have sex. 'Going out' was something that began only afterward, and even then it was always accompanied by ironic scare quotes.

Against this background, it is hardly surprising that so many young women reached out for *The Rules*. Many feminists had already noticed, early on, that 'free love' had opened the door to the sexual exploitation of women in our society on a massive scale. The initial feminist assumption had been that because men were the oppressors, all of the rules governing relations between the sexes had to have been rigged to the man's advantage. The fact that many of these rules were obviously for the defence of women, designed to protect them from men, somehow escaped notice. Camille Paglia caused a furore in the '80s when she pointed out that many of these fussy old social conventions actually had the rather important function of reducing the risk of rape. Similarly, the old 'shotgun wedding' rule forced men to take some responsibility for the children they fathered. The erosion of this norm has been one of the main factors contributing to the widespread feminisation of poverty in the Western world.

In fact, if you were to ask a group of men to think up their ideal set of dating rules, they would probably choose something very much like the 'free love' arrangement that emerged out of the sexual revolution. You only have to tour a gay bathhouse to see how men choose to organise their sex lives when they don't have to cater to feminine sensibilities. Yet these possibilities were all ignored, primarily due to the power of the countercultural analysis: women are an oppressed group, it was argued, and social norms are the mechanism of oppression. Therefore the solution is to abolish all the rules. Freedom for women thus becomes equated with freedom from social norms.

In the end, this was a disastrous equation. Not only did it set up a completely unobtainable state as the ideal of liberation, but it created a tendency to dismiss as 'co-optation' or 'selling out' any acceptance of reforms that might actually lead to tangible improvements in women's lives. How could we have gone so far astray?

The countercultural analysis that comes out of the '60s takes as its point of departure an extremely important question: Why do we need rules? Long ago, Jean-Jacques Rousseau observed that 'man is born free, yet everywhere he is in chains'.[1] The 'chains' he referred to were not just the laws of the state, but also the informal social norms and conventions that govern every minute of our waking lives. Whether it's walking down the street, riding the bus or having a conversation at the water-cooler, our social interactions are all highly structured. There is a very rigid formula that specifies what you can and cannot do in such situations: what topics can be discussed, what movements are considered appropriate, what gestures are expected. Much of the observational humour in *Seinfeld* consisted of drawing our attention to these little rules: how we strive to avoid being a 'close talker', a 'double-dipper' or a 're-gifter'.

Why are our lives so structured? Why can't we all be free simply to do as we choose?

Rousseau himself never doubted that we were in need of *some* rules. His only question was how these rules could and should be rendered 'legitimate'. In a sense he took the rules for granted and merely set out to justify them (and to reform them in cases where such justification was found wanting). But the countercultural analysis throws the very existence of the rules into question. Countercultural rebels began to suggest that *nothing* justifies the rules. Rules may be nothing other than a structure of repression. Thus, in the '60s, Rousseau's question began to be posed in a far more radical way: Why do we need rules at all?

It is no accident that the United States served, throughout the 20th century, as the driving force of countercultural thinking. While European intellectuals were constantly trying to graft countercultural criticism onto older theoretical traditions – Marxism in particular – Americans were far more likely to treat the countercultural idea as a self-standing political programme. This is due, in part, to the fact that the hippie counterculture shared many of the individualistic and libertarian ideas that have always made neoliberalism and free-market ideology such a powerful force on the right wing of the American political spectrum. This individualism has profound roots. One can find countercultural ideas clearly prefigured in the work of mid-19th century thinkers like Ralph Waldo Emerson and Henry Thoreau. Both Emerson and Thoreau were members of a group known as the New England transcendentalists, whose members shared a common faith in the essential goodness of nature, combined with a widespread dissatisfaction over the values of their civilisation. They were romantic individualists who valued self-reliance and were possessed of a grand contempt for mass society. As Thoreau, who is best known for spending two years 'roughing it' in a cabin on Walden Pond (his mother actually brought him regular meals and did his washing), famously wrote, 'The mass of men lead lives of quiet desperation.'[2]

Emerson, the acknowledged leader of the group, was exasperated by a society that preached 'democracy' but in fact demanded conformity to depersonalising custom and habit. His famous dictum that 'a foolish consistency is the hobgoblin of little minds'[3] is frequently cited as a celebration of irrationality, but that misses the point. Emerson ridiculed society as 'a joint stock company in which the members agree for the better securing of his bread to each shareholder, to surrender the liberty and culture of the eater. The virtue in most requests is conformity. Self reliance is its aversion.'[4] As he saw it, the demand that people be consistent in their habits and beliefs was simply a way of using the past to exercise tyranny over the present. Self-reliance is the only response, and 'whoso would be a man must be a non-conformist'.

This sort of romantic individualism can easily be given either a right-wing or a left-wing spin. The basic right-wing argument takes this individualism and uses it to attack 'interventions' by government in daily life. This is founded upon the view that individuals, when left to their own devices, are able to achieve better outcomes than those that would be obtained when imposed in a top-down manner. Society is naturally self-organising. Government is an artificial imposition, invented by those who have an interest in domination and control. (One can find the clearest expression of this view in the theory of 'spontaneous order' developed by Friedrich von Hayek.)[5]

It is not far from the idea that we do not need government to the idea that we do not need any rules at all. This argument was developed most forcefully in the work of Ayn Rand. In Rand's view, the invisible hand of the market reconciles self-interest with the common good, and so eliminates the need for any rules or restrictions on the individual. There is no need for government, and no need for self-restraint. Even the restrictions of everyday morality are portrayed by Rand as yet another system of repressive limitations on individual freedom. Altruism, in Rand's view, is a conspiracy perpetrated by the weak upon the strong, an attempt to handicap those whose natural superiority makes them a threat. The heroes of Rand's novels are all surrounded by scheming parasites – men of compromise and compassion – trying to drag them down to their level. Yet the heroes eventually triumph, achieving the Nietzschean ideal of transcendence, or going 'beyond good and evil'. This ultimate freedom from morality is one that Rand takes very seriously. Her male protagonists in *The Fountainhead* and *Atlas Shrugged* both commit acts that we ordinary mortals would describe as 'rape'. Yet for Rand, such standards do not apply – the whole concept of 'rape' is, for her, simply a rule concocted by the weak, designed to fetter the powerful sexual drive of the free individual.

One need only compare the rape scenes in Rand's novels to Lester's seduction of his daughter's high school friend in *American Beauty* to see the parallels that exist between right-wing libertarian ideology and left-wing countercultural theory. In both cases, deeply exploitative sexual acts are rationalised on the grounds that they are a part of the protagonist's emancipation from the socially imposed repression of his sexuality.

The key difference between left-wing and right-wing individualism concerns the status of private property. In the right-wing view, it is market exchange that creates mutual benefit, and thus supplies the incentives necessary for harmonious cooperation. The left-wing countercultural theorists took things one step further. They claimed that you could have 'spontaneous order' even without the invisible hand of the market, without any property rights to speak of. Property rights, they reasoned, are necessary only among people who are unwilling to share. If we transform people's consciousness, in order to free them from the narrow 'possessive individualism' imposed by the capitalist system, then the need for even the minimal constraints of property will be removed. When the Beatles sang 'All you need is love', many people took it quite literally.

A serious proposal for the establishment of a global community based on love can be found in Duane Elgin's extremely influential book *Voluntary Simplicity*.[6] Elgin suggests that there are three legitimate contenders for the foundation of a cohesive global order: force, law and love. Force could be effective (assuming that nuclear holocaust is avoided), except that the lasting peace could be obtained only through the construction of a monolithic military-political hegemony on a planetary scale. Order would be based entirely upon a psychology of fear. The result would be a system wholly at odds with the needs of the human spirit for freedom and creativity. Given the massive armaments that would be required to make any threat credible, Elgin claims, the result would be, for the living, barely more than 'only not dying'.

A global order founded on law, in Elgin's view, would not be much different. Humanity could establish a set of global rules of conduct that could allow peaceful interaction between nations and humans, with minimal coercion and maximum freedom, to be administered through something like the United Nations. Yet even a peaceful legal order would require a massive bureaucratic foundation, equally serving to dampen the 'vitality, vigour, and creativity of civilisational growth'. Therefore, the only possible foundation of a global community consistent with personal freedom and creativity is love or compassion. As a practical basis for human relations, love has a number of advantages. It is non-coercive, and thus tends to 'touch the world more lightly and gently'. This will temper the violence done by the limited bureaucracy that will still be necessary, and permit the emergence of a global family.

Elgin's thinking reveals quite clearly the close connection that has always existed between countercultural politics and political anarchism. Throughout the Cold War, most American radicals found communism and capitalism equally unpalatable. Unlike European thinkers, American radicals were more likely to see that communism had simply substituted the tyranny of the state for the tyranny of the market. Furthermore, with no domestic communist or even socialist party making a play for their allegiance, there was little to block a move toward anarchism. By denouncing the two great evils of the day – the market and the state – anarchism seemed to be at least innocent of the accusation of worshipping false gods. Of course, traditional anarchism was concerned only with coercive authority structures – the power of the state, in essence. But it was not difficult to generalise this opposition and blend it with the countercultural opposition to any form of rule or regulation. The ubiquitous '60s slogan 'Question authority' demonstrates how the two preoccupations could become almost imperceptibly fused.

Thus, despite variations in the formula, anarchism has always formed the core of countercultural politics. It was thematised more explicitly in the punk subculture, with bands like Crass and Black Flag directly campaigning under the anarchist banner. But anarchism did not start with the Sex Pistols. If anything, the Sex Pistols simply took anarchist ideas that were pervasive in the hippie subculture and gave them a more negative spin (and thereby tapped into an enormous pool of frustration over the failure of the '60s countercultural project to yield tangible results). Since the efforts to build a new society based upon free love and communes had proved to be such an ignominious failure, the Sex Pistols suggested that it might be more useful to focus on destroying the old society. In a sense, their efforts simply accentuated the failure of the countercultural movement to produce a coherent vision of a free society.

The basic goal of anarchism is to eliminate coercion from society. Initially this may not seem entirely far-fetched. After all, why is coercion needed in the first place? The only time that coercion is ever justified is when it is required in order to prevent people from inflicting greater harm upon others. Thus coercion is only necessary because of prior injustice. Simply put, bad people try to hurt others, and society has to prevent them from doing so. Yet what motivates these bad people? Usually it is that they themselves have suffered from coercion or injustice. They steal because they are poor. They attack because they have been attacked. Perhaps it is all just a vicious circle. So instead of punishing these people and perpetuating the cycle, we might be better off addressing the 'root causes' of their anger. Through better education – more effective socialisation – and the elimination of social injustice, it should be possible to remove the need for state coercion later on.

So what is wrong with this idea? The standard 'realist' response is simply to denigrate the plan as 'pie in the sky', pure utopian fantasy. 'Out of the crooked timber of humanity', as Immanuel Kant said, 'nothing straight was ever made'.[7] There will always be bad people, doing bad things. Countercultural theorists, according to this view, deny the reality of 'evil'. They are all just bleeding hearts and social workers. Show them a depraved criminal and they will explain it all away as the effects of a bad childhood. They are too weak to face up to the hard truth: that some people are just born bad and need to be controlled or put down. (One can see a remarkable dialogue between these two perspectives in the way that Oliver Stone – still the countercultural ideologue – tried to rework Quentin Tarantino's script for *Natural Born Killers*.)

This is why, to this day, Republicans in the United States go to almost comical lengths to denounce the enemies of America as 'evil'. In their minds, they are striking a rhetorical blow against the counterculture, which they believe denies the reality of evil. (As usual, American politics is dominated by the compulsion to refight the battles of the '60s.) What conservatives fail to observe is that this rhetoric directly feeds the countercultural idea that they are so desperate to oppose. 'We need to get tough', the conservatives claim. 'We need to use force, because our enemies are evil.' What they tacitly admit, thereby, is that if their enemies *weren't* evil, then there would be no need for the use of force. This sets things up for the argument that the enemies in question are not actually evil, they're just misunderstood. And so there is no need for coercion! Thus the conservative backlash feeds the countercultural ideas whose conclusions it tries so hard to oppose.

What both sides in this debate fail to consider is that coercion may be necessary even in the absence of evil. Perfectly free and equal individuals often have an incentive to adopt coercively enforced rules of conduct to govern their interactions. So the existence of coercion in society is not always a sign of domination, of the need to control evil or of one group imposing its will upon another. Often everyone is better off when everyone is governed by a set of enforced rules. Indeed, when left to do as they please, people will tend to generate their own rules and create a new social order, complete with its own system of punishment and reward. They do so because these types of systems are in their interest, both as individuals and as a group.

This is the lesson that should have been learned from the commune experiments of the '60s. Nearly every one of these communes was founded with the goal of creating a harmonious living space based upon mutual sharing and cooperation. Naturally, it was assumed that with everyone committed to the project, there would be no reason for explicit rules and regulations. Everything could be organised informally; people would pitch in to do the necessary work and would take out no more than their fair share. Yet the reality proved to be much different. No matter how much goodwill went into creating these communes, a completely open system inevitably led to conflict. As a result, people who wanted to keep the group functioning smoothly had to start creating rules. And these rules, once created, had to be enforced. In other words, communal living arrangements tended either to fall apart or to start reproducing many of the features of mainstream society that they had been created in order to avoid.

The central mistake they made was to assume that because a particular group of people have a collective interest in securing a certain outcome, each individual in that group will also have an individual interest in doing what is necessary to achieve that outcome. It is natural to assume that because we, as a community, need food and shelter, people will spontaneously do what is necessary to secure food and to keep the shelter in good repair. The problem with this assumption is that individual incentives are often not aligned in such a way as to promote the collective good. In particular, because everyone is a little bit lazy, there is a tendency to hang back a little bit before doing any work, in the hope that someone else will come along and do it. Everyone who has lived with roommates knows the pattern. Why do the dishes right away, when someone else may get fed up and do them first? Why replace the milk you drank, when someone might be going to the store? Why sweep the stairs ...?

Of course, if everyone thinks this way, then the dishes will never get done, no milk will be bought and the stairs will never get swept. In fact, life among roommates often becomes something of a contest to see who will be the first to break down and clean up. The person with the highest tolerance for filth has the advantage and will usually be able to get away with doing the least work. Even then, the level of cleanliness in the house will usually be lower than *anyone* would like, including the most filth-tolerant. The problem is that, in the absence of rules, no one has an incentive to invest an optimal level of effort in the task.

Situations of this type are known as 'collective action problems' – cases where everyone would like to see a particular outcome but no one has the incentive to do what is necessary in order to bring it about. The most well-known example of such a situation is the now famous 'prisoner's dilemma'. The name refers to a story that is used to illustrate the situation: Imagine you and a friend rob a bank. The police know that you've done it, but they don't have enough evidence to convict you. They do, however, know about your little drug habit, and so they raid your apartment one day and find enough evidence to charge you and your friend with possession of narcotics. They wheel you both down to the station, put you in separate interrogation rooms. After a slight delay, a cop comes in and says, 'You're looking at one year in prison for the drug-possession charge. We are, however, reasonable men. If you are willing to testify against your accomplice in the bank robbery, we would be willing to let those charges drop. Think about it for a few minutes. I'll be back.'

Initially, the offer looks quite attractive. Because of your rights against self-incrimination, your testimony against your partner in the bank robbery cannot be used against you. So if you testify, then there is a chance that you will be able to get away scot-free. Of course, you suspect that the police are off in the other room making exactly the same offer to your friend. But even if he does testify against you, you are still better off testifying against him. That way you only have to do time for the robbery and can avoid the conviction for drug possession. So no matter how you slice things, if you want to minimise your own jail time, you should testify. In fact, your four options are as follows (in order of preference):

1 You testify, he doesn't testify. Jail time: zero.
2 You don't testify, he doesn't testify. Jail time: one year.
3 You testify, he testifies. Jail time: five years.
4 You don't testify, he testifies. Jail time: six years.

Unfortunately, the exact same process of reasoning that leads you to want to testify against your partner will also lead him to testify against you. Thus there seems to be something collectively self-defeating about your decisions. By attempting to minimise your jail time, you will both wind up spending five years in jail for robbery instead of one year for drug possession. The attempt to minimise jail time has the perverse effect of maximising it. You both prefer outcome 2 to outcome 3. Sadly, you don't get to choose between 2 and 3, you only get to choose between 1 and 2, or between 3 and 4 (depending upon what your friend does). So you choose to testify, he chooses to testify, and you both wind up with outcome 3.

The important point about this little dilemma is that you don't get into the mess because either of you is interested in harming the other one. You get into it simply because you care *less* about the consequences that your action has for the other than you do about the consequences that it has for yourself. This is pretty natural. One can see, however, the seeds of a solution to the problem here as well. If it were possible to make testifying a less attractive option, then you would both stand to benefit. There are many ways of doing this: The two of you might adopt a 'code of silence' – a rule that states, in effect, that you both promise to go to jail rather than turn the other one in. You could then find some member of the criminal underground to enforce it. You might like to join a gang, for instance, that has a standing policy of killing anyone who 'rats out' another member. Even though this seems rather draconian, it is in fact mutually advantageous. If you are each too afraid to testify against the other, then you can expect to spend only one year in prison instead of five.

This is why petty crime has a tendency to become organised crime. Everyone can benefit from having some rules, even those who are doing their utmost to break the rules of society.

*

When we examine the rules of everyday social interaction more closely, we can see that a surprising number of them have as their purpose the elimination of collective action problems. Queuing, for example, is a source of constant annoyance, whether it is at the bank, at the supermarket or on the on-ramp to the expressway. Economists constantly condemn this as an unproductive use of time and energy. Yet the primary function of queues is to speed up the process of moving everyone through. Each individual has an incentive to rush to the front of the line and cut in ahead of the others. But if everyone does so, then the resulting crush slows everyone down, so that the entire group gets through more slowly. Single file is faster than 'single pile'. This becomes tragically apparent when there is a fire in a crowded building and those who are trying to escape fail to form an orderly queue at the exits. As a result, many more die than would otherwise have been necessary.

This is a form of prisoner's dilemma. Rushing the front of the queue is like testifying against your partner – it improves your situation, but only by creating greater costs for others. When the others turn around and do the same thing to you, the result is worse for everyone. The institution of queuing is thus in everyone's interest (even though it may not feel that way some days). The rules that govern turn-taking in a conversation have much the same structure (everyone wants to get a word in, but no one can hear if everyone talks at once). It's also why you're not supposed to talk during movies, not supposed to enter a junction unless you're sure you can clear it, not supposed to lie, not supposed to urinate in public places, not supposed to litter in parks, not supposed to play loud music at night, not supposed to burn leaves in the garden, and so on and so forth. The examples could be multiplied indefinitely.

The important point about these rules is that they all represent instances in which everyone benefits from the constraints the rules impose. Thus, far from repressing our fundamental needs and desires, these rules are precisely what enable us to satisfy them. The two suspects in the prisoner's dilemma do not want to go to jail. A code of silence is the best way of satisfying this desire. Of course, once the code has been adopted, it does constrain the prisoners, by preventing them from adopting the 'free rider' strategy of testifying against one another. But it is essential to see that this constraint is not one that runs contrary to their interests. Sometimes we need the threat of external coercion in order to achieve outcomes that we ourselves would all like to see.

From this perspective, one can already see how perverse many of the forms of rebellion promoted by the counterculture have been. The faceless masses, patiently standing in line, have for decades served as an object of contempt and derision – as the emblem of everything that is wrong with mass society. How often have we seen the comparison between the masses and a herd of sheep or cattle being led to the slaughter? Or people queuing being fed through an assembly line, deprived of their individuality by the anonymity of the machine? Or dressed in identical business suits, going up an escalator or getting off a train? (The movie *Koyaanisqatsi* represents an especially obvious example.) The hero is inevitably the one who breaks free from the queue, who refuses to accept the 'mindless' conformity of the masses. Yet is this conformity really so mindless?

It is often observed that all social norms are enforced, in one way or another. People will display their anger toward the person who interrupts them when they are speaking; they will confront the person who queue-jumps; they will sound their horn at the person who blocks a junction when the light turns red. All of these are ways of expressing social disapproval, of punishing the offender. And yet the mere fact that the rules are enforced does not mean that they are repressive or that they represent an intolerable limitation of the individual's freedom. Whenever there is a collective action problem, there will be a motive to free-ride. If everyone else is going to be queuing patiently, then the incentive to sneak in at the front is even greater. Some kind of social control is required in order to maintain the system that generates the mutual benefits – hence the punishments for disobedience. Yet this does not mean that all social norms are tyrannical or coercive, and it does not mean that those who obey are simply conformists or cowards. They are also known as 'good citizens'.

Thus it is important to draw a distinction between acts of rebellion that challenge senseless or outdated conventions and those that violate legitimate social norms. We must distinguish, in other words, between *dissent* and *deviance*. Dissent is like civil disobedience. It occurs when people are willing in principle to play by the rules but have a genuine, good-faith objection to the specific content of the prevailing set of rules. They disobey *despite* the consequences that these actions may incur. Deviance, on the other hand, occurs when people disobey the rules for self-interested reasons. The two can be very difficult to tell apart, partly because people will often try to justify deviant conduct as a form of dissent, but also because of the powers of self-delusion. Many people who are engaged in deviant conduct genuinely believe that what they are doing is a form of dissent.

For example, during the '60s, many of the social norms that governed relationships between the sexes came under sustained criticism. Traditional male 'gallantry' involved showing a somewhat exaggerated concern for the health and well-being of women: opening doors for them, offering them one's coat during inclement weather, paying for their meals and so forth. Feminists argued that these norms, far from helping women, served only to reinforce the conviction that they were helpless and unable to care for themselves. So, many people began to dissent from this pattern of behaviour, adopting more egalitarian norms in its stead. Yet this dissent was also accompanied by a considerable amount of straightforward social deviance. Men took the criticism of the older male obligations as a licence to do whatever they wanted. This gave rise to the widely noted epidemic of yobbishness in the male population. Rather than finding alternative ways of expressing concern and respect for women, a lot of men have simply stopped paying any attention to the needs of women at all. For these men, equality means 'I look after myself, she looks after herself.'

This sort of confusion was positively courted by the countercultural critique. One way of articulating the central idea of the counterculture is simply to say that it collapsed the distinction between deviance and dissent (or, more accurately, that it *began treating all deviance as dissent*). How else can one explain the parallel that so many people saw between, on the one hand, Martin Luther King, the civil rights movement and freedom riders and, on the other hand, Harley-Davidson choppers, cocaine smuggling and easy riders? The freedom to resist tyranny, to fight against unjust domination, is not equivalent to the freedom to do whatever you want, to have your own interests prevail. Yet the counterculture assiduously eroded this distinction.

It is interesting to compare the political programmes of Martin Luther King and Abbie Hoffman. In his famous 'Letter from Birmingham City Jail', written in 1968 while he was imprisoned for participating in a civil rights march in Alabama, King explicitly draws attention to the deviance/dissent distinction: 'In no sense did I advocate evading or defying the law as the rabid segregationist would do. This would lead to anarchy. One who breaks an unjust law must do so *openly*, *lovingly* … and with a willingness to accept the penalty. I submit that an individual who breaks a law that his conscience tells him is unjust, and willingly accepts the penalty by staying in jail to arouse the conscience of the community over its injustice, is in reality expressing the very highest respect for the law.'[8]

Contrast this with the politics of the 'yippie'. Officially, the term was a derivation of 'Young Internationalist Party', although Hoffman claimed that it was coined when he and some friends were rolling around on a floor, stoned, yelling 'yippee!' The yippies invaded the Democratic National Convention in Chicago in 1968, and they got a lot of publicity for their proposals to nominate a pig for president, to spike the Chicago water supply with LSD and to have squads of yippie men and women seduce delegates and their families while giving them all doses of acid.

Is this deviance or dissent? There is one very simple test that we can apply in order to tell the two apart. It may sound old-fashioned, but it is still helpful to ask the simple question, 'What if *everyone* did that? – would it make the world a better place to live?' If the answer is no, then we have grounds to be suspicious. A lot of countercultural rebellion, as we shall see, fails to pass this simple test.

This analysis allows us to see quite clearly Freud's great mistake in his diagnosis of the dynamic between civilisation and barbarism. The problem can be drawn out by contrasting Freud's analysis of the 'natural condition' of humanity with that of Thomas Hobbes. Freud agreed whole-heartedly with Hobbes's assessment that without the rules and regulations that govern civilised man, life would be 'solitary, poor, nasty, brutish and short'.[9] Although primitive man had greater instinctual freedom, Freud argued, 'his prospects of enjoying this happiness for any length of time were very slender.'[10] In contrast to Hobbes, however, Freud claimed that the insecurity of man's natural condition reflects a deep fact about the human psyche. Given that there are such obvious gains to be had from cooperation, Freud argued, the insecurity of the natural conditions reveals how powerful the instinct for aggressive or violent behaviour must be.

In *Civilisation and Its Discontents*, Freud writes that 'in consequence of this primary mutual hostility of human beings, civilised society is perpetually threatened with disintegration. The interest of work in common would not hold it together; instinctual passions are stronger than reasonable interests.'[11] The argument here is flawed, but flawed in a highly instructive way. Freud observes that we have an enormous amount to gain from 'work in common'. Thus 'reason' tells us that we should behave in a civilised fashion and do our part to participate in cooperative projects. The fact that we so often *fail* to cooperate, and that we have difficulty working together, shows that our more antisocial tendencies – our aggressive instincts – are extremely powerful. If these 'instinctual passions' were not so powerful, they would be unable to overcome our interest in the enormous gains that come from cooperation. The task involved in building a civilisation must be a very great one indeed, since we must seek to repress these extremely powerful instincts.

Freud's overall view, therefore, is one in which all of the violence that exists in the state of nature is a direct expression of our aggressive and destructive instincts. These instincts cannot be eliminated; they can only be sublimated or repressed. So the level of violence never changes. It is simply redirected – given an inward, rather than an outward, expression. Instead of attacking other people, we develop more and more sophisticated forms of psychological self-torture. In keeping with Freud's 'pressure-cooker' model of the mind, the violence that is internalised never goes away. When we look at a contemporary civilised person, we know that behind the calm facade there is a seething cauldron of anger and resentment just waiting to boil over. This is why, in Freud's view, the state of nature can be said to reveal a deep fact about humanity – the overt violence tells us something about our underlying instinctual nature.

For Hobbes, on the other hand, the crucial feature of the violence that exists in the state of nature is that it does *not* reveal anything deep about human nature. In Hobbes's view, the violence is produced by superficial features of our social interactions. Freud assumes that because we have a common interest in cooperating with one another, 'reason' must tell us to do so. Hobbes, however, sees that in the absence of rules, the fact that we have a common interest in cooperating does not necessarily translate into an individual incentive to do so. Reason often tells us to steal the neighbour's vegetables rather than grow our own; to lie rather than tell the truth; to shirk rather than toil. Reason, in other words, leads us into collective action problems. Furthermore, in the absence of rules and regulations, we often have no guarantee that others will live up to their end of agreements. We have no guarantee that they will not attack us while we sleep or steal the fruits of our labour. This tends to make everyone very jumpy. Thus, people who themselves have no hostile intent will often engage in pre-emptive strikes against their neighbours in order to stave off anticipated attacks. In Hobbes's terms, people invade one another not only for gain, but also for safety.

There is therefore no need to assume, in Hobbes's view, that men are governed by any deep-seated love of violence or aggression. Hobbes insists that even though the state of nature is violent, this is not because human beings are fundamentally aggressive. The problem in the state of nature is simply that we cannot *trust* one another. Thus we adopt an aggressive stance toward one another, and we adopt exploitative strategies – but not because of some fundamental need to exploit other people. We do so primarily as a way of protecting ourselves against exploitation by others. If you suspect, in a prisoner's dilemma, that your partner is going to testify against you, then you would be crazy not to testify against him. So you both screw each other, not because of any deep desire to do so, but simply to avoid being screwed yourselves. This isn't evidence of some unruly 'death instinct' trumping our rational faculties; it is simply a rational response to a situation of mutual distrust.

As a result, Hobbes regards the task involved in the construction of civilisation in significantly more modest terms than Freud does. Most of the violence that we see in the state of nature is simply a product of insecurity. People are afraid of one another, and so they are prone to attack. But if you eliminate the source of the insecurity, then you also eliminate the motivation for most of the violence. Thus the creation of order does not require massive repression of our instinctual nature; it simply requires the application of enough force to align individual incentives with the common good. Because the problem is superficial – arising out of the structure of social interaction – the solution can also be superficial. We do not need to transform human consciousness in order to correct the problem; all we need to do is realign people's incentives. In other words, both the problem and the solution arise at a strictly institutional level. Civilisation is essentially a technical fix to the problems of social interaction; it does not require any deeper transformation of human nature. Freud, therefore, massively overestimates the amount that we must give up in order to enter into society, and thus the amount of repression that civilisation requires.

To see how the Hobbesian and the Freudian analyses of the state of nature differ, consider the very concrete example of an arms race. As everyone knows, violence has a tendency to escalate when left unchecked. Military preparations exhibit the same tendency. When stockpiling weapons, the basic goal is to have a larger and more deadly arsenal than another who is likely to attack you. When two countries fear attack from one another, this desire to have more weapons than the other generates a collective action problem. As soon as one country gains any advantage, this just encourages the other to redouble its efforts. Soon the advantage will be eliminated and both countries will be back where they started, except that their level of military expenditure will be higher. Furthermore, since massive investment in weapons spending generates some pressure to use those weapons, such stockpiling can reduce the overall level of security.

Consider the dilemma of a statesman faced with a choice between adopting a 'high' or 'low' level of military expenditure. Here are the possible outcomes, again in order of preference:

1   You choose high, your rival chooses low. Security level: high.
2   You choose low, your rival chooses low. Security level: medium.

3   You choose high, your rival chooses high. Security level: lower.
4   You choose low, your rival chooses high. Security level: lowest.

As in the prisoner's dilemma, you have a choice between 1 and 2, or between 3 and 4. You will choose a high level of military spending, as will your rival, and so you will wind up with outcome 3. In other words, you wind up spending a lot of money yet getting a lower overall level of security.

But this is only the beginning of the problem. Suppose that you choose a high level of military expenditure and that there is something of a delay before your rival can respond in kind. This means that, for a brief moment, you will enjoy a high level of security (outcome 1). However, as soon as your rival's spending begins to kick in, you will experience a decline in relative security. At this point, rather than accept the inevitable (outcome 3), there is a temptation to escalate the rivalry by choosing to spend even more. This transforms the collective action problem into what is known as a 'race to the bottom'. Here the inferiority of the outcome associated with the collective action problem, rather than giving people an incentive to stop what they are doing, gives them an incentive to redouble their efforts, thereby exacerbating the very problem that they were hoping to solve (like when, in order to drown out your neighbour's music, you turn up your own stereo). Eventually, the outcome becomes so bad that both parties are 'locked in' to the conflict – they cannot pull out, simply because the stakes have become too high.

Thus military expenditures have a well-known tendency to degenerate into arms races. From an external perspective, the results seem completely irrational. And yet the parties involved are often locked into them, so that even as the sacrifices that the arms race imposes upon the population become greater and greater, it becomes increasingly difficult to drop out of the race. This is why many of the countries in the world that can least afford it spend huge percentages of GDP on armaments. Eritrea and Ethiopia, for example, have been locked into an arms race for years because of an unresolved border dispute. Despite widespread famine and lack of even rudimentary government services, Eritrea spends upward of 25 per cent of its GDP on armaments. And, of course, there was the mother of all arms races: the Cold War between the United States and the Soviet Union. The Soviet Union essentially bankrupted itself through defence spending. And even a decade after the collapse of the Soviet Union, the United States retains an astronomical level of military expenditure – spending as much as the rest of the world combined.

The important point about these arms races is that, from the outside, they appear irrational. During the '60s, when the Cold War began in earnest, the logic of these conflicts was not well understood. Thus it was easy to conclude that politicians and military leaders had gone somewhat mad (or that the state had fallen under the sway of the 'military-industrial complex'). Various Freudian analyses of this madness had enormous influence. The arms race was presented as an example of our aggressive instincts overpowering our rational faculties. The 1964 movie *Dr Strangelove* provided the classic articulation of this view (and drew all of the usual parallels between sexual repression, German fascism and American nuclear escalation). Building weapons was essentially a form of sublimated aggression. The constant increase in size and payload could be explained as a neurotic reaction to the discipline that military production imposed upon society. The demand for more weapons means more discipline in the factory, more deferred gratification. This increase in psychic repression creates increased aggression, and thus the need for more sublimation – more weapons. The feedback relationship between the two creates the logic of increased escalation, inevitably culminating in nuclear holocaust.

From this Freudian perspective, an arms race reveals something *deep* about human nature. The fact that human beings feel the need to build 100-megaton nuclear bombs shows just how scary our instincts are. It shows that, deep down, to want to use such weapons against one another, we must be extraordinarily violent creatures.

The Hobbesian analysis, on the other hand, denies that arms races reveal any such deep tendencies. It is possible for two countries to get into an arms race even though neither of them has any serious plans to attack the other one; they only need to believe that the other one intends to attack them. It is precisely this lack of trust that triggers the race to the bottom. One country starts stockpiling weapons in order to deter a perceived threat. The other regards this as a threat, and so increases its own level of expenditure. The cycle continues, with each one perceiving the other's defensive move as an offensive one. The important point is that, in a prisoner's dilemma, there is no difference between the two moves – either way, the arms race gets escalated. Thus the Soviet Union and the United States both claimed, throughout the Cold War, that their preparations were entirely defensive in nature. But since neither believed the other, the lack of aggressive intent did nothing to stop the arms race.

Now that the Cold War is over, it is possible to look back and see that the Hobbesian analysis was essentially correct. If the Freudian analysis had been right, then the Cold War would never have ended (or it certainly would not have ended in the way that it did). Both the Soviet Union and the United States were motivated less by hatred of one another than by fear of each other's intent. All it took to end the conflict was the essentially unilateral decision by Mikhail Gorbachev to call the whole thing off. In so doing, he showed that the arms race was based much less on aggression between the two parties than simply upon a lack of trust.

What can we conclude from all this? Freud argued that civilisation creates unhappiness, by repressing some of our most powerful instincts. What is the evidence that we have such instincts? The evidence is that when you leave people free to do whatever they want, things quickly degenerate into violence. According to Freud, this shows that, at some fundamental level, we are all bloodthirsty creatures. Hobbes proposes a far more simple explanation. People often treat others poorly not because of any desire to inflict suffering, but out of a desire to avoid being treated poorly themselves. It is like the couple who break up not because they do not like each other, but because each believes that the other is about to break things off, and would rather be the 'dumper' than the 'dumpee'. Their problem is simply a lack of trust.

The contrast between the Hobbesian and the Freudian analysis reminds us that psychologically deep explanations are not better merely by virtue of their depth. Sometimes a cigar is just a cigar. And sometimes a missile is just a missile. The exaggerated consequences of the kind of military escalation seen during the Cold War can be explained without positing a crazed inner child, hell-bent on destruction. Nuclear escalation is certainly an undesirable outcome, but it is produced through a *rational* response to a situation characterised by distrust and insecurity. Thus, eliminating the race to the bottom, replacing mutually assured destruction with 'nuclear sanity', does not require repression of our instincts. If a coercively imposed solution is able to create the necessary level of trust, there is no reason that it cannot be enthusiastically embraced by all parties.

More generally, Hobbes's argument shows that not all rules are bad, and that people who follow the rules are not merely repressed conformists. There is a middle road between Colonel Fitts's neurotic demand for 'structure' and Lester Burnham's puerile rejection of all social norms. It is possible to be a normal, well-adjusted adult, simply by following the rules that promote the general interest while conscientiously objecting to those that are unjust. Yet this option is one the countercultural critique has studiously ignored.

It's easy to forget how rule-governed everyday life is. For the most part, we are all so well socialised that the thought of breaking the rules does not even occur to us. And since we never think of breaking them, and pretty much no one else does either, we quickly lose sight of the fact that there are any rules at all. And yet they are still present. If you need to be reminded of the fact, just try breaking a few. Next time you get on a crowded bus, try sitting down in someone's lap. Or next time you go to the corner store, try negotiating a lower price for the milk. In a crowded elevator, stand facing the back. Or queue-jump at the cinema. Or stare straight into the eyes of everyone you pass on the street. People will not merely be surprised, they will get very upset. This kind of social deviance is normally met with reactions ranging from expressions of disapproval to outright punishment.

The social order, in other words, is enforced. Even the weakest, most well-socialised members of society will eventually get around to taking action in the face of blatant disregard for the basic rules of social order. This is exploited to great comic effect in *Fight Club*, when Tyler Durden sends the new recruits out with instructions to get themselves beaten up. The caveat: they aren't allowed to throw the first punch. So there is a montage of clips showing fight club members repeatedly queue jumping, stealing sweets from babies and pointing a hose at a nerdy businessman. The initial reaction is always an almost apologetic confusion, followed by anger, then finally violence.

The responses portrayed in *Fight Club* are not so different from the reactions that were elicited in several important sociological experiments conducted during the '60s. At the time, there was considerable interest in the way that conformity to social norms is enforced. Some of the most provocative investigations were conducted by California sociologist Harold Garfinkel. Garfinkel sent his students out to conduct what he called 'breaching experiments'. They were instructed to violate a set of conventional expectations, then record the response. For example, students were instructed to spend between fifteen minutes and an hour acting as though they were boarders in their home, not family members. Thus they were 'to avoid getting personal, to use formal address, to speak only when spoken to' and to otherwise be 'circumspect and polite'. In a small minority of cases, family members dismissed the unusual behaviour as 'a joke'. In the remainder of cases, the behaviour provoked a serious breakdown of social relations. Many family members reacted with overt hostility to this deviation from the 'normal' pattern of conduct:

> *They vigorously sought to make the strange actions intelligible and to restore the situation to normal appearances. Reports were filled with accounts of astonishment, bewilderment, shock, anxiety, embarrassment, and anger, and with charges by various family members that the student was mean, inconsiderate, selfish, nasty, or impolite. Family members demanded explanations: What's the matter? What's gotten into you? Did you get fired? Are you sick? What are you being so superior about? Why are you mad? Are you out of your mind or are you just stupid? … One mother, infuriated when her daughter spoke to her only*

when she was spoken to, began to shriek in angry denuncia-
tion of the daughter for her disrespect and insubordination and
refused to be calmed by the student's sister. A father berated his
daughter for being insufficiently concerned for the welfare of
others and of acting like a spoiled child.[12]

Garfinkel's overall conclusion is that 'being normal' is not simply a characteristic that people have, it is a status that we all actively try to achieve and maintain. Furthermore, we expect others to act normally. It is a standard that we hold them accountable to: when they fail to act normally, we demand an explanation, and we break off relations or otherwise punish them if they are unable to supply a satisfactory one.

One very important point about 'being normal' is that it significantly reduces the cognitive strain that one's behaviour puts on other people. In a typical social situation – say, walking down a city street – there is simply too much going on for anyone to pay proper attention to all of the possibilities. Normally, the cars stay on the street and the people stay on the pavement. And people normally walk along the pavement, maintaining a discreet distance (not pulling up right beside one another, not talking to strangers, etc.). In principle, any one of these rules could be violated at any time. Yet we routinely ignore these possibilities. People stand waiting on the curb as a bus passes by within two feet of their face. Imagine if they were standing in an open field and a bus passed by so close to them! In this case, the extraordinary physical danger that the vehicle poses to the pedestrian would be palpable. Yet in the city we routinely ignore it. We take it for granted that the bus driver will do what 'normal' bus drivers do everywhere, and avoid running down pedestrians. It is only when a vehicle swerves unexpectedly that we are jolted out of these expectations and have to start worrying about our safety.

This is why the culture shock that people experience in new or unfamiliar social environments is such a consistent and well-documented phenomenon. Culture shock is, in essence, the effect of cumulative frustration and anxiety stemming from the loss of the familiar signposts used to manage social interactions. A large part of the strain comes from not knowing what is 'normal' and what is 'abnormal'. Although initially a foreign environment can be new and exciting, after a certain period of time the difficulty that people experience trying to get even very simple things done begins to wear on them. Their inability to detect and respond to social cues – how to buy something, and whether the price is reasonable; whether people are being serious or joking, rude or polite; how to make conversation, and what to talk about; whether people are laughing with you or at you – makes them feel childlike and incompetent. Initially, a surplus of goodwill is enough to smooth over these difficulties, but eventually everyone longs for a return to a 'normal', less demanding interaction style.

Garfinkel concluded, on the basis of such observations, that the dense network of rules that govern our daily lives serves as the 'routine ground of everyday activities'. Its most important function is to maintain and reproduce a system of generalised trust. In effect, the only way we are able to go about our business in society is by trusting other people. We have to trust that drivers will not try to run us over, that strangers will not all try to rip us off, that cooks will not try to poison us, and so on. But usually we have no specific evidence of this – especially in a large city, where we have never met most of the people we interact with on a daily basis. So how do we avoid the intense anxiety that such interactions can provoke? What we need to believe is that others will obey the rules.

One way in which people establish the requisite trust is by demonstrating their willingness to play by the rules in small symbolic ways. This is the core function of courtesy and good manners. Greeting someone politely, holding the door open, using the correct salad fork and adopting a benevolent demeanour all help to reassure others that there are no nasty surprises in store – that the interaction will unfold pretty much as it is supposed to. Thus, all the dumb little rules that we are supposed to follow, far from serving as simply a constraint on individuality, freedom and self-expression, actually turn out to serve a valuable function. Every little action serves as a cue, allowing others to infer what is likely to follow.

It is precisely this trust mechanism that is exploited by the best con artists and psychopaths, who are invariably charming and polite. Strictly speaking, it is a false inference to conclude that people who play by the rules when it comes to the small stuff will also play by the rules when it comes to the big stuff. Con artists prove this, by doing the former and not the latter. Yet does this mean that we should all stop making that inference, that we should all stop trusting one another? If we did, it would make almost all social life impossible. Life without culture, in other words, would be a state of permanent culture shock.

So what can we say about the demand for conformity to social norms? Is this the tyranny of the majority? Is this mass society, trying to dominate the individual and to punish any sign of uniqueness or creativity? Absolutely not. The countercultural rebels took the observation that all social norms are enforced, and concluded, on this basis, that all of culture is a system of domination. A continuum was posited between Adolf Hitler and Emily Post – both were regarded just as fascists, trying to impose their rules on people in order to deny them pleasure. Any rebellion against any sort of social norm was therefore positively valued. Yet the primary consequence of this analysis has been a shocking decline in civility, most of all in the United States (where people now routinely respond to 'thank you' by grunting 'uh-huh'). It's enough to make anyone think twice. The decline in manners, far from setting anyone free, seems to have simply played into the hands of those with antisocial attitudes (and political platforms).

Anyone who has ever dabbled in subculture will have first-hand experience of the many subtle ways in which social norms are enforced. As a former punk rocker coming from a small town, I know all about it. I actually got into the whole punk business somewhat by accident. For the most part, I was a quiet kid. I started out the first couple of years of high school minding my own business, hanging out in the computer room playing Dungeons and Dragons. This was back in the days before cyberpunk and hackers, so the computer-room crowd was all just a bunch of nerds, without delusions of grandeur and with no prospects of ever achieving coolness.

My high school was sort of on the wrong side of the tracks, and it tended to be where they sent all the kids with discipline problems, to give them one last chance before reform school. One day a girl got transferred in who had a completely tricked-out punk-rock haircut – bleached out on one side, black on the other. Everyone was talking about it. The principal took one look at her and told her to dye her hair back to 'normal' or face expulsion. She refused, and so that was it for her. No one ever saw her again. I thought this was a bit heavy-handed, so as a gesture of solidarity, I showed up at school a couple of days later with my hair dyed exactly the same way. I was interested to know whether the principal would also expel one of his best students for having dyed hair, or if he expelled just the ones he didn't like.

The principal didn't do anything about it other than give me dirty looks. But some things did change. Although punks were a stigmatised minority in Canada at the time – getting beaten up for looking like a punk was as easy as falling down – it was also widely understood to be extremely cool. The sense of persecution in many ways just contributed to the exclusivity of the club. And so, with my new punk haircut, I found myself suddenly getting access to a social circuit that I would never have had a chance at before. It meant making friends with people who would never have spoken to me, finding out about all sorts of great music, getting invited to cool parties and, most importantly, being able to score with girls who had been way out of my league just a few months before.

The other thing that I noticed was just how differently other people started treating me, especially strangers in public. Old ladies would scowl at me in the street, rednecks in pickup trucks would scream obscenities at me as they hurtled by, security guards would begin not-so-subtly tailing me as I wandered through the grocery store, and Christians on the street corner would make an extra effort to press copies of their magazines upon me. In other words, people overreacted. From this, it was not difficult to conclude that I was doing something genuinely radical, that I was challenging people's expectations, freeing their minds, shocking the masses out of their conformist stupor. I was just the thin edge of the wedge, the beginning of a larger revolution, the most visible sign of the impending collapse of Western civilisation.

I remember describing this feeling once to a friend of my mother's, a woman who could best be described as a hardcore hippie (at the time, somewhere around 1984, she still routinely referred to police as 'the pigs' and used the word 'fuck' more than anyone else I have ever met). She said, 'I know what you mean. When I was your age I felt exactly the same way. People used to call us "dirty hippies," throw us off the bus, refuse us service at restaurants. But now no one cares.'

This hadn't been what I was expecting to hear. And it raised some uncomfortable questions. After all, just how many times can the masses be shocked out of their conformist stupor before we begin to wonder whether they were ever in a conformist stupor to start with? John Ralston Saul claims that we live in an 'unconscious civilisation', all victims of conformity and groupthink.[13] We need to wake up, smell the coffee and start acting as genuine individuals. Yet thousands of people read his book, without many feeling that the description applied to them. After all, it's never *you* who's unconscious; it's always the guy next to you or the guy who lives down the street. If everyone thinks that everyone else is unconscious, perhaps it's time to consider the possibility that we are all wide awake. Perhaps calling other people unconscious is just a way of dismissing the fact that *not everyone thinks the same way you do.*

For a long time, I bought into the countercultural theory, which held that the system was just demonstrating its enormous ability to co-opt dissent. Yet as time passed, the more obvious explanation became increasingly difficult to resist. People initially respond to unusual social conduct with expressions of disapproval. This is how human culture works. It's also a perfectly understandable response. When someone who is visibly deranged gets onto the subway, no one rushes to sit down next to him. This is not so much due to any specific fear, but simply because the other passengers do not know what to expect, and they don't need the hassle. Yet subcultural rebellion is not random; it fits a very tightly scripted pattern. This is what allows hippies or punks to 'make a statement' with their appearance and not simply be dismissed as lunatics. In other words, it is the alternative norms of the subculture that identify it as a movement of *dissent* and not merely social deviance. But precisely because of that fact, people eventually get used to it. It becomes 'normal' to have a few punks hanging out at the mall. As a result, the adverse reactions go away; people learn what to expect from them. This is how culture changes. It's not co-optation – it's a simple mechanism of adaptation.

Here I think we can see the basic error in countercultural thinking. Countercultural rebels take the fact that social norms are enforced and interpret this as a sign that social order as a whole is a system of repression. They then interpret the punitive response elicited by the violations of these norms as confirmation of the theory. The result, too often, is simply a glamorisation of antisocial behaviour – transgression for the sake of transgression. In everyday life this is usually harmless, but politically this mode of thinking can be disastrous. It leads countercultural activists to reject not just existing social institutions but any proposed alternative as well, on the grounds that the alternative would also need to be institutionalised and thus coercively imposed. This is what underlies the countercultural dismissal of traditional leftist politics as 'merely institutional'.

The tendency to reject institutional solutions to social problems leads directly to the cardinal sin of the counterculture. Countercultural activists and thinkers consistently reject perfectly good solutions to concrete social problems, in the name of 'deeper', 'more radical' alternatives that can never be effectively implemented. As the following chapters will show, this cardinal sin contaminates every field of countercultural politics. It shows up among culture jammers and the anticonsumerism movement, among critics of the education system, in the environmentalist movement, the antiglobalisation movement and the feminist movement, and among adherents of 'New Age' religious beliefs. By rejecting any proposal that stops short of a total transformation of human consciousness and culture, countercultural activists too often wind up exacerbating precisely the problems they are hoping to solve.

Notes

1   Jean-Jacques Rousseau, 'On Social Contract', *Rousseau's Political Writings*, ed. and trans. Alan Ritter and Julia Conaway Bondella (New York: Norton, 1988), 85.

2   Henry David Thoreau, *Walden* (1854; Boston: Beacon, 1997), 6.

3   Ralph Waldo Emerson, 'Self-Reliance', in *Ralph Waldo Emerson*, ed. Richard Poirier (Oxford: Oxford University Press, 1990), 137.

4   *Ibid.*, 133.

5   Friedrich von Hayek, *The Road to Serfdom* (Chicago: University of Chicago Press, 1994).

6   Duane Elgin, *Voluntary Simplicity* (New York: William Morrow, 1981), 203.

7   Immanuel Kant, 'Idea for a Universal History with a Cosmopolitan History', in *Kant: Political Writings*, ed. Hans Reis, trans. H. B. Nisbet (Cambridge: Cambridge University Press), 46.

8   Martin Luther King, 'Letter from Birmingham Jail', in *Law and Morality*, ed. David Dyzenhaus and Arthur Ripstein (Toronto: University of Toronto Press), 459.

9   Thomas Hobbes, *Leviathan*, ed. Richard Tuck (Cambridge: Cambridge University Press, 1996), 89.

10 Freud, *Civilization and Its Discontents*, 52.

11 *Ibid.*, 49.

12 Harold Garfinkel, *Studies in Ethnomethodology* (Cambridge: Polity Press, 1984), 48.

13 John Ralston Saul, *The Unconscious Civilization* (Concord, ON: Anansi, 1995).

4

I hate myself and want to buy

Do you hate consumer culture? Angry about all that packaging, all those commercials? Worried about the quality of the 'mental environment'? Well, join the club. Anticonsumerism has become one of the most important cultural forces in the more affluent parts of the world, across every social class and demographic. Sure, as a society we may be spending record amounts of money on luxury goods, vacations, designer clothing and household comforts. But take a look at the non-fiction best-seller lists. For years they've been populated by books that are deeply critical of consumerism: *No Logo*, *Culture Jam*, *Luxury Fever*, *Fast Food Nation*. Two of the most popular and critically acclaimed Hollywood films in the past decade were *Fight Club* and *American Beauty*, which offered almost identical indictments of modern consumer society.

What can we conclude from all this? For one thing, the market obviously does an extremely good job at responding to consumer demand for anticonsumerist products and literature. But how can we all denounce consumerism yet still find ourselves living in a consumer society?

The answer is simple. What we see in films like *American Beauty* or books like *No Logo* is not actually a critique of consumerism; it's merely a restatement of the critique of mass society. The two are not the same. In fact, the critique of mass society has been one of the most powerful forces driving consumerism for the past forty years.

That last sentence is worth reading again. The idea is so foreign, so completely the opposite of what we are used to being told, that many people simply can't get their head around it. So here is the claim, simply put: Books like *No Logo*, magazines like *Adbusters* and movies like *American Beauty* do not undermine consumerism; they reinforce it. This isn't because the authors, editors or directors are hypocrites. It's because they've failed to understand the true nature of consumer society. They identify consumerism with conformity. As a result, they fail to notice that it is rebellion, not conformity, that has for decades been the driving force of the marketplace.

Over the past half-century, we have seen the complete triumph of the consumer economy at the same time that we have seen the absolute dominance of countercultural thinking in the 'marketplace of ideas'. Is this a coincidence? Countercultural theorists would like to think that their rebellion is merely a *reaction* to the evils of the consumer society. But what if countercultural rebellion, rather than being a consequence of intensified consumerism, were actually a contributing factor? Wouldn't *that* be ironic?

They say that money can't buy happiness. That may be so, but it's hardly enough to make the case for poverty. Most people feel, quite rightly, that there is some connection between material prosperity and happiness, however tenuous. And many studies bear out this conviction. People in wealthy industrialised societies are, on average, much happier than people in poor ones. It is not hard to imagine why. With greater wealth comes a greater ability to satisfy our needs and desires, to alleviate suffering and illness, and to carry out our life projects.

From this, we might reasonably conclude that economic growth is a good thing. Unfortunately, there is an unexpected twist in the story. While economic development has been shown to generate a steady increase in average happiness levels, after a certain level of development has been reached the effect disappears completely. The rule of thumb among economists who study the subject is that once GDP reaches about £5,000 per capita, further economic growth generates no gains in average happiness.[1] In North America we hit that level long ago. So despite spectacular economic growth since World War II, there has been no overall increase in happiness. Some studies even show a decrease.

There is something very puzzling about this. It would not be surprising to find that as a country becomes richer and richer, additional economic growth generates increasingly smaller improvements in average happiness levels. What is shocking is the discovery that growth ceases to produce any improvements at all. Every year our economy pumps out more cars, more houses, more consumer electronics, more labour-saving appliances, more restaurant meals, more of everything. Furthermore, the quality of these goods increases dramatically, year after year. Looking around a typical suburban home, the most striking feature is the sheer abundance of material goods. How could all of this stuff fail to please?

Yet in the middle of all this wealth, the middle classes continue to feel 'squeezed' economically. People are working harder, are under more stress and are finding themselves with less free time. It is no wonder that they are not especially happy. But how could more wealth bring about such consequences? Now that we're richer, shouldn't we all be working less?

The situation is bad enough to make some people question the value of economic growth altogether. After all, we make serious sacrifices as a society in order to maintain a high growth rate. Unemployment, job insecurity, social inequality and environmental degradation are just some of the things that we tolerate in order to keep the economic pump primed. But if growth isn't making us any happier, then what is the point? At the very least, it would seem that, as a society, we have our priorities confused.

Consider what the future was supposed to have in store for us. Factory automation and labour-saving appliances were supposed to have all but eliminated the need to work. Yet in the past twenty years there has been no change in the average number of hours worked in the United Kingdom (and an alarming *increase* in the United States). Productivity gains were supposed to create universal affluence, to eliminate poverty as we know it. Yet since the expansion of the welfare state in the '60s and '70s levelled off, there has been no reduction in the level of 'basic needs' poverty, even in the face of spectacular economic growth. And what about those flying Jetsons cars, or at least clean high-speed trains? Commuting has become a nightmare for most city-dwellers.

Who could seriously have predicted, thirty years ago, that this is how things would play out? How is it that we can produce so much more wealth and yet fail to secure any measurable improvement in satisfaction? We constantly hear about how, as a society, we can no longer 'afford' health care or State education. But if we can't afford them now, how could we afford them thirty years ago, when the country produced only half as much wealth? Where did all the money go?

The answer to this question is in fact quite straightforward: the money is being spent on private consumption goods. Yet if this pattern of expenditure is not making us happier, why are we doing it? There seems to be something pathological about consumption habits in our society. We are obsessed with acquiring more and more consumer goods, even though this leads us to make unreasonable sacrifices in other areas of life. It is this compulsion that critics refer to as 'consumerism'.

But identifying the compulsion is not the same thing as explaining it. If consumerism is so bad for us, why do we keep doing it? Are we just like kids at a birthday party, eating too much cake even though it will give us a tummy-ache later on?

One of the most talked-about cinematic set pieces in recent memory is the scene in *Fight Club* where the nameless narrator (played by Ed Norton) pans his empty apartment, furnishing it piece by piece with Ikea furniture. The scene shimmers and pulses with prices, model numbers and product names, as if Norton's gaze were drag-and-dropping straight out of a virtual catalogue. It is a great scene, driving the point home: the furniture of his world is mass-produced, branded, sterile. If we are what we buy, then the narrator is the Allen-key-wielding corporate-conformist drone.

In many ways, this scene is just a CGI-driven update of the opening pages of John Updike's *Rabbit, Run*. After yet another numbing day selling the MagiPeel Kitchen Peeler, Harry Angstrom comes home to his pregnant and half-drunk wife, whom he no longer loves. Harry takes off in his car, driving aimlessly south. As he tries to sort out his life, the music on the radio, the sports reports, the ads, the billboards, all merge in his consciousness into one monotonous, monolithic brandscape.

It may give us pause to consider that, though *Fight Club* was hailed as 'edgy' and 'subversive' when it appeared in 1999, *Rabbit, Run* had enjoyed enormous commercial success when it was first published – in 1960. If social criticism came with a sell-by date, this one would have been removed from the shelf a long time ago. The fact that it is still around, and still provokes awe and acclaim, makes one wonder if it is really a criticism or, rather, a piece of modern mythology.

What *Fight Club* and *Rabbit, Run* have in common is that they both posit an indissoluble connection between consumer society and mass society. The alienation that leads the narrator of *Fight Club* to blow up his apartment, along with all of his worldly possessions, is no different from the suppressed rage that leads him to create the clandestine fight club, where men get together in the middle of the night to beat each other senseless. Both are a revolt against the repressive conformity of modern society.

This identification of the consumer society with mass society is so complete that many people have difficulty imagining it otherwise. Say the word 'consumerism', and what image comes to mind? Most people think, once again, of the classic American suburb from the '50s. They see shiny Buicks with tail fins, white picket fences, cookie-cutter homes, men in gray flannel suits and skinny ties. They think of people trying to 'keep up with the Joneses', trying to impress the neighbours with the latest gadget, parking their shiny new cars in the driveway and obsessing over their status in the community. Above all, they imagine a society of compulsive conformists, a herd of sheep, subject to eternal manipulation by advertisers and corporations.

Yet the idea that consumerism is driven by a desire to *conform* is not obvious. Kids sometimes demand a particular style of jeans or a given brand of trainers, on the grounds that 'all the other kids have them'. They want to fit in, to be accepted. But how many adults act this way? Most people spend the big money not on things that help them to fit in, but on things that allow them to stand out from the crowd. They spend their money on goods that confer *distinction*. People buy what makes them feel superior, whether by showing that they are cooler (Nike shoes), better connected (Cuban cigars), better informed (single-malt Scotch), more discerning (Starbucks espresso), morally superior (Body Shop cosmetics) or just plain richer (Louis Vuitton bags).

Consumerism, in other words, would appear to be a product of consumers trying to outdo one another. It is competitive consumption that creates the problem, not conformity. If consumers were just conformists, then they would all go out and buy exactly the same stuff, and everyone would be happy. Furthermore, there would be no reason to go out and buy anything new. Thus the desire to conform fails to explain the compulsive character of consumer behaviour – why people keep spending more and more even though they are overextended, and even though it brings them no happiness in the long run.

So why do we lay the blame for consumerism on those who are struggling to 'keep up with the Joneses'? The fault would appear to lie with the Joneses. They're the ones who started it all, by trying to one-up their neighbours. It's their desire to stand out from the crowd, to be better than everyone else, that is responsible for ratcheting up consumption standards in their community.

In other words, it's the nonconformists, not the conformists, who are driving consumer spending. This observation is one that anyone working in advertising will find crushingly obvious. Brand identity is all about product differentiation; it's about setting the product apart from others. People identify with brands because of the distinction that they confer.

So how could social critics have got it so wrong? Where does the idea come from that consumerism is driven by a quest for conformity?

★

Jean Baudrillard's 1970 book *The Consumer Society* is a classic in the field of cultural studies and social criticism. Drawing upon the work of Guy Debord, Baudrillard argues that the commodity has become so abstract that the economy is now nothing but a system of signs. The 'needs' that we express in the marketplace are not a reflection of any underlying set of real desires; they are simply a way of conceptualising our participation in the symbolic system. In fact, the idea that we have 'needs' is a type of 'magical thinking', produced by the same illusion that makes us believe we are consuming 'objects'.[2]

This analysis offers a convenient explanation for why modern consumer society fails to produce any happiness. It is because the 'needs' that it satisfies are simply a 'function (induced in the individual) by the internal logic of the system'.[3] If the system could function without feeding its workers, Baudrillard argues, there would be no bread. And, similarly, if the system could function without consumers with 'needs', there would be no needs. Thus 'there are only needs because the system needs them'.[4]

Yet when Baudrillard tries to provide some illustrations of these supposedly fictitious needs, the book becomes inadvertently comical. In a section dedicated to a discussion of '*le gadget*' – the functionally useless object that serves as a marker of social status – one of the items that he singles out for special ridicule is the two-speed windshield wiper.[5] Apparently, back in 1970, this little innovation struck certain French intellectuals as being ostentatious.

How things have changed in thirty years. One can only wonder how Baudrillard would feel about modern cars, with their variable-speed windshield wipers, not to mention the exotic 'intermittent' setting. Is all this just useless gadgetry? Who would buy a car today that *didn't* have variable-speed wipers? Can we conclude from this that our needs are entirely ephemeral, part of an ideological system driven by the interest of capital (or automobile manufacturers)? Could it not be that variable-speed wipers are genuinely *handy*?

The deeper issue raised here concerns the standpoint of the critic. Who is to say what is useful and what is not, which needs are genuine and which are false? Simply saying that all needs are ideological doesn't help. Where does Baudrillard get off telling us that we are 'naive' for thinking that we need variable-speed windshield wipers? As one reads *The Consumer Society*, it is difficult not to imagine him in his crumpled black suit, hauling on a Gauloise, sitting out on the *ter-*

rasse at Les Deux Magots, scowling at the traffic, complaining about Americans and their fancy windshield wipers.

The naivety, it would seem, is on the side of those who accept this critique of the consumer society. Whenever you look at the list of consumer goods that (according to the critic) people don't really need, what you invariably see is a list of consumer goods that *middle-aged intellectuals* don't need. Budweiser bad, single malt Scotch good; Hollywood movies bad, performance art good; Chryslers bad, Volvos good; hamburgers bad, risotto good and so on. Furthermore, intellectuals have a natural bias against consumer goods in general, precisely because they are people who tend to be more engaged and stimulated by ideas than by goods.

Consumerism, in other words, always seems to be a critique of what *other people buy*. This makes it difficult to avoid the impression that the so-called critique of consumerism is just thinly veiled snobbery or, worse, puritanism. It is important to remember that there has always been a very powerful streak of anticonsumerism in the Christian tradition, beginning with Jesus himself, who famously claimed that it was easier for a camel to pass through the eye of a needle than for a rich man to enter the kingdom of God. This is because the rich are self-sufficient in material needs, and the material world is traditionally regarded as a realm of corruption and sin. The true Christian must elevate his or her sights and focus on finding happiness in the spiritual.

Obviously, if the critique of consumerism was just more of the same, it would never have gained much credibility with the radical left. What made the theory more attractive to many people was an argument, derived from the work of Marx, which gained considerable influence during the '60s. One can see it quite clearly in Baudrillard's work. According to Marx, capitalism suffers from periodic crises of overproduction. As the factory owner goes about his business, he is constantly trying to lower his costs of production. He does so by introducing the techniques of mass production. He therefore increases the quantity of goods produced, and introduces machines as a substitute for human labour (which allows him both to lay off workers and to drive down wages). Marx's (seemingly plausible) observation is that these two strategies are contradictory. Mass production increases the supply of goods, yet it also reduces the income of workers, leading to a shortfall in demand. So at the end of the day the capitalist is left with a mountain of unsold goods, having deprived the working class of the revenue needed to buy them. The result is a crisis of generalised overproduction.

Marx thought that this tendency toward overproduction was responsible for the business cycle. The economy generated more and more stuff, which accumulated until there was simply too much. At this point profits would collapse, all economic activity would slacken, a recession would set in and the excess wealth would be destroyed. This would reset the system, so that a new cycle of production could begin. Thus, as Baudrillard writes, capital 'confronted by its own contradictions (over-production, falling rate of profit), tried at first to surmount them by totally restructuring its accumulation through destruction, deficit financing, and bankruptcy. It thus averted a redistribution of wealth, which would have placed the existing relations of production and structures of power seriously in question.'[6]

Yet after the World War II, most Western nations enjoyed two decades of almost uninterrupted growth. The economic crises that Marx had diagnosed appeared to have been, at the very least, tamed. This created something of an explanatory challenge for Marxists. After all, mass production and mechanisation had accelerated in the '50s. Capitalism appeared to be 'overproducing' as much as ever. So how to explain the attenuation of the business cycle?

One answer, which acquired growing popularity during the '60s, was that advertising had been introduced in order to resolve the crisis of overproduction. The solution to the 'contradiction' of capitalism, Baudrillard argues, is to transform the worker into a *consumer*. The way to get rid of all those excess goods is to trick the workers into wanting more and more. Convince them that they absolutely can't live without a new car or a fancy home in the suburbs. Thus, capitalism instils what Baudrillard calls 'a compulsion to need and a compulsion to consume'[7]: 'The industrial system, having socialised the masses as a labour force, was forced to go further, in order to finish the job, and socialise them (which is to say, control them) as a consumption force.'[8] This form of mandatory desire is initially instilled through co-optation, yet someday the violence inherent in the system may be revealed: 'One can imagine laws sanctioning such constraint one day (an obligation to change cars every two years).'[9]

There is one little glitch. Because it is mass production that creates the surplus of goods, the desires that are to be instilled in the workers cannot be individual or idiosyncratic. The goods produced are all entirely homogenous, and so the desires that are created must also be homogenous. As Stuart Ewen argues in *Captains of Consciousness*, 'The control of the masses required that people, like the world they inhabited, assume the character of machinery – predictable and without any aspirations toward self-determination. As the industrial machinery produced standardised goods, so did the psychology of consumerisation attempt to forge a notion of the "mass" as "practically identical in all mental and social characteristics".'[10]

Consumerism must therefore be a system of rigid conformity. It cannot tolerate any deviation from the norm, because the false needs that are instilled in the population are required in order to relieve the excess of commodities generated by mass production. Thus consumerism arises out of what Baudrillard calls the 'attempt to massify men's consumption in step with the requirements of the productive machinery'.[11] It is here that the 'totalitarian logic' of the system is revealed. Because consumption needs are dictated by the functional requirements of the production system, 'the system can only produce and reproduce individuals as elements of the system. It cannot tolerate exceptions.'[12]

This is the point of contact between the critique of consumerism and the theory of countercultural rebellion. According to this view, the system cannot tolerate exceptions, either on the factory floor or in the supermarket. It requires an absolutely uniform system of functionally imposed 'needs' in order to absorb the excess of commodities produced through mass production. As a result, non-standard acts of consumption come to be seen as *politically radical*. Just as the worker can disrupt the entire assembly line by refusing to do the job that he has been assigned to, so the consumer can disrupt the system simply by refusing to shop where she has been told to.

Here we witness the birth of *the rebel consumer*.

This is a nice theory. It is also one that a lot of smart people have found persuasive. There is only one problem: it is based upon an elementary economic fallacy. There is no such thing as generalised overproduction. Never was, never has been.

No modern economist, left or right, endorses Marx's claim that capitalism is subject to crises of overproduction. Unfortunately, someone forgot to inform the critics of consumerism. So theories like Baudrillard's and Ewen's continue to circulate and are taken seriously, even though they are based upon the academic equivalent of an urban myth.

The problem with Marx's theory is that it ignores the fact that a market economy is fundamentally a system of exchange. Although we sell goods in return for money, the money itself is not consumed; we simply use it in order to purchase other goods from other people. As a result, the supply of goods *constitutes* the demand for other goods. Total supply and total demand always add up to the same amount, simply because they are the *same thing*, seen from two different perspectives. So while there can be 'too much' of one particular good relative to other goods, there cannot be an excess of goods in general.

This relationship is not only obscured, it is also complicated by the fact that we use money to mediate our exchanges. So it is helpful to start by setting aside the question of money and imagining a pure barter economy. In such an economy, total supply is always identical to total demand, simply because goods are always exchanged for other goods. Suppose I decide to start making shoes. Each pair that I produce increases the overall supply of commodities in the economy. Yet my plan is obviously not to give them away. If I am to sustain my shoe operation, I will need to exchange the finished product for food, shelter, clothing and all of the other necessities of life. As a result, when I go into the marketplace with my shoes to sell, not only do I increase the supply of goods, but I also increase the demand for other goods by precisely the same amount. This relationship is not causal, it is conceptual. The reason that the increase in supply of one good creates an increase in demand for other goods is that the supply of the one *is* the demand for the others. Goods are exchanged for goods.

Of course, the precise amount by which the shoes that I sell will increase supply and demand will be determined by how much other people *want* shoes, and therefore how much they are willing to give up to acquire them. This is what determines the shoes' price. Not enough demand for shoes, and the price will drop. Not enough supply, and the price will go up. This is why we speak of *local* over-production or underproduction. Yet because total supply and total demand for all goods must be the same, it is meaningless to speak of *global* overproduction or underproduction. There can be too many shoes, but there cannot be too many goods.

This explains why economists can use either of two methods to calculate a nation's GDP. They can add up the total value of goods and services sold in the economy, or they can add up the total amount of income earned. The two must come to the same figure, simply because one person's purchase is someone else's income. It is also why, for example, immigration does not create unemployment. The new immigrant's willingness to supply labour represents an increase in demand for other goods in the economy of precisely the same magnitude. So while immigration can create too much supply of one particular *type* of labour, it cannot produce too much labour *in general*.

Consider, in this light, the Marxian claim that capitalists, by depressing wages, deprive themselves of markets for their own products. This may be true of individual capitalists, but it cannot be true of capitalists as a whole. Suppose one capitalist is in the business of making bread. He introduces a new automated mixer, which allows him to lay off employees and reduce his wage bill by £1000 a week. Naturally, since his workers eat bread, this reduction in wages reduces demand for the capitalist's own product. Is this the beginning of a vicious spiral? Is the capitalist caught in a 'contradiction', as Marx suggested?

Not at all. The £1000 that is cut out of the wage bill does not disappear. It is presumably taken by the capitalist in the form of profits. What does he do with this money? He either spends it or saves it. While cutting wages may reduce the demand for bread, when the capitalist spends the money he increases the demand for other products produced by other firms. Thus the cut to the wage bill does not deprive the economy as a whole of £1000 worth of demand, it simply shifts it out of one sector into another (that is, away from the goods that workers tend to buy, toward the goods that capitalists like to buy). The situation is not much different if he saves it. Banks take money that is deposited and lend it out again, either to investors, who spend it on capital goods, or to other consumers, who simply spend it. Either way, total demand for goods remains unaffected by the wage reductions; it is simply shifted out of one sector into another.

One could tell exactly the same story if, instead of reducing the wage bill by £1000, the capitalist introduced new mass production technology that allowed him to produce £1000 worth of additional bread while leaving all other costs unchanged. This does not create a disequilibrium in the economy (and it certainly does not mean that 'the system' needs to brainwash consumers into wanting to consume more in order to absorb this extra bread). If people don't want more bread, then the new technology won't allow him to produce an extra £1000 worth of bread, it will only allow him to produce an extra £500, or £100, or £5 worth. In any case, there is no point tracking down the ultimate fate of every breadcrumb just to make sure that there will be sufficient demand to absorb this increase in supply. We know that there must be because the two are an accounting identity.

The principle that I am appealing to here is known to economists as Say's law. Unfortunately, Say's law is widely viewed as having been discredited, after John Maynard Keynes launched a blistering attack against it in the '30s. Keynes's view has, however, been widely misunderstood. What Keynes showed was that when money is introduced into the economy, things become significantly more complicated. Money is not a purely transparent medium; it can also serve as a store of value. If people think that prices are going to drop, for example, they may decide to hold on to their cash instead of spending it right away. As a result, if you treat money as something separate from all the other commodities in the economy, a sudden increase in the demand for money will appear to be a sudden decline in the demand for all other commodities. In other words, a spike in the demand for money *looks like* an excess of supply of all other goods. This is what misled Marx into thinking that recessions were caused by generalised overproduction. Keynes showed that recessions were not caused by 'too many goods', but rather by 'not enough money'. The solution to such a shortfall in demand was therefore not to instil new needs in consumers in order to increase overall demand for goods – this would have absolutely no effect. It was simply to put more money into circulation. This is precisely the remedy that was adopted, in one form or another, by Western nations after World War II, allowing them to more successfully manage the business cycle. Advertising had nothing to do with it.

The Keynesian diagnosis has unfortunately made it extremely common to talk about 'stimulating demand' during recessions, as though there really were a total shortage of demand in the economy relative to supply. In fact, during periods of recession there is really only a slackening of the volume and number of exchanges, combined with a shortage of demand for all other goods except money. When politicians encourage consumers to go shopping in order to help the economy, they are not really trying to create new demand (since every increase in demand corresponds to an increase in supply of the same magnitude); their goal is simply to get money back into circulation.

Sadly, the majority of politicians, to say nothing of the general public, don't understand this. This creates fertile ground in which the Marxian theory of consumerism has flourished. Critics of consumerism insist on treating consumption and production as though the two processes were completely independent of one another. *Adbusters* magazine, for example, has attracted worldwide attention with its campaign to institute an annual Buy Nothing Day. This ignores the fact that, one way or another, your total income gets spent. If you don't spend it, you put it in the bank and someone else spends it. The only way you can reduce consumption is by reducing your contribution to production. Yet somehow an annual Earn Nothing Day doesn't have the same ring to it.

A similar fallacy is at work in the arguments of those who *defend* consumerism on the grounds that it creates jobs for others.

They accuse those who cut back their spending of creating unemployment. They forget that simply cutting back your own spending will not reduce aggregate demand for labour – the money you save will simply be spent by someone else. The only way to genuinely cut back is to work less and reduce your own income. In this case, you are reducing demand for labour, and thus 'creating unemployment' – but it is your own job that you are cutting back, not anyone else's. The idea that *your* consumption helps other people is wishful thinking, pure and simple. Giving food to charity is not morally equivalent to eating it yourself, no matter how much we might like it to be so.

Part of the attraction of the consumerism-as-conformity thesis is that it helps to explain why consumer goods fail to generate any lasting satisfaction. If we don't really need any of these things in the first place, then it's a bit easier to understand why we find ourselves unhappy at the end of the day. Yet there are other, more plausible explanations available. First, it is worth noting that in developing countries, economic growth does an enormous amount to promote overall happiness. It is only once a society has become quite wealthy that growth no longer delivers increased happiness. Second, there is still a fairly strong correlation between *relative wealth* and happiness, even in very rich societies. While money doesn't buy happiness, having more money than your neighbours does significantly improve your prospects.

This observation is at the heart of the critique of the consumer society developed by Thorstein Veblen in the late 19th century. In many respects, Veblen's analysis is far more penetrating than any of the theories developed in the 20th century. In Veblen's view, the fundamental problem with the consumer society is not that our needs are artificial, but that the goods produced are valued less for their intrinsic properties than for their role as markers of relative success. When a society is very poor, an increase in productive capacity is almost entirely directed toward producing 'staple' goods: clean water, nutritious food, decent shelter, and so on. Thus economic growth initially produces tangible, permanent gains in individual satisfaction. However, once these more elementary needs are satisfied, goods become valued increasingly for their 'honorific' properties. Clothing becomes more ornately decorated, houses become larger, food preparation becomes more elaborate and jewellery begins to make its appearance. All of these goods serve as markers of social status.[13]

The problem is that while an increase in 'material' goods can generate increased happiness for everyone, status is an intrinsically zero-sum game. In order for one person to win, someone else must lose. Moving up necessarily involves bumping someone else – or everyone else – down. So the time and effort invested in the production of prestige goods is, according to Veblen, 'wasteful'. Veblen is careful to point out, however, that to call such expenditures wasteful 'implies no deprecation of the motives or ends sought by the consumer'.[14] The reason it is wasteful is that when everyone does it, everyone winds up right back where they started. Thus the expenditure of time and energy does not generate any improvements in 'human well-being on the whole'.[15]

This is not puritanism. In Veblen's view, consumerism is essentially a collective action problem – a prisoner's dilemma. To see how this argument works, consider the case of two doctors, each of whom drives to work in a modest Honda sedan. Suppose they both believe the 'King of Real Estate' Buddy Kane's thesis that in order to succeed, 'one must project an image of success at all times'. They also know that patients are likely to be suspicious of a doctor who doesn't drive at least a BMW. Of course, they also know that they should be saving some of their income for retirement. But that seems a long way away. Furthermore, buying the new car now should improve business, making it easier to save that much more later.

In this way, it is easy for either doctor to talk himself into buying the BMW. But does this improve business? The strategy only works if not all the doctors do it. If every doctor runs out and buys a BMW, then patients still have no basis for choosing one doctor over another. The situation is the same as it was when they were all driving Hondas, except that now everyone is saving less and spending more on their car payments. Soon enough, the BMW comes to be seen as merely an entry-level car. Of course, in this situation, the only way to improve one's position is to go out and buy a Mercedes or a Jaguar. Yet this just forces the others to make the same expenditure in order to keep up. Again, everyone winds up back where they started, and there is no overall increase in happiness.

Thus, as society as a whole grows wealthier, consumer behaviour increasingly acquires the structure of an arms race. It's like turning up your stereo in order to drown out the neighbour's music. At first, this produces a genuine improvement in welfare – you no longer have to listen to the noise coming from next door. The problem arises only when the neighbour, in response, turns her stereo up even higher. The same principle applies to consumers. Their consumption decisions generate no lasting increase in happiness, but this does not mean that consumers are stupid, irrational or brainwashed. It simply means that they are stuck in a collective action problem.

Yet the competition is not limited to status seekers and social climbers. People who are not particularly interested in outdoing their neighbours, but who want to maintain a 'respectable' living standard, wind up having to spend more year after year. Their consumption takes the form of 'defensive consumption', since they are for the most part just trying to avoid humiliation. In other words, they are trying to keep up with the Joneses. But as the example of the arms race illustrates, it doesn't matter whether armaments are acquired for defensive or for offensive purposes – the consequences are the same. One person's attempt to retain a decent living standard merely forces the others to spend more in order to acquire superior status. Consumption habits therefore tend to be propagated downward through the social hierarchy, as they become increasingly emulated by those in the lower ranks.

When it comes to explaining the nature of modern consumerism, Veblen obviously hit the nail right on the head. His theory is almost freakish in its prescience. And not only is his diagnosis of the problem dead on, but his theory also suggests a number of extremely practical ways of reducing its severity. Yet despite this, the progressive left has spent most of the 20th century trying to resist Veblen's ideas. The entire critique of mass society is, in a sense, an attempt to salvage Marx's view and to defend it against Veblen's.

Why this animus toward Veblen? In the eyes of the left, Veblen commits one cardinal sin: *he blames consumers for consumerism*. More specifically, he argues that the existing social hierarchy is actively maintained by competitive consumption *among all classes of society*. Thus, consumerism, far from being something that is inflicted upon the working classes by the scheming bourgeoisie, is something that the working classes actively participate in maintaining – even though it is not in their collective interest to do so. If the working classes had wanted to buy out the capitalists, they could easily have done so by now, simply by saving a fraction of the wage increases that they have received over the years. But instead they have chosen to max out their spending on consumer goods.

In fact, if we regard the propensity to spend now rather than save for later as the hallmark of rampant consumerism, then consumerism is much worse among the poor than among the rich. Average propensity to save is much higher among the wealthy than among the broad middle class (who have significant disposable income). Veblen's theory provides an elegant explanation for this. Social status, like everything else, is subject to diminishing marginal utility – the less you have of it, the more you are willing to pay to get some. Thus lower-status groups are willing to dedicate a greater percentage of their income to competitive consumption than are high-status groups. People in the upper class already have so much status that they're not willing to make any great sacrifices to obtain more of it. The lower classes, on the other hand, are.[16]

This is an explosive suggestion, and it has brought forth heated denials. The primary strategy for dismissing Veblen involves a variation on the consumerism-as-brainwashing theory. The naive version suggests that people like to buy expensive cars because they are programmed by advertising to want them. Veblen suggests that they want these cars because they are embroiled in a competition with other consumers. The sophisticated version of the brainwashing theory acknowledges this, but then counters with the claim that consumers are only embroiled in this competition because they have been programmed by advertising to be competitive. Thus it is claimed that advertising *creates* competitive consumption, by stimulating envy or by encouraging an unhealthy preoccupation with social status. Status-seeking is regarded as another artificial need, instilled in consumers by 'the system'.

This argument also leads to the unhelpful suggestion that it is possible to 'opt out' of competitive consumption, simply by avoiding any overt preoccupation with status. Just ignore the Joneses, and you will be striking a blow against consumerism. Unfortunately, things are not so simple. Even if envy and status-obsession were purely an artefact of the capitalist system (which is highly doubtful), there is often no way to opt out. When most people think of competitive consumption, they think of 'offensive' strategies. Consider the person who goes overboard and buys everyone in the family a more expensive Christmas present than the norm. This makes her seem more generous, more loving, but at the expense of everyone else, who now appears less so. This offensive strategy calls for defensive measures. Next year, everyone in the family may have to spend more on their gifts. They do so not because they want to engage in one-upmanship, but simply to regain the position they once had. (This 'arms race' may continue to escalate, until eventually an arms control pact may be required – such as a 'secret Santa' protocol.)

It only takes one person, one act of 'offensive' consumption, to trigger such an episode. The other people in the family are not obsessed with status; they simply want to avoid seeming cheap. But in Veblen's view, the motives that drive competitive consumption at the level of society are usually just as innocent. The average level of consumption serves as a point of reference that determines what Veblen called 'the pecuniary standard of decency' – the minimum level of expenditure below which a person comes to be the object of either contempt or pity. For over thirty years, social scientists have been tracking what people consider to be the 'absolute minimum' required to live a decent life. The amount has ratcheted up steadily over time, mirroring the overall rate of economic growth almost precisely. Thus even the very poor are chasing a moving target.

Furthermore, a lot of defensive consumption has nothing to do with status. We are often forced into competitive consumption just to defend ourselves against the nuisances generated by other people's consumption. In many parts of North America, for example, the number of big four-wheel drives on the road has reached the point where people are forced to think twice before buying a small car. When there is a fatality in a collision between a four-wheel drive and a car, 80 per cent of the time it is the person in the car who dies.[17] The four-wheel drives make the roads so dangerous for other drivers that everyone has to consider buying a larger car just to protect themselves.

This is why expecting people to simply opt out of all competitive consumption is unrealistic. The cost to the individual is just too high. Four-wheel drives present a clear race to the bottom. In an accident, it's much better to be in a vehicle that is heavier than the one you hit. As a result, everyone tries to get a vehicle that's heavier than everyone else's, and the average size of vehicles steadily increases, making the road more dangerous for everyone. It's all well and good to say that someone should put an end to this competition. But in the meantime, heavy four-wheel drives are not about to disappear from the roads. So are you willing to endanger your children's lives by buying a runaround?

Because so much of our competitive consumption is defensive in nature, people feel justified in their choices and blameless for the consequences that ensue. Unfortunately, everyone who participates contributes just as much to the problem, regardless of his or her intentions. It doesn't matter why you bought the four-wheel drive—because you want to intimidate other drivers or because you want to protect your children – you still made it harder for other drivers to opt out of the automotive arms race. When it comes to consumerism, intentions are irrelevant. It is the consequences that count.

★

It is a commonplace observation that property prices are determined by 'location, location, and location'. We sometimes forget the extent to which this is true. My house in central Toronto is over 100 years old, just slightly over 15 feet wide, and has about 1200 square feet of interior space. It's a generic three-storey row house, virtually identical to the twenty-two other houses on my side of the block. The property market has been quite robust lately, so houses in my row have been selling for over $400,000 (£178,000). Needless to say, the same house in another location would not be worth quite as much. In fact, just down the road, in the city of Hamilton, Ontario, you can buy an identical house on a lot of the same size for around $60,000 (£27,000).

Obviously, the price of property in the centre of town has very little to do with the materials that go into the construction of a dwelling. It has to do with how many other people want to live there. This is easy to notice when you buy a house in the city, because there are often multiple bids on houses in attractive locations. Thus the eventual sale price of the house will be determined entirely by how much it takes to outbid the other potential buyers. Yet while it is possible for developers to respond to rising house prices by building more houses, it is impossible to create more good locations. Property in the centre of town is intrinsically scarce simply because the centre is where most people want to be (if they didn't, then it wouldn't be the centre). As a result, the quest for location, like the quest for status, is very close to being a zero-sum game. It's even worse in the United Kingdom, where the perceived quality of State schools varies enormously between boroughs and so consumers are also competing with one another to get into good school catchment areas. In the end, those who buy into good districts inexorably squeeze out those who are unable or unwilling to pay. Thus access to desirable property is determined by one's *relative* ability to pay. For every winner, there must be a loser. And what is this if not competitive consumption?

This doesn't happen only in inner city areas. People who buy in the suburbs are generally looking for easy access to the city, combined with the open space and quality of life associated with the country. Yet because this can only be achieved at the outer perimeter of the city, each new suburban development leapfrogs existing suburbs, creating the familiar expanding-doughnut pattern of urban growth. Urban sprawl, in other words, is a race to the bottom driven by the quest for a good location. (Even those who try to 'get away from it all' are embroiled in a competition. Each person who stakes out a piece of unspoiled wilderness or an isolated tract of land makes it that much harder for anyone else to do the same. It's like wanting to drive on an open road.)

What these examples show is that competitive consumption often has nothing to do with people's motives; it is often imposed by the very nature of the goods that are sought. In *The Social Limits to Growth*, Fred Hirsch argues that we should distinguish 'material' goods from 'positional' goods. Things like paper, houses, petrol and wheat – material goods – are scarce only because they require time, energy and effort in order to produce. As a result, if we are willing to invest more time, energy or effort, we are able to produce more of them. Other goods, however, are intrinsically scarce – we could not produce more of them even if we wanted to. Because the quantity is fixed, access to these positional goods will always be determined by one's relative ability to pay. Status is simply one type of positional good. Property is another.

Of course, most goods have both material and positional qualities. We can think of every good as carrying a 'competitive premium'. If a restaurant is very popular, it will become crowded, and customers may find it difficult to get a table. The management may respond by raising prices in order to thin out the crowds. Thus a meal at the restaurant will now come with a competitive premium: one portion of the bill is spent on the food; another portion goes toward keeping out other people who would like to eat there. In the city, this sort of competitive premium exists everywhere you turn – at the gym, the movie theatre, the hairdresser. In many ways, the city simply *is* one giant competition. Find anything desirable and you will also find a dozen other people crowding in on it, trying to get some as well. If you sit down and add it up, it's easy to see that the average city-dweller's income is almost entirely absorbed into competitive consumption. The competitive premium on my house – the amount that I pay for the location – is at least $350,000 (£156,000). This means that, on a monthly basis, about half of my take-home income is absorbed into pure competitive consumption – I am literally paying to keep out all of the other people who would like to live where I live.

I would move, except that I really enjoy being able to walk to work. As it stands, I am just a fifteen-minute stroll from the campus where I teach. Of course, there are hundreds of thousands of people who also work in central Toronto who would also love to walk to work. But that just isn't possible unless we are willing to pave over all the nice leafy neighbourhoods and build back-to-back residential skyscrapers. So how do we decide who will have the pleasure of being able to live in a leafy neighbourhood *and* walk to work? We start bidding against one another. We drive up the price of residential properties. As the bidding goes higher, the people who can't afford it or who are not willing to pay that much for the pleasure of walking to work start to drop out. How high does the bidding go? Depends how much people are willing to pay for this particular luxury. There is no upward limit. Some quick arithmetic shows that the implicit cost of my little walk to work is well over £45 per trip.

The point of this exercise is to show that the question of whether you are engaged in competitive consumption has absolutely nothing to do with whether you *think* you are engaged in competitive consumption. Competitive consumption is not necessarily conspicuous consumption, and it need not be motivated by envy. It would be much cheaper for me to buy a larger house in the suburbs, along with a Porsche as compensation for having to drive to work. This would be highly conspicuous, and I would certainly get disapproving stares from all of my colleagues as I pulled up to work. Yet walking to work is far more expensive. It is simply a very inconspicuous form of competitive consumption – so inconspicuous that most people don't even notice it or think of it as consumption.

Given the importance of access to positional goods in determining our quality of life, it is easy to see why economic growth eliminates the connection between happiness and absolute wealth. In a very poor country, the basic problem is that people lack material goods. Economic growth is able to expand the supply of these goods and thus to generate lasting improvements in people's welfare. In our society, by contrast, material scarcity has been almost completely eliminated, and so the typical consumer's income is spent mostly on positional goods. Yet because these goods are intrinsically scarce, economic growth does nothing to increase their supply. An increase in my salary does not help me to buy a nicer house, or a more luxurious car, when all my neighbours receive the same; it simply increases the price. Furthermore, we may all consume more and more in a quest to achieve these positional goods. We commute farther and farther. We enrol our children in a hundred different extracurricular activities. We redecorate the home more and more often. Economic growth begins to resemble a giant arms race rather than a system of production aimed at satisfying human need.

This is why, according to Hirsch, economic growth in our society, rather than reducing the frustration of the middle classes, has tended rather to exacerbate it. Early industrialisation created unrealistic expectations by permitting the population at large to enjoy many of the privileges that had once been reserved for the wealthy. Those days are now long gone. 'What the wealthy have today can no longer be delivered to the rest of us tomorrow, yet as we individually grow richer, this is what we expect.'[18] By the time you can afford a Gucci bag, the world will have moved on to Prada. By the time you can afford an Armani suit, Canali will be the next big thing. This is not an accident. It's what drives the economy.

Ever notice that the masses have incredibly bad taste? Admit it. Take a look at a painting by Thomas Kinkade ('Painter of Light') the best-selling visual artist in the United States. His work is so awful, it must be seen to be believed. Or go down to one of those discount furniture warehouses, the kind that is constantly advertising 'no payment until 2037'. Try to find a single piece that you would be willing to put in your living room. Or listen to an entire album by Kenny G, the best-selling instrumentalist in the world. Your typical urban sophisticate would find this experience not just unpleasant, but positively harrowing.

I've been in a fair number of mobile homes across North America. I've also been to quite a few New York City apartments. Most of the mobile homes are considerably more spacious and comfortable than the New York City apartments. Yet the average New York apartment-dweller would be driven mad living in a caravan park. Why? Because the entire environment – from the linoleum in the bathroom to the wagon wheels out on the front lawn to the neighbour's mullet – is irredeemably *tacky*. The question is: which came first? Is it because the poor are poor that they have such bad taste? Has poverty deprived them of aesthetic experience, and thus prevented them from developing sound judgment? Or is it perhaps the other way around? Are certain styles considered tacky precisely *because* the affluent want to distance themselves from the choices made by the poor?

The popular view of aesthetic judgment is dominated by what sociologist Pierre Bourdieu calls 'the ideology of natural taste'. According to this view, the difference between beautiful and ugly, tasteful and vulgar, stylish and tacky, resides in the object. Bad art really *is* bad, it's just that only people with a certain background and education are able to recognise it as such. Yet, as Bourdieu points out, this ability to detect bad art is distributed in an almost miraculously class-specific fashion. In fact, only a tiny percentage of the population has it. And as Bourdieu documents quite exhaustively, this capacity is almost entirely concentrated among the high-status members in society. The lower classes uniformly love bad art, while the middle classes have resolutely 'middle-brow' taste.[19]

Anyone with an even moderately critical turn of mind can see the obvious explanation for this pattern. Veblen noticed long ago that 'the superior gratification derived from the use and contemplation of costly and supposedly beautiful products is, commonly, in great measure a gratification of our sense of costliness masquerading under the name of beauty.'[20] One can see this clearly in our appreciation of flowers, where 'some beautiful flowers pass conventionally for offensive weeds; others that can be cultivated with relative ease are accepted and admired by the lower middle class, who can afford no more expensive luxuries of this kind; but these varieties are rejected as vulgar by those people who are better able to pay for expensive flowers and who are educated to a higher schedule of pecuniary beauty in the florist's products.'[21]

Bourdieu argues that aesthetic judgment is always a matter of *distinction* – it involves separating out that which is superior from that which is inferior. Thus, much of good taste is defined negatively, in terms of what it is *not*. 'Tastes', says Bourdieu, 'are perhaps first and foremost distastes, disgust provoked by horror or visceral intolerance of the tastes of others.'[22] For taste in music, what you listen to is in many ways less important than what you *don't* listen to. It's not enough to have a few Radiohead CDs in your collection; it is also essential that you *not* have any Celine Dion, Mariah Carey or Bon Jovi. When it comes to art, it is okay to have a few tasteful reproductions, nothing too mainstream. Dogs playing poker are completely impermissible.

Because it is grounded in distinction, aesthetic judgment plays an extraordinarily strong role in reproducing status hierarchies in society. Taste involves not merely an appreciation of that which is tasteful, but also a deprecation of that which is tacky (and, by implication, of those who lack the ability to draw such distinctions). Good taste confers a sense of almost unassailable superiority upon its possessor. This is the primary reason that, in our society, people from different social classes do not freely interact with one another. They cannot stand each other's taste. More specifically, the people who are higher up in the social hierarchy are utterly contemptuous of everything that the people beneath them enjoy (movies, sports, television shows, music, etc.). 'Aesthetic intolerance', Bourdieu reminds us, 'can be terribly violent. Aversion to different lifestyles is perhaps one of the strongest barriers between the classes; class endogamy is evidence of this.'[23]

In cases where members of superior social classes do consume aesthetically inferior goods, it is essential that they do so ironically – so that everyone knows that they know that these goods are in bad taste. This is the essence of kitsch. This ironic distance allows them to enjoy the inferior goods while avoiding the taint of inferiority associated with their consumption. The ironic distance allows them to preserve their distinction so that they will not be confused with those who simply *like* black velvet paintings or Arborite tables or

Tom Jones songs. The kitsch consumer, usually through an exaggerated consumption style, shows everyone that he is 'in on the joke', and thus preserves the sense of superiority or distinction that elevates, or 'aestheticises', the goods he is consuming.

Because taste is grounded in the sense of distinction, it follows that not everyone can have good taste. It is a conceptual impossibility (just as not all students can have above-average grades). Through public art galleries and subsidies to producers, modern governments have invested significant resources in promoting the aesthetic education of the public. Yet has this improved the overall calibre of popular taste? Of course not. When an artistic style becomes popular, as with the Group of Seven in Canada or Salvador Dali in the United States, it is simply demoted in the canons of aesthetic judgment. Precisely because of their popularity, an appreciation of these styles no longer serves as a source of distinction. Thus 'good taste' shifts toward more inaccessible, less familiar styles.

Good taste, in other words, is a positional good. One person can have it only if many others do not. It is like belonging to an exclusive yacht club, or walking to work in the centre of town, or hiking through untouched wilderness. It has an inherently competitive logic. Thus any consumer who buys an object as an expression of her style or taste is necessarily participating in competitive consumption.

Whenever goods serve as a source of distinction, it means that at least part of their value stems from their exclusivity. Because not everyone has them, these goods identify the owners as members of a small club (those who are in the know) and distinguishes them from the masses (those who do not have a clue). Conformity and distinction thus always go hand in hand – one conforms to the habits and standards of the exclusive club in order to distinguish oneself from the great unwashed. Critics of mass society, unfortunately, have focused on the wrong side of the equation. It is not the desire to conform that is driving the consumption process, but rather the quest for distinction. The value of a good comes from the sense of superiority associated with membership in the club, along with the recognition accorded by fellow members. Yet once the word gets out and more people begin to acquire the good, the distinction that it confers is slowly eroded. The quest for distinction is therefore collectively self-defeating – everyone strives to get what not everyone can have.

Of course, the result of this competition is that consumers all wind up with roughly the same commodities at the end of the day. But this sort of conformity was never part of their intention. Consumers are like crabs stuck in a bucket, each one trying to escape but getting pulled back in by the others. It's not that the crabs want to stay in the bucket. It's just that as soon as any one crab makes any progress toward the rim, the others try to crawl over it, using its progress as a way of furthering their own escape. As a result, they all wind up back where they started.

Bourdieu's analysis of aesthetic judgment shows how naive it is to think we can opt out of consumerism, and avoid the problems that Veblen diagnosed, simply by avoiding status-seeking and envy. The sense of distinction permeates all of our aesthetic judgments: what is beautiful or ugly, charming or tacky, cool or uncool. Anyone who cares about style is *eo ipso* committed to competitive consumption. The only way to opt out is to refrain from allowing any such judgments to inform our purchasing decisions.

The year 2000 was the high water mark of the Burberry brand. The classic Burberry plaid began showing up everywhere, as a subtle accent: an elegant wool scarf, the lining of a jacket, a small hand clasp. The brand has its origins in the Burberry trench coat, which was developed for officers during World War I. It subsequently developed an association with the genteel lifestyle of the English countryside. Burberry was reinvigorated in the late '90s through a brilliant marketing campaign featuring aristocrat-turned-model Stella Tennant (granddaughter of the Duke and Duchess of Devonshire). Soon, exclusive retailers began stocking the full line of Burberry clothing, sunglasses, purses, shoes and dog collars.

Yet, within two years, Burberry was struggling. As brand strategist John Williamson puts it, 'As soon as you go down the mass market road you lose control of who wears your product.'[24] The low water mark for Burberry in the UK came when a contestant on the reality TV show *Big Brother 4*, Tania Do-Nascimento, paraded about in a Burberry bikini and bandanna, week in and week out, in front of an audience of millions. Good exposure for the brand? Hardly. Nascimento attracted attention mainly for boasting about her sexual exploits and vowing, if she won, to spend the prize money on breast implants.

The problem, as the brand consultants put it, is that Burberry was supposed to be an 'aspirational' brand. The aristocratic pedigree of the line allowed it to serve as a marker of social class. Wearing Burberry said, 'I am more concerned with classic elegance than I am with fashion.' Of course, in the early years of the brand renaissance, the overwhelming majority of the population didn't know the difference between Burberry and any other plaid. Those who were 'in the know' wore Burberry in order to telegraph a message to other people who were 'in the know', to exchange subtle glances of mutual recognition. Burberry served as a source of *distinction*. Distinction always involves both inclusion and exclusion. It involves reaffirming one's membership in the superior in-group and, at the same time, disavowing membership in the inferior out-group.

The most important thing about class is that not everyone can have it. Burberry might have protected the exclusivity of its brand by keeping prices very high, except that it is very difficult to enforce a trademark on a plaid. As a result, anyone and everyone began to produce Burberry knockoffs. The plaid became instantly available to the great unwashed – people like Nascimento – whose concept of 'classy' is very much contrary to the brand image Burberry hoped to cultivate. And the thought that wearing Burberry might telegraph the message 'I like reality TV and boob jobs', instead of 'I prefer classic elegance', is enough to scare most members of the social elite off the brand.

Another way of formulating the problem is to say that Burberry became too mainstream and thus ceased to serve as a source of distinction. And it is here that we can see the obvious point of contact between the critique of mass society and the problem of consumerism. The traditional critique of mass society suggests that most people are members of the herd, cogs in the machine, victims of mindless conformity. They lead vacuous, hollowed-out lives ruled by shallow, materialistic values. They are manipulated to serve the functional requirements of the system, and so will never experience true creativity, freedom or even complete sexual fulfilment. That having been said, who could possibly want to be a member of mass society? If anything, people should be desperate to prove that they are *not* victims of conformity, that they are *not* merely cogs in the machine. And of course, as the critique of mass society became increasingly widespread, this is precisely what people tried to do.

Thus countercultural rebellion – rejecting the norms of 'mainstream' society – came to serve as a source of considerable distinction. In a society that prizes individualism and despises conformity, being 'a rebel' becomes the new aspirational category. 'Dare to be different', we are constantly told. In the '60s, becoming a beat or a hippie was a way of showing that you were *not* one of the squares or the suits. In the '80s, dressing like a punk or a goth was a way of showing that you were not one of the preppies or the yuppies. It was a way of visibly demonstrating one's rejection of mainstream society, but it was also a tacit affirmation of one's own superiority. It was a way of telegraphing the message that '*I*, unlike *you*, have not been fooled by the system. I am not a mindless cog.'

The problem, of course, is that not everyone can be a rebel, for the same reason that not everyone can have class and not everyone can have good taste. If everyone joins the counterculture, then the counterculture simply becomes the culture. Then the rebel has to invent a *new* counterculture, in order to re-establish distinction. Countercultural style begins as a very exclusive thing. It starts out 'underground'. Particular symbols – a love bead, a safety pin, a brand of shoes or cut of jeans, a Maori tattoo, a body piercing, an aftermarket muffler – will serve as points of communication among those who are 'in the know'. Yet as time passes, the circle of those who are 'in the know' expands, and the symbol becomes increasingly common. This naturally erodes the distinction that these markers confer – in the same way that Nascimento cheapened the Burberry brand. 'The club' becomes less and less elite. As a result, the rebel has to move on to something new. Thus the counterculture must constantly reinvent itself. This is why rebels adopt and discard styles as quickly as fashionistas move through brands.

In this way, countercultural rebellion has become one of the major forces driving competitive consumption. As Thomas Frank writes:

> With the 'alternative' facelift, 'rebellion' continues to perform its traditional function of justifying the economy's ever-accelerating cycles of obsolescence with admirable efficiency. Since our willingness to load up our closets with purchases depends upon an eternal shifting of the products paraded before us, upon our being endlessly convinced that the new stuff is better than the old, we must be persuaded over and over again that the 'alternatives' are more valuable than the existing or the previous. Ever since the 1960s, hip has been the native tongue of advertising, 'antiestablishment' the vocabulary by which we are taught to cast off our old possessions and buy whatever they have decided to offer this year. And over the years the rebel has naturally become the central image of this culture of consumption, symbolising endless, directionless change, and eternal restlessness with 'the establishment' – or, more correctly, with the stuff 'the establishment' convinced him to buy last year.[25]

Of course, in order to preserve the ideology that sustains this consumption, it is essential that the mass-marketing of rebellion be described as 'co-optation'. In this way, the perpetual cycles of obsolescence can be blamed upon the system rather than seen as a consequence of competition for a positional good.

The myth of co-optation thus serves to conceal the fact that 'alternative' is, and always has been, good business. Casual inspection of any Urban Outfitters store should be enough to confirm the impression. Furthermore, because the critique of mass society treats the entire culture as a system of repression and conformity, the number of rebel styles is potentially infinite. Find anyone who is breaking any kind of rule and you have marketing potential. The sartorial preferences of drug dealers, for example, have been driving 'urban' style for decades. Standing on the street corner all night selling dime bags gets pretty cold. Better put on a puffy down jacket and a pair of Timberlands. Everyone knows the look, not because they buy a lot of drugs, but because they know hip hop style. They see what NBA players are wearing, and they're familiar with Tommy Hilfiger's latest collection.

Or consider skateboarding. The same month that *Adbusters* magazine featured a special on skateboarding subculture, the number-one movie at the box office in North America was *Jackass*, a film that originated from the same subculture. A photo spread in *Adbusters* emphasised the subversive character of boarders by featuring close-up photographs of pavilions, stairs and walkways worn down and damaged by their boards. But skateboarders do not target corporate headquarters for abuse; they are just as happy damaging public property. And, as *Jackass* showed, the market for random stupidity and destruction is vast indeed. The film earned over US$64 (£35) million in cinemas.

'When we first uncovered the creative genius of the underground skateboard mentality of *Jackass*, we knew it would resonate with our young adult audience', said Brian Graden, MTV's president of programming. Right he was. But is it plausible to say that MTV and Johnny Knoxville 'co-opted' skateboard culture? In order to co-opt, there has to be something there to be co-opted in the first place. The tradition of 'jackassing' around is certainly an integral part of boarding subculture. All that Knoxville and the gang did was to start videotaping it. Jackassing is, in a sense, anti-authoritarian. There is no question that you are breaking the rules – doing everything that your parents told you not to do. What's more, passing businesspeople will probably give you disapproving stares. Security guards may chase you off the property. But is it subversive? Of course not. At best it's a form of mild social deviance.

It's important to remember that the first skateboarding fad came and went in the mid-1970s. (Who can forget the banana board?) It fizzled out, largely because of the backlash against roller skating (which was, in turn, associated with disco). From there, it went 'underground' (i.e. became less popular). By that time, many towns and cities had got around to passing ordinances prohibiting skateboarding on sidewalks, in courtyards and in malls. This in turn gave boarding something of a rebellious edge, as cops and security guards began cracking down on boarders, chasing away 'those damn kids', and so forth. This is precisely what was needed for skateboarding to stage a comeback.

Since then, the rebel style associated with skateboarding has become a massive driving force in the sports industry (not to mention its offshoot, snowboarding, which injected literally billions of dollars into the moribund ski industry). People complain about Nike 'co-opting' '60s rebellion by using the Beatles song 'Revolution' in their ads or by hiring William S. Burroughs as a spokesperson. But what about Vans, a company that has built a £166 million-a-year business entirely on the basis of 'alternative sports'? Is there any difference between building skateboard parks and tennis courts? It's all big business. In the United States, it is estimated that more than one thousand skate parks were built in the eighteen-month period from January 2001 to June 2002. One thousand skate parks in eighteen months? That's big business. Is it also the co-optation of a subculture? No. It's called 'responding to popular demand'. It's what companies are supposed to do. Will it destroy the subculture? Certainly. That's because there is nothing really 'extreme' about extreme sports. Nothing that boarders do in a half-pipe is even remotely as dangerous as playing rugby. Extreme sports are just sports for people who don't want to be mistaken for jocks. Once the jocks start doing them, the distinction will be lost, and so it will be time to move on to something new.

Thanks to the myth of counterculture, many of the people who are most opposed to consumerism nevertheless actively participate in the sort of behaviour that drives it. Consider Naomi Klein. She starts out her book *No Logo* by decrying the recent conversion of factory buildings in her Toronto neighbourhood into 'loft living' condominiums. She makes it clear to the reader that her place is the real deal, a genuine factory loft, steeped in working-class authenticity yet throbbing with urban street culture and what she calls a 'rock-video aesthetic'. Klein also drops enough hints about her neighbourhood that any reader familiar with Toronto would know that she was in the King-Spadina area. And any reader with a feel for how social class in Canada works would know that at the time Klein was writing, a genuine factory loft in the King-Spadina area was possibly the single most desirable piece of property in the country – comparable to a SoHo loft in Manhattan.[26]

Yet unlike merely expensive neighbourhoods in Toronto, such as Rosedale and Forest Hill, where it is possible to buy your way in, genuine factory lofts in Klein's neighbourhood could be acquired only by people with superior social connections. This is because they contravened zoning regulations, and so could not be bought or leased on the open market. Only the most exclusive segment of the cultural elite could get access to them.

Unfortunately for Klein, the City of Toronto, as part of a very enlightened and successful strategy to slow urban sprawl, decided to rezone all the central neighbourhoods to permit mixed usages. King-Spadina was rezoned to permit any combination of industrial, commercial and residential use. Before long, an enormous revitalisation of the neighbourhood began, as old warehouses and factories were renovated, condominium complexes were built, new restaurants opened and so forth.

Yet from Klein's perspective, this was a disaster. Why? Because the rezoning allowed yuppies to buy their way into her neighbourhood. What's wrong with yuppies? Other than being yuppies, what crime did these newcomers commit? Klein claims they brought with them 'a painful new self-consciousness' to the neighbourhood. But, as the rest of her introduction to *No Logo* demonstrates, she too is conscious – painfully so – of her surroundings. She describes her neighbourhood as one where 'in the twenties and thirties Russian and Polish immigrants darted back and forth … ducking into delis to argue about Trotsky and the leadership of the International Ladies' Garment Workers' Union.' Emma Goldman, we are told, 'the famed anarchist and labour organiser', lived on her street! How exciting for Klein! What a tremendous source of *distinction* that must be.

It is here that we can see the true nature of Klein's complaint. The arrival of yuppies led to an erosion of her social status. Her complaints about commercialisation are nothing but an expression of this loss of distinction. A few years back, saying 'I live in a loft at King-Spadina' sent a very clear message to anyone with ears to listen. It said, 'I am extremely cool. Quite possibly cooler than you.' But with a dozen new condominium complexes, the noise threatens to drown out the signal. How will people know that you live in a 'real' loft, and not just one of those yuppie ones?

Klein can see only one solution. If the landlord decides to convert her building to condominiums, she will have to move out. She discusses this as though it were self-evident. Yet if the landlord decided to convert her building, why wouldn't she just buy her loft? (It's not as though she couldn't afford it.) The problem, of course, is that a loft-living condominium doesn't have quite the cachet of a 'genuine' loft. It becomes, as Klein puts it, merely an apartment with 'exceptionally high ceilings'.

Thus, the real problem becomes clear. It is not her landlord who threatens to drive her from the neighbourhood; it is her fear of losing her social status. What Klein fails to observe is that the cachet associated with her neighbourhood is precisely what is driving the property market, what creates the value in these dwellings. People buy these lofts because they want to be cool like Naomi Klein. Or more specifically, they want some of her social status. Naturally, she is not amused.

Here we can see the forces driving competitive consumption in their starkest form. The extraordinary thing is that they passed unnoticed, even though they occur in the introduction of a book that has been adopted as the bible of the anticonsumerism movement.

Notes

1   See Bruno S. Frey and Alois Stutzer, *Happiness and Economics: How the Economy and Institutions Affect Human Well-Being* (Princeton, NJ: Princeton University Press, 2002).

2   Jean Baudrillard, 'The Ideological Genesis of Needs', trans. Charles Levin, *The Consumer Society*, ed. Juliet B. Schor and Douglas B. Holt (New York: Free Press, 2000), 63.

3   *Ibid.*, 73.

4   *Ibid.*, 73.

5   Jean Baudrillard, *La Société de Consommation* (Paris: Éditions Denoël, 1970), 170.

6   Baudrillard, 'Ideological Genesis of Needs', 75.

7   *Ibid.*, 74.

8   Baudrillard, *La Société de Consommation*, 115 (our translation).

9   Baudrillard, 'Ideological Genesis of Needs', 74.

10 Stuart Ewen, *Captains of Consciousness: Advertising and the Social Roots of the Consumer Culture* (New York: Basic Books, 1976), 84.

11 *Ibid.*, 44.

12 Jean Baudrillard, 'Ideological Genesis of Needs', 77.

13 Thorstein Veblen, *Theory of the Leisure Class: An Economic Study in the Evolution of Institutions* (New York: Penguin, 1994), 33.

14 *Ibid.*, 98.

15 *Ibid.*, 97.

16   Robert H. Frank, *Choosing the Right Pond: Human Behavior and the Quest for Status* (Oxford: Oxford University Press, 1985).

17   For discussion, see Keith Bradsher, *High and Mighty: SUVs – The World's Most Dangerous Vehicles and How They Got That Way* (New York: Public Affairs, 2002), 166–206.

18   Fred Hirsch, *Social Limits to Growth* (Cambridge, MA: Harvard University Press, 1978), 67.

19   Pierre Bourdieu, *Distinction: A Social Critique of the Judgement of Taste*, trans. Richard Nice (Cambridge, MA: Harvard University Press, 1984), 126.

20   Veblen, *Theory of the Leisure Class*, 128.

21   *Ibid.*, 132.

22   Bourdieu, *Distinction*, 56.

23   *Ibid.*, 56.

24   Quoted in Richard Fletcher, 'Burberry Takes a Brand Check', *Daily Telegraph*, June 22, 2003.

25   Thomas Frank, 'Alternative to What?' in *Commodify Your Dissent: Salvos from 'The Baffler,'* ed. Thomas Frank and Matt Weiland (New York: Norton, 1997), 151.

26   *No Logo*: Naomi Klein, *No Logo: Taking Aim at the Brand Bullies* (Toronto: Knopf, 2000), xiii–xv.

5

Extreme rebellion

The Industrial Revolution and its consequences have been a disaster for the human race. They have greatly increased the life expectancy of those of us who live in 'advanced' countries, but they have destabilised society, have made life unfulfilling, have subjected human beings to indignities, have led to widespread psychological suffering (in the Third World to physical suffering as well) and have inflicted severe damage on the natural world. The continued development of technology will worsen the situation. It will certainly subject human beings to greater indignities and inflict greater damage on the natural world, it will probably lead to greater social disruption and psychological suffering, and it may lead to increased physical suffering even in 'advanced' countries.

We therefore advocate a revolution against the industrial system. This revolution may or may not make use of violence: it may be sudden or it may be a relatively gradual process spanning a few decades. We can't predict any of that. But we do outline in a very general way the measures that those who hate the industrial system should take in order to prepare the way for a revolution against that form of society. This is not to be a political revolution. Its object will be to overthrow not governments but the economic and technological basis of the present society.[1]

These lines are from the opening paragraphs of the 'Unabomber Manifesto'. In the 1980s and 1990s, the Unabomber gained national notoriety by mailing parcel bombs to prominent research scientists, engineers and industry lobbyists throughout the United States – those responsible for the reproduction of the 'technological basis' of society. The bombs were elaborately concealed, often in everyday objects. Many of these were cigar boxes or books, with triggers that detonated them when opened. In one case, the bomb contained a pressure-sensitive trigger designed to explode the parcel when an aircraft carrying it reached a certain altitude.

Police had no success in the Unabomber case for over fifteen years. The break came in 1996, when the bomber anonymously contacted authorities, offering to stop his campaign if the *New York Times* or the *Washington Post* would print his manifesto. In a controversial move, the two papers agreed. Once the manifesto was printed, the Unabomber's brother recognised the work and contacted police. The tip led police to a tiny shack near Lincoln, Montana, where Theodore Kaczynski had been living the life of a hermit since 1979, with no electricity, growing his own vegetables, hunting rabbits and crafting homemade bombs.

When the Unabomber Manifesto was published, many people on the left, somewhat to their surprise, found that there was very little in it to disagree with. The text contained familiar elements of the countercultural critique. Modern technology has created a system of total domination and control? Sure. Nature is being systematically destroyed? Check. Industrial society provides nothing but substitute gratifications? Right. The masses are oversocialised, compulsive conformists? Tell me something I don't know.

In fact, many people found their differences with Kaczynski to be more tactical than substantive. (A popular Internet quiz that challenged readers to distinguish quotes from Al Gore's *Earth in the Balance* from Kaczynski's manifesto proved surprisingly difficult.) They agreed with his beliefs – they simply didn't approve of mail bombs. Yet even there, Kaczynski's thoughts on violence were not all that far from the positions taken by a number of '60s icons, from Jean-Paul Sartre and Frantz Fanon to Malcolm X.

Thus the Unabomber case forced many people to confront a question that partisans of the countercultural critique had studiously avoided for decades. Where do we draw the boundary between transgression and pathology? When does 'thinking outside the box' shade over into mental illness? What is the difference between engaging in antisocial behaviour and rebelling against society? At what point does alternative degenerate into just plain crazy?

★

Every radical political movement attracts its share of kooks and misfits. Yet still, countercultural rebellion movements seem to have had somewhat more than their fair share. From the Jonestown cult and the Manson family to the Nation of Islam and the Society for Cutting Up Men, '60s radicals seem to have been peculiarly susceptible to the siren songs of lunatics and madmen. *Morning of the Magicians*, ufology, ancient space god theory, Druidic rituals, the search for Atlantis, theosophy, Scientology, Rosicrucianism – there seemed to be no limit to the credulity of the countercultural rebels.

The explanation for this is not hard to find. While countercultural rebellion probably attracts no more kooks than any other movement, it is peculiarly ill-equipped to deal with them once they arrive. This is because the countercultural critique essentially denies the distinction between social deviance and dissent. Since the entire culture is regarded as a system of repression, anyone who breaks any rule, for whatever reason, can claim to be engaging in an act of 'resistance'. Furthermore, anyone who criticises these claims will automatically be attacked as just another stooge of 'the system', another oppressive fascist trying to impose rules and regulations upon the rebellious individual.

For this reason, the counterculture has always had a tendency to romanticise criminality. From *Bonnie and Clyde* to *American Psycho*, the temptation has been to reinterpret (and intellectualise) theft, kidnapping and murder, and treat them as forms of social criticism. Punitive drug laws in the United States exacerbated this tendency. If it was easy to see the cocaine dealers in *Easy Rider* as striking a blow for freedom, then why not Mickey and Mallory from *Natural Born Killers*? Before long, we had people arguing that the Columbine school shootings were a critique of the mass education system. (Dylan Klebold and Eric Harris refused to conform to the tyranny of the jocks and preps!) Lorena Bobbitt wasn't just blowing off some steam when she cut off her husband's penis; she was making a feminist statement. (She refused to be a victim!) And, of course, O.J. was framed.

In each of these cases, ordinary (and sometimes extraordinary) criminal acts were taken up, given a political interpretation and then either defended or excused as acts of protest against 'the system'. The template for this interpretive strategy was forged in the late '60s. One can see it quite clearly in the indulgence shown to the Hell's Angels (which led directly to the disastrous Rolling Stones concert at Altamont in 1969). Of much greater political significance was the popular reaction to the riots that swept through hundreds of black neighbourhoods in the United States (most notably Watts and Detroit) in the late '60s. The dominant tendency among white radicals was to see these riots as merely an extension of the civil rights movement, not as a separate phenomenon. Blacks had tried peaceful protest under King, it was argued, but change had been too slow in coming. As frustration built, blacks turned to more radical leaders, such as Malcolm X and Stokely Carmichael. And they started to express their protest in more violent ways – through riots. Thus the Watts riots, according to one civil rights activist, showed that black Americans refused 'to walk peacefully to the gas chambers'. They were a response to 'the outrage of unemployment and hopelessness that pervades the ghetto.'[2]

This interpretation has since been canonised by filmmakers like Spike Lee (in his *Do the Right Thing*). The problem is that it has no empirical foundation. At the time of the catastrophic Detroit riot, for example, the auto industry was booming and black unemployment in the city was only 3.4 per cent. Average black family income was only 6 per cent lower than that of whites, and the home-ownership rate among blacks was the highest in the country. The images of the Detroit ghetto that we are now so familiar with – miles of empty lots and vacant buildings – were a *consequence* of the riots, not one of the causes.

Furthermore, the riots did not coincide with any shift toward support for more radical 'black power' leaders. The radical stances adopted by men like Malcolm X and Bobby Seale always appealed more to white countercultural radicals than to members of the black community. During his lifetime, Malcolm X's popular approval ratings among blacks never got out of the single-digit range (even in his base, New York City), while his disapproval ratings were at 48 per cent. A later survey of blacks showed 'black power' leaders Carmichael and Rap Brown each receiving an approval rating of 14 per cent, with a disapproval rating of 35 per cent for Carmichael and 45 per cent for Brown. Yet the sight of black militants marching into the California assembly armed with M1 rifles proved irresistible to many white radicals, who wanted nothing less than a total revolution against the social order. For them, Martin Luther King's integrationism was just one more instance of the system 'co-opting' dissent.

So the counterculture reinterpreted the development of American race relations to suit their own political predilections. Rather than seeing the civil rights movement as a battle for legally constituted rights, they encouraged everyone to regard it as the opening salvo in a total rebellion against American culture and society. But in so doing, they created a pattern of tolerance for criminal behaviour in black neighbourhoods that, in many ways, exacerbated conditions in the American inner city. To this day, the progressive left in the United States is deeply confused about where they should draw the line between deviance and dissent in African-American culture. An enormous amount of hip hop, for example, is a celebration of frankly antisocial behaviour and attitudes, yet many people feel comfortable criticising this only when the words come from the mouths of white rappers. (Eminem is surely right to point out the hypocrisy of his critics, who take him to task for lyrics that are often mild by the standards of much contemporary black hip hop.)

Even when criminal behaviour is not being treated as a form of protest, it is often 'politicised' by those who claim that it is a reaction to repressive social conditions: while the rioters may not have been protesting poverty and racism, their riot was nevertheless *caused* by these conditions. So even though the rioters were not consciously articulating a particular political agenda, the only way to respond to the riot is to address this political agenda.

This is the famous 'root causes' theory of crime. Like most theories, it has a grain of truth in it. It gets problematic only when taken too far – when it is imagined that *all* crime, or *all* antisocial behaviour, could be eliminated through political measures aimed at correcting social injustice. This ignores the underlying free-rider incentives that any social order invariably generates. Most of the time, crime actually does pay. People derive tangible benefits from it. Thus there will always be a need for a punitive social response to the behaviour of those who choose to harm others in order to benefit themselves, and always a need for some criteria for distinguishing antisocial behaviour from social protest.

Yet the countercultural critique makes it all but impossible to distinguish between 'good' repression – enforcement of the rules that enable mutually beneficial cooperation to emerge – and 'bad' repression – gratuitous violence inflicted upon the weak and disadvantaged. And when 'root causes' theory gets stirred into the mix, the results can be intellectually debilitating. If society is a giant system of repression, then every act, no matter how violent or antisocial, can be seen either as a form of protest or as 'blowback' caused by excess repression in the system. Thus the blame for anything bad that happens ultimately lands on 'the system', never upon the individuals who perpetrate it.

One can see the baleful influence of root-causes theory in Michael Moore's Academy Award-winning documentary *Bowling for Columbine*. The Columbine High School massacre was a criminal act in at least one obvious sense. Among adolescents who have been persecuted in high school, the fantasy of killing off a few jocks and blowing up the school is almost universal. Who didn't love the scene in *Heathers* when Christian Slater's character kills two jocks then dismisses his girlfriend's objections with the claim that since football season was over, the two 'had nothing left to offer the school except for date rape and AIDS jokes.' The difference between Klebold and Harris and most other kids in their situation is not that they *had* these fantasies, but that they acted upon them. In this respect, they are like all other criminals, who for the most part simply do what most of us are only ever *tempted* to do.

Yet for Moore, the Columbine massacre was not simply a criminal act, it was an indictment of all American society and history. The documentary starts out predictably enough, with a focus on the guns that Klebold and Harris used and how easy they were to obtain in the United States. But, slowly, the argument of the film takes a strange twist. The absence of gun control, it seems, is merely a superficial element of the problem. Canadians, Moore claims, have all sorts of guns, but almost no gun violence. Thus we need to look deeper to find the 'root causes' of the problem. The culprit, Moore claims, is a 'culture of fear' that exists in the United States.

At this point, Moore feels the need to retell the entire history of the United States, from the pilgrims to the present age. We hear about the history of slavery, lynchings and the KKK, the Spanish-American War, CIA-sponsored coups in South America, the invasion of Grenada, right through to the NATO bombing of Serbia. The 'culture of fear', in the end, has its origins in a deep-seated fear of blacks, reflecting the slave owner's fear of the slave rebellion, amplified by the military-industrial complex, America's paranoid pursuit of nuclear hegemony, and right-wing talk television. This is also, in some way, connected to unemployment and poverty.

In the end, Moore winds up taking a position *against* gun control. Gun control is too superficial. Gun control is what Roszak would call a 'merely institutional' solution to the problem of gun violence in American society. It doesn't get to the root of the problem. Moore will not settle for anything less than a total transformation of American culture and consciousness. Here we can see Moore committing the cardinal sin of the counterculture. He passes up a perfectly workable solution to the problem that he is confronting – a solution that would demonstrably improve the lives of his fellow citizens – on the grounds that it is not radical or 'deep' enough. Not only does he insist upon a revolutionary change in the culture, *he rejects anything less*. This is extreme rebellion.

Upon closer examination, Moore's argument against gun control turns out to be entirely specious. Gun violence is a classic example of a Hobbesian race to the bottom. Each individual can increase his or her own personal security by acquiring a gun, but everyone who does so also becomes more of a danger to the neighbours. The net effect is collectively self-defeating – everyone winds up endangering each other, lowering the average level of personal security. The solution is the same among individuals as it is among nations locked into an arms race. People need an arms control agreement, to dampen the competition. This is precisely what gun-control laws provide.

Moore claims that gun-control laws are unimportant, because Canada has millions of guns but almost no gun violence. This argument is disingenuous to the point of dishonesty. Moore fails to mention that Canada has extremely strict gun laws. There may be eight million guns in Canada, but they are almost all single-shot rifles and shotguns, locked away in gun cabinets in rural areas. There are almost no handguns, no semi-automatics and absolutely no assault rifles. The TEC 9 pistols used by the Columbine shooters are unobtainable in Canada. No citizen can carry a loaded gun around in a Canadian city, for any reason. Moore shows footage from a shooting range in Sarnia, Ontario, but fails to mention that none of the men there is allowed to take the handguns out of the building.

In other words, the primary difference between Canada and the United States is not cultural, it is institutional. If anything, differences in the culture are a *consequence* of the differences in laws and institutions. Canadians don't live in a culture of fear, not because they watch different TV shows than Americans or because they are exempt from the legacy of slavery, but because they don't have to worry about getting shot all the time.

If countercultural thinking has led to a certain naivety when it comes to crime, it has encouraged an almost unconscionable glamorisation of mental illness. From *One Flew over the Cuckoo's Nest* to Michel Foucault's *Madness and Civilisation* and R. D. Laing's *The Politics of Experience*, the suggestion is repeatedly made that crazy people are not really crazy, they're just different. They aren't sick, they're nonconformists, drugged up and incarcerated to prevent them from asking too many difficult questions.

Norman Mailer drew this connection as early as 1957, arguing that 'the hipster', in his disregard for social convention, is essentially a type of psychopath. In the modern world, the acceleration of everyday life has created a situation in which 'the nervous system is overstressed beyond the possibility of such compromises as sublimation'.[3] Thus neurotic repression of instinctual energy tends to be replaced by psychopathology, as the social control system loses its grip upon the individual. The only difference between the hipster and the garden-variety psychopath is that the former 'extrapolates from his own condition, from the inner certainty that his rebellion is just, a radical vision of the universe which separates him from the general ignorance, reactionary prejudice, and self-doubt of the more conventional psychopath.'[4]

The connection that Mailer sees between countercultural rebellion and madness actually follows quite directly from the core premises of the countercultural critique. If *all* rules are repressive constraints – limitations on the freedom and creativity of the individual – one cannot fail to notice that rationality itself is a system of rules. According to Mailer, there are only two types of people: those who are Hip ('rebels') and those who are Square ('conformists'). It's no surprise then that rationality ends up being for Squares. What is the principle of noncontradiction other than a socially enforced rule that constrains our speech? What are scientific facts other than beliefs that have received the official seal of bureaucratic approval? What is linguistic meaning other than the dead hand of past prejudices and conventions, weighing down upon us, constraining what we can say and think? What is grammar, even, if not a straitjacket that limits our spontaneity, creativity and freedom?

We can see all this in the work of artists who, in order to truly express themselves, freely break all of these rules. Yet if rationality is nothing but a system of rules, and freedom lies in the spontaneity of individual self-expression, then freedom itself must be a kind of irrationality. If reason is Apollo, then madness must be Dionysus. As Foucault wrote, madness 'rules all that is easy, joyous, frivolous in the world. It is madness, folly, which makes men "sport and rejoice".'[5]

In order for reason to establish its hegemony, reason must therefore 'subjugate non-reason'. It must eliminate madness in order to establish order and control. In the Middle Ages, the Church needed to burn heretics in order to maintain its grip over the hearts and minds of the people. In a secular era, reason has displaced religion as the hegemonic cultural system. It is lunatics, therefore, not heretics, who pose the greatest threat to the system.

Foucault claims that the modern era began with what he calls 'the great confinement'. Social misfits of every stripe were rounded up and consigned to prisons, asylums, workhouses and hospitals. In Foucault's view, these institutions became the pillars of order in modern society. He consistently draws the analogy between prisons and asylums: prisons punish those who refuse to *act* like everyone else; asylums control those who refuse to *think* like everyone else. The repressive society that George Orwell imagined in his book *1984*, where 'thought police' patrol the streets arresting those who commit 'thought crimes', is already upon us, according to Foucault. We simply fail to recognise it because the prisons are labelled 'hospitals' and the police are called 'doctors'.

Of course, it must be acknowledged that in the Soviet Union, political dissidents *were* routinely confined to psychiatric institutions, just as the communist government of China sent an extraordinary number of people to 're-education camps'. Furthermore, until quite recently, Western psychiatry did contain a number of very dubious diagnoses (such as the classification of homosexuality as a mental illness). Yet this hardly warrants the conclusion that asylums are merely prisons under a different name. There is an enormous difference between doubting that homosexuality is a mental disorder and doubting that schizophrenia is a mental disorder. Yet in the '60s, this is precisely what many prominent intellectuals began to do. In his best-selling 1967 book *The Politics of Experience*, Laing claimed that schizophrenics were on a 'journey of discovery', attempting to undo all of the normalising structures imposed by the socialisation process. While he did not deny that this journey involved great suffering, he argued that schizophrenics were on the road to discovering their most authentic human self. If all socialisation is essentially coercive, then freedom must lie in the undoing of all of its effects. This requires a rejection of the socially imposed distinctions between inner self and outer world, past and present, real and imaginary, good and evil. 'Normal' society perceives this as a disrupted thought pattern precisely because it constitutes a break with the conventional social order. But what it actually reveals is the impossibility of genuine freedom within the confines of 'normal' society.[6]

The arguments of the anti-psychiatry movement were eagerly lapped up by hippies and other countercultural rebels. Apart from *One*

Flew over the Cuckoo's Nest, one can find an especially clear formulation of the theory in the 1972 film *The Ruling Class*. Peter O'Toole plays Jack, the fourteenth Earl of Gurney, a lunatic who believes himself to be Jesus Christ. He is released from the asylum upon inheriting the family fortune, but mortifies the relatives by espousing brotherly love and threatening to give away his estate to the poor. The family hires a quack, who through a series of unorthodox treatments, including powerful electrical shocks, manages to reorient Jack's delusions so that he now believes himself to be Jack the Ripper. Yet in this new guise, Jack is able to move through British society with great success. His madness goes undetected as he takes his place in the House of Lords.

The message of the film is clear: madness is in the eye of the beholder. Who are we to say what's real and what's not, or what's right and what's wrong? If Jesus came into the world today, he would have been institutionalised. Yet homicidal maniacs walk the corridors of power. Scientists, bureaucrats and pharmaceutical companies conspire to control the public, dulling their senses with a variety of unguents and potions. For those most easily duped by the falseness and artifice of modern life, there are consumer goods. When that fails, there is Prozac to dull the pain. And for those who still cannot find satisfaction or meaning, it's time to bring in the Haldol. We secretly cheer for the psychiatric patient who pretends to swallow his pills only to reveal them a few minutes later, artfully concealed beneath his tongue (so that we are mildly shocked, in *Girl, Interrupted*, when Angelina Jolie's character turns out to be a genuine sociopath rather than just an assertive female oppressed by a patriarchal society).

Madness itself becomes widely regarded as a form of subversion, and mad ideas, whatever their content, as subversive. In the same way that a psychoanalyst takes anger and defensiveness on the part of the patient as a sign that therapy is starting to 'get somewhere', the social critic takes being called crazy as a sign that his questions and theories are getting close to some uncomfortable truths. The correct response must be to press these inquiries further, rather than to pull back.

★

To see the extent to which the romanticisation of insanity has persisted in countercultural thinking, one need only skim through some of the publications produced by the Disinformation Company. A classic example of countercultural entrepreneurship, the Disinformation Company could best be described as a wholesale retailer of alternative culture. A recent profile of company founder Richard Metzger describes him as a man who 'wants to be big business: the Ted Turner of freak-out journalism and counterculture: He makes his living selling counterculture, or, rather, selling the titillating, mind-blowing thrill some people get when they watch social taboos being blown wide open.'[7] His goal is nothing less than the branding of subversion.

The Disinformation Company's publications are usually for the most part simply a grab bag of 'alternative thinking'. The problem is that 'alternative thinking' here is taken to mean anything that is contrary to 'mainstream thinking' – becoming a category that therefore includes everything from radical social criticism to the delusions of madmen. Thus critics like Noam Chomsky and Arianna Huffington (who, despite being strident, are nevertheless serious) find themselves thrown together with articles claiming that humans are routinely being cloned, aspartame is toxic, ancient North America was inhabited by pygmies and the universe is sentient. Any signal present is quickly lost amidst all the noise.

The quest for the weird becomes even more extreme in the TV show called *Disinformation*, produced by Metzger and aired in the UK. At this point, Disinformation veers off into a 'Ripley's Believe It or Not' celebration of weirdness for its own sake, combined with a Fox Television-like fascination with 'stupid behaviour caught on tape'. This includes 'transgressive footage' of rednecks setting each other on fire, a woman having her labia sewn shut, an interview with a CIA mind-control slave, discussions with the inventor of a time machine, and so forth. And of course, there is the cash cow of the Disinformation Company's business model: ufology. Alternative entrepreneurs have made so much money off public fascination with UFOs that the entire racket is quickly becoming mainstream.

Most of what Disinformation presents is not much weirder or grosser than what anyone can see on 'mainstream' TV, where contestants on *Fear Factor* routinely eat live centipedes or immerse themselves in vats of cockroaches, and where alien abductions now rival tough inner-city cops as the most overworked theme. But, unlike reality TV, the Disinformation Company takes itself very seriously. They believe that their work is political – it is pushing back the boundaries, challenging the mainstream and thereby subverting the system. Their products are received with utmost seriousness as well. In a review of *Disinformation: The Interviews*, the *LA Weekly* insisted that beneath all the emphasis on cranks and kooks, there lies a serious intent:

> *This emphasis on the magical alteration of reality through force of will may seem whimsical at first glance, but points up an essential aspect of the disinformation agenda. Where dissection of propaganda and exploration of alternative theories awaken individuals to the web of fictions that surrounds them, the examples of pranksters and deviants empower them to put their own, competing fictions into play. This is William Burroughs-style magic, exploiting whatever current technology works best – culture jamming, ad busting, or hacking a hole in the prevailing consensus.*[8]

One can see the theme from Guy Debord and Jean Baudrillard lurking in the background. We live in the society of the spectacle, a world in which everything is merely a representation, an illusion. The Matrix is real; it is all around us. So who cares what is true and what is false? It is all simply a struggle over who will have the power to define reality.

The problem is that this sort of 'subversion' has been going on for over forty years without any noticeable effect. Nothing that Disinformation has coughed up is much weirder than what anyone can find on cable access. And yesterday's 'alternative' is simply today's mainstream. It is instructive, in this context, to note that the 'zine scene – which is essentially what Disinformation draws upon – has played the role of farm team for the literary establishment since the early '60s. And the same radical claims – 'hacking a hole in the prevailing consensus' – have been made since its inception. In 1968,

Douglas Blazek wrote that 'literature is now a wheel of fire and it's burning a new cycle into the skulls of more people than ever before – mostly young people who first heard of gas chambers instead of jolly ice cream cones & Ferris wheels.'[9] He went on to review some of the more prominent 'zines: 'ENTRAILS is edited by Mike Berardi in lieu of Gene Bloom (busy proselytising inmates of Sing Sing while serving out a grass bust) & is simply loaded with insanity, ennui slayers & dementia cacklers. Read about the new identification procedure called "Dickprinting". Read about the hilarious judge who said "1 to 3 years, Sing Sing". Read about the nun who said "FUCK". Read a review of the 1967 Spring/Summer Sears Catalogue.'[10]

How many times can the system be subverted without any noticeable effect before we begin to question the means of subversion? If insanity truly is doing the same thing again and again while expecting a different result, then it must be madness to think that any of this radicalism is going to undermine the system. How many more decades will it take before we realise that nuns who say 'fuck' are not radical, they are simply entertainment?

Here's a quick list of things that, in the past fifty years, have been considered extremely subversive: smoking, long hair for men, short hair for women, beards, miniskirts, bikinis, heroin, jazz music, rock music, punk music, reggae music, rap music, tattoos, underarm hair, graffiti, surfing, scooters, piercings, skinny ties, not wearing a bra, homosexuality, marijuana, torn clothing, hair gel, Mohicans, afros, birth control, postmodernism, plaid trousers, organic vegetables, army boots, interracial sex. Nowadays, you can find every item on this list in a typical Britney Spears video (with the possible exception of underarm hair and organic vegetables).

Countercultural rebels have become like doomsday prophets, forced to constantly push back the date on which the world is supposed to end, as one deadline after another passes by uneventfully. Each time a new symbol of rebellion gets 'co-opted' by the system, countercultural rebels are forced to go further and further to prove their alternative credentials, to set themselves apart from the despised masses. Punks started out with multiple ear piercings. When that became too common, they moved on to nose piercing, then eyebrow, tongue and navel piercing. When high school girls started getting those, the rebels moved into 'primitive' styles, like Balinese ear blocks or ampallangs.

One can see a self-radicalising tendency at work here that is highly characteristic of countercultural movements. The fundamental problem is that rebellion against aesthetic and sartorial norms is not actually subversive. Whether people have piercings and tattoos, what kind of clothes they wear, what music they listen to, simply does not matter from the standpoint of the capitalist system. Corporations are fundamentally neutral when it comes to gray flannel suits and biker jackets. No matter what the style, there will always be merchants lined up to sell it. And any successful rebel style, because it confers distinction, will automatically attract imitators. Because there is no genuine subversion involved, there is nothing to stop everyone from adopting the same style. Anyone can get a piercing or grow their hair long. So anything that is 'alternative' or 'cool' and has the least bit to recommend it will inevitably be 'mainstreamed'.

This creates a dilemma for the rebel. Sartorial markers that once served as a source of distinction find their significance eroded. This leaves the rebel with two choices: accept the inevitable and be overtaken by the masses, or resist further, by finding some new, more extreme style, one that has not yet attracted as many imitators and thus can still serve as a source of distinction. What the rebel is looking for, in the end, is the unco-optable subculture. Like the gambler in the Leonard Cohen song, looking for the card so high and wild he'll never need to play another, the countercultural rebel is looking for a path that no one else will follow, a look so extreme that it will never be mainstream.

The problem is that by the time the imitators start to fall away, it's usually for a pretty good reason. Take the example of music. Everyone wants to listen to fabulous 'underground' bands. As Hal Niedzviecki writes in his lengthy lament on the subject, 'we all want to cast off the shackles of TV, or fast food, or pre-packaged snacks and predetermined outfits.' Yet 'in the mediocre world of top-forty crapola, in our made-in-Taiwan-product-ridden universe, there is … precious little room for the individual as anything other than a buyer.' And so we strike back against the tyranny of the machine, searching for creativity and expression, fighting back against the 'rigid, profit-obsessed market economy that would turn all creative expression into widgets rolling off the assembly line.'[11]

What Niedzviecki doesn't notice is that while we may all want to rebel in this way, we can't all succeed. If we all turn our backs on 'top-forty crapola' and start listening to alternative music, then those alternative bands will *become* the new top forty. This is precisely what happened to Nirvana. Furthermore, given the structure of the music industry, where it costs a lot to produce an album but very little to make additional copies, this is going to be extremely profitable for whomever most people wind up listening to. The idea that the music industry is 'rigid' or that it produces 'widgets' could appeal only to someone in the grip of a theory. Has Niedzviecki never heard of Death Row Records? Has he never seen Christina Aguilera's 'Dirrty' video? Who's calling who a widget?

Undaunted, Niedzviecki sets off on a quest to find the holy grail of alternative music – the sound that can't be assimilated. He finds it, at least temporarily, in a Toronto band called Braino. They become the heroes of his narrative, with their 'muted howl of rebellion', their 'mournful, elegiac articulation of inner despair'. He describes with evident satisfaction the band's performance at their CD launch party, as they play 'staccato blasts that unnerve the scattered chattering poseurs and scare the unprepared'.

Reading between the lines of Niedzviecki's account, however, we are able to acquire some further intelligence about why Braino is so unco-optable. It quickly becomes apparent that Braino will never be mainstream *because they suck*. Their music is unlistenable. This is inti-mated at the outset of his narrative, when Niedzviecki describes the Braino sound as 'a self-conscious, ironic mélange of avant-jazz, rock, punk, soundtrack, and barbershop'. This does not sound promising. He later describes Braino as making a 'big, awkward, painful noise'. Later he simply admits, 'It's annoying music. You want to walk out'.

So there you have it. In an effort to avoid the tyranny of mass society, the rebel finds himself in a half-empty bar listening to music that he himself acknowledges to be 'annoying', feeling superior to the poseurs. (The presence of startled poseurs in Niedzviecki's account is essential. Taste involves distinction, and distinction involves separating 'us' – those who are in the know – from 'them' – those who serve as the object of scorn and contempt.)

The worst thing about Niedzviecki's predicament is his failure to recognise that it's all been done before. The ultimate alternative album has already been issued, back in 1975. It's called *Metal Machine Music*, by Lou Reed, a double album made up entirely of unlistenable guitar feedback and white noise (in a final irritating touch, the B side of the second album contains a locked groove, so that the last sequence plays indefinitely, until the needle is physically lifted from the vinyl). Most people who bought it demanded their money back, and it still tops many rock critics' lists as the worst album of all time. Nevertheless, there is an elite group of critics and fans who admire the work, finding it 'mesmerising', a 'continually-simmering blast of squawking energy ripples screeching over half-heard tremolos and snaking rivulets of molten guitar strings' and, perhaps more honestly, 'an acquired taste'.

If you really want alternative music, there it is. Everything else is easy listening.

After examining all of these tendencies in the counterculture, it is perhaps easier to see how a person could end up living in a cabin in the woods with no electricity. Most of the measures that are popularly promoted as 'anticonsumerist' are useless. Often they have the exact opposite effect, promoting competitive consumption. One can see this with perfect clarity in the bakery industry. In the '60s, many people started baking their own bread as a reaction against the soul-destroying uniformity of the Wonder bread society. Yet there is a reason that, throughout most of history, people have gone to bakers to buy bread. Preparing and cooking bread in small batches is extremely inefficient, expensive and time-consuming (not to mention bad for the environment). Home bread-baking, in other words, is an activity that is necessarily reserved for the privileged few (those with an excess of either wealth or leisure). As a result, it was not long before markets began appearing for 'home-style' bread, along with bakers willing to supply them. Thus the decline of white bread coincided with a boom in so-called artisan bakeries, along with the growth of powerful franchises like the Great Harvest Bread Company. And because these bakeries were not using mass production techniques, their loaves cost significantly more than Wonder bread. But there was no shortage of consumers willing to pay premium rates in order to avoid being victims of consumerism and mass society. Again the counterculture proved to be the vital spark driving consumer trends. It is not an accident that San Francisco is the home of both the £2 latte and the £3 loaf of sourdough bread.

People who take the critique of mass society seriously are forced into increasingly extreme measures in order to escape from the clutches of 'the system'. First of all, as has already been mentioned, it is useless to reduce your own consumption unless you also reduce your income. Everything you earn gets saved or spent, and anything that you save just gets spent later, by you or someone else. Changing your spending pattern will put a dent in the amount consumed only if it allows you to reduce your income.

One of the most prominent advocates of this sort of 'downshifting' of consumption and income is Juliet Schor. In *The Overspent American*, Schor offers a profile of a typical downshifter – a pretty photograph of a young woman carrying groceries, with little arrows pointing out the various ways in which she is fighting consumerism. As one looks over these points, it is easy to see what a difficult task this budding downshifter faces. Here is a sample: [12]

- 'Buys organic food'. How does this combat consumerism? Our downshifter is certainly going to have to earn a lot more money if she intends to pay two to three times more for all of her groceries. Organic food is simply the latest category of 'premium' consumer goods. Like artisan bread, espresso coffee and handmade carpets, it is more labour-intensive to produce. Super-markets around the world are cashing in on the organic craze. Organic food is one of the major forces driving the return to an almost aristocratic class structure in the United States, in which the wealthy no longer eat the same food as the poor.

- 'Carrying *The Time Dollar*, a book for getting the local barter economy off the ground.' The idea that a local barter economy is somehow less 'consumerist' than the national monetary economy is just bizarre. All goods are exchanged for other goods. The only advantage of a barter economy is that it facilitates tax avoidance, which is not something that the left should be advocating.

- 'Gave up gym membership to walk with spousal equivalent in the evenings.' This is why leisure goods retailers have been selling so many £150 pairs of high-tech walking boots rather than cheap, less rugged gym shoes. People with gym member-ships enter into a cooperative arrangement in which they agree to share exercise equipment. Outdoor enthusiasts, being such individualists, inevitably buy all their own gear. This is why the market for outdoor leisure goods is so much richer. Engaging in 'virtuous' activities is one of the major psychological devices that consumers use to grant themselves permission to overspend.

- 'Lives in the moment.' This sounds great, but how does it help? Aren't people who live in the moment more likely to purchase things on impulse, things they don't really need? Doesn't living in the moment imply saving nothing?

- 'Repairs rather than buys' (carrying a hammer). Great. Do it yourself, and you'll need your own set of tools. You'll need books to tell you how it's done. You'll need to attend seminars to learn techniques. This is the entire business model of DIY stores.

- 'Makes own clothes, cards own wool, shears own sheep.' This is obviously intended as a joke. But once you get your laughter under control, you realise with a sinking feeling that of all the points listed, this is the only one that is actually likely to do anything to reduce 'consumerism'. And if living like the Amish is the only way to avoid consumerism, then it really forces us to wonder what is wrong with consumerism in the first place.

All of this advice on downshifting is based upon the countercultural faith that changing society is ultimately a matter of changing our own consciousness. As a result, it generates a set of highly individualised strategies. The average number of hours worked has been on the rise over the last few decades. And given the number of people who report increased difficulty achieving work–family balance, there is no question that much of this is involuntary. Most of it is due to the competitive structure of the workplace. If everyone else is working a sixty-hour week, then your chances of being promoted are close to zero if you kick off work at 5 p.m. in order to go home to the kids. Schor is absolutely right in claiming that Americans are overworked, but there are very simple, 'superficial' remedies for this problem. One is simply to impose further legislative limits on the workweek, to extend mandatory vacations and to have lengthy, paid maternity and parental leave. (Americans now have 'casual Fridays', where people are encouraged to shed their suits and ties at work, in order to create a more weekend-like atmosphere. In France they have a much better solution. They call it 'not working on Fridays'.) These sorts of institutional changes would do far more to combat consumerism than any of the downshifting strategies recommended by Schor.

Meet Michelle Rose. A forty-one-year-old mother of three living in Vermont, Rose suffered a series of personal tragedies, including a bad marriage and an abusive relationship. But all that has changed now. She has turned her life around. The turning point occurred when she lost all of her earthly possessions in a fire that burned her house to the ground. This was the wake-up call that she needed. This was when (according to her profile in *Real Simple* magazine) 'she realised that all she really needed was the earth itself'.[13]

The above seems like the beginning of a wholesome tale about how one woman learned to transcend materialist values and escape from the rampant consumerism that dominates our culture. An accompanying photospread shows Michelle working in her garden:

'Gingerly, she lowers the plants into their new homes, then slowly presses dirt around them. Her movements are tender, almost maternal. Here, in the dirt, she is her truest self.'

A bit further in, however, the story takes a strange twist. It turns out the 'dirt' in northern Vermont is not quite up to Rose's specifications. Her little garden, where she goes to escape from her cares, is actually in Kauai, 'one of Hawaii's least developed and lushest islands'. She commutes to it – driving to Burlington, flying to Chicago, grabbing a few more connecting flights, then driving another hour to get to her land. She takes the trip several times a year, 'to clear and prepare her ten acres for the tea, sandalwood and bamboo she has begun to cultivate.' When her children finish high school, she plans to 'simplify' her life by living on the island full-time.

Welcome to the new consumerism. There used to be a time when people moved to northern Vermont to get away from it all. As a result, northern Vermont has obviously become a bit too crowded. So, what's next? A remote island in the Pacific. Of course, these islands are also in short supply. But so far, Rose has managed to stay ahead of the pack. 'Unlike the timeshare visitors who come to the increasingly popular island for Mai Tais and luaus', we are told, 'Michelle comes for the dirt'. In case anyone misses the point, Michelle provides added emphasis. 'Most people who come on vacation like the south side of the island', she says, where the climate is sunnier. Her property, on the other hand, is part of a rain forest. 'We like the moisture in the air', she says. Naturally. It's not the exclusivity or the feeling of moral superiority that draws her to the other side of the island, away from all the tourists. It's the *moisture*.

And the plan to grow tea? That's not really capitalism. 'An acre can yield one to two tons of tea … That's not a lot if you're Lipton, but if you're selling organic tea locally, it's quite a few pots.' Besides, the plan is probably not very economical. It turns out that Michelle has a full-time employee, who takes care of her 'dirt' while she is away. She also hired a contractor to build three buildings on the acreage out of 'teak-stained cedar'– one of them for the organic tea that she intends to cultivate. The style is both 'primitive and elegant'. How does she afford all this? Turns out she received a rather generous divorce settlement. And the buildings were lovingly designed by her new husband, who (it is mentioned in an aside) happens to be both an architect and a college professor. Isn't it amazing how much you can learn by having all of your material possessions destroyed?

Obviously there is something wrong with this picture. For someone who professes antimaterialist values and endorses the ideal of 'simple' living, Michelle sure seems to be spending an awful lot of money. Some might call it 'the paradox of antimaterialism'. In the past forty years, antimaterialist values have been one of the biggest cash cows of American consumer capitalism. The simple fact is, not everyone has the time to grow their own organic tea. Some people have jobs. But while they may not have the time or the money to share Rose's lifestyle, they can at least endorse her values, and embrace her aesthetic, by purchasing organic tea. Here's the rub: The values that *Real Simple* magazine promotes have superior prestige precisely because they are antimaterialist. Growing your own tea, rather than buying the cheap mass-produced stuff, makes you seem like a better person, more in touch with the earth. Thus 'dropping out' of the tea market in order to make your own does not really strike a blow against consumerism; it just creates a market for more expensive, 'all-natural' organic tea for those who do not have the time to grow it themselves. In other words, it exacerbates competitive consumption rather than reduces it.

This is why the hippies didn't need to sell out in order to become yuppies. It's not that the system 'co-opted' their dissent, it's that they were never really dissenting. As Michelle Rose and others have proved, rejecting materialist values, and rejecting mass society, does not force you to reject consumer capitalism. If you really want to opt out of the system, you need to 'do a Kaczynski' and go off and live in the woods somewhere (and not commute back and forth in a Range Rover). Because the everyday acts of symbolic resistance that characterise countercultural rebellion are not actually disruptive to 'the system', anyone who follows the logic of countercultural thinking through to its natural conclusion will find herself drawn into increasingly extreme forms of rebellion. The point at which this rebellion becomes disruptive generally coincides with the point at which it becomes genuinely antisocial. And then you're not so much being a rebel as you are simply being a nuisance.

Notes

1   Theodore Kaczynski, 'Industrial Society and Its Future' (aka 'The Unabomber's Manifesto'). This document is widely available on the Internet. It was published in its entirety in *The Washington Post* on September 19, 1995, as an eight-page pullout. The *Post* split the cost of publication with the *New York Times*.

2   Stephan Thernstrom and Abigail Thernstrom, *America in Black and White* (New York: Simon & Schuster, 1997), 142; data on economic conditions in Detroit, 162; support for radical black leaders, 167–68.

3   Norman Mailer, 'The White Negro', *Advertisements for Myself* (New York: Putnam, 1959), 345.

4   *Ibid.*, 343.

5   Michel Foucault, *Madness and Civilization*, trans. Richard Howard (New York: Pantheon, 1965), 25.

6   R. D. Laing, *The Politics of Experience* (New York: Ballantine Books, 1967), 107.

7   Lianna George, 'Corporate Avant-Garde Market Radicalism,' *National Post*, March 15, 2003.

8   Doug Harver, 'Pranksters, Deviants and SoCal Satanists: The Interviews', *LA Weekly*, November 29, 2002.

9   Douglas Blazek 'THE little PHENOMENA', in *The Portable '60s Reader*, ed. Ann Charter (New York: Penguin, 2003), 267.

10 *Ibid.*, 267.

11   Hal Niedzviecki, *We Want Some Too: Underground Desire and the Reinvention of Mass Culture* (Toronto: Penguin, 2000), 2–11.

12   Juliet Schor, *The Overspent American: Upscaling, Downshifting, and the New Consumer* (New York: Basic Books, 1992), 112.

13   All citations are from Jenny Allen, 'Endless Summer', *Real Simple*, June/July 2003, 198–204. Used by kind permission of Time Warner Inc.

Part II

Uniforms and uniformity

One of the most arresting features of the *Star Trek* universe is the complete absence of branded consumer goods. It goes beyond the fact that everyone in the show wears a uniform almost all of the time. What they eat and drink, the equipment and products they use for work and for entertainment, their computers, tricorders, weapons and so on – all are free of any sort of corporate trademarks, logos and brand names. Furthermore, everything lacks the variation and diversity of design and customisation we take for granted in the artefacts of our world. In almost every way, the *Star Trek* universe is uniform. In this respect, *Star Trek* is notably different from most contemporary science fiction. In films such as *Blade Runner*, and in books from authors such as William Gibson and Neal Stephenson, the near future is a high-powered form of information capitalism dominated by corporations, franchises and consumer goods.

Not so in *Star Trek*, where the impact of information technology, markets and consumer goods, so central to the subgenre of cyberpunk, is almost completely ignored. Did Jean-Luc Picard ever hope that a short and decisive battle against the Borg would restore consumer confidence within the Federation? For all his vanity, did James T. Kirk ever show the slightest interest in fashion? In this indifference to consumer culture, *Star Trek* has always resembled the science fiction of the '50s, which foresaw a future dominated by military competition between governments and ideologies, not by market-based competition between corporations and among consumers.

The *Star Trek* future is clearly one in which American values are triumphant, at least within the Federation. As many commentators have pointed out, the politics of each incarnation of the show tend to mirror the era in which it was made, with the muscular militarism and red-baiting of Captain Kirk giving way to the touchy-feely multiculturalism of Picard and Janeway. It is tempting to view the absence of consumer products and consumerist values from the series as just bad writing and failure of imagination on the part of the show's writers. But that would be too quick and easy a conclusion. Another way of looking at it is as political allegory, of an enlightened future in which the citizens of the Federation have found a way of being individuals without being rebels, of wearing uniforms without succumbing to a deadening existential uniformity.

We live in a society that is the exact opposite. We are all, to an unparalleled degree, self-conscious about what we wear, and the counterculture has played an enormous role in heightening this self-consciousness. Even now, many alternative newsweeklies run little 'style' features that show a picture of a local scenester along with a painstakingly minute inventory of his or her clothing and accessories, detailing the provenance of each. The competitive structure of this self-presentation is never far from the surface. Each item must be acquired in an exotic locale, or in an offbeat manner, or for an exceptionally low price. Each item must be unique; it must have its own special story. The overall arrangement must be eclectic, yet not garish.

How did it come to this? What ever happened to our *Star Trek* future?

From a purely practical perspective, clothes are for covering up. They keep us warm, keep the sun off, keep insects out and generally protect the parts of us that need protecting, support the parts that need supporting and otherwise make it easier for us to get on with the business of living. This much is obvious. Yet, just as obviously, clothes are more than that. People have always used clothing not only (or even primarily) for covering, but for communicating. The symbolic use of clothing is in many ways like a language, with a grammar or syntax that allows for a range of expressive acts. And what a rich language it is, with regional and demographic dialects sophisticated enough to permit jokes, ironic statements, even slang and metaphor.

What we wear speaks volumes about who we are. Our clothes reveal our age and income, our education and our social class; they reveal our current attitudes and political beliefs, our gender and even our sexual orientation. They play an extraordinarily important role in mate selection. Clothing is also an extremely accurate guide to the time in which we live – notice how clothing (along with hairstyles) is the easiest way to date old photographs. In short, who we are is firmly wrapped up in what we wear.

None of this will strike many people as terribly controversial. But if clothing is a form of expression, then, like speech, it can be more or less free; and just as restricting what people can say or hear is often seen as a way of restricting what they can think, so it would seem that restrictions on what people can wear might serve to limit who they can be. This idea is what motivates the widespread hostility to uniforms in our society. The argument is simple: uniformity of dress leads inevitably to uniformity of mind; if you are conforming to the sartorial dictates of others, then you are conforming to an externally determined way of being. In *The Language of Clothes*, Alison Lurie sums up the countercultural analysis of uniforms: 'No matter what sort of uniform it is – military, civil, or religious; the outfit of a general, a postman, a nun, a butler, a football player, or a waitress – to put on such livery is to give up one's right to act as an individual – in terms of speech, to be partially or wholly censored.'[1]

This sort of thinking goes a long way toward explaining the hostility, which begins with the hippies, not only to the military and the police, but to just about every bureaucratic organisation. If we regard any sort of standardised dress as a uniform, then it is easy to treat the man in the gray flannel suit as equivalent to the National Guardsman. The natural alliance within capitalism of the military-industrial complex is thus revealed through the fact that everyone involved is wearing a uniform of some sort. Here come the cops, here come the suits, here comes The Man. The uniform becomes the common thread running through all of these institutions, which permits them to be decoded.

Of all uniforms, none was subjected to more vicious and sustained criticism than the school uniform. It is not hard to see why. The standard countercultural view held that the purpose of the bureaucratic state was to 'administer consciousness' to the individual, such that one becomes entirely subordinate to a particular role or function, identified with one's place in the system. In *The Greening of America*,

Charles Reich argues that in such a system, man 'walks through the remainder of his days mindless and lifeless, the inmate and instrument of a machine world.'[2] The gray flannel suit becomes a symbol of the essential one-dimensionality of life in the technocracy. It is through the education system that students are first indoctrinated, where they learn to accept their functional role. In describing education as a way of 'indoctrinating the inmates' into 'a role-prison', Reich betrays his fondness for correctional metaphors, but his belief that the point of schooling is to create 'the Organization Child' is widely held.

For an entire generation, the school uniform came to symbolise everything soul-destroying about contemporary society. Desecration of this uniform became one of the most powerful symbols of youthful rebellion. Angus Young, the age-old guitarist for AC/DC, still performs in his signature schoolboy uniform – a near-religious invocation of the anarchic soul of rock and roll, one that is far more effective than the strict iconoclasm of Madonna or Sinead O'Connor. This is a constant theme in rock. In the movie version of *The Wall*, a chorus of uniformed schoolboys sings Pink Floyd's famous denunciation/identification of education and thought control, as they are slowly fed into a meat grinder, emerging as hamburger out the other end. This happens after one schoolboy has been mocked then beaten by the schoolmaster for daring to write poems in class. Into the meat grinder with them all! Creativity and imagination must be crushed at all cost. How else will we keep the factories running smoothly?

And yet something strange happened in the '90s, when the offspring of the baby boomers reached high school. The forces of reaction had always strongly favoured uniforms, arguing that they improved discipline and encouraged more respect among students. Military academies and most private schools never gave up the uniform. But this opposition merely reinforced the belief, treasured among countercultural radicals, that eliminating uniforms would be emancipatory, would lead to a new era of creativity and freedom. Yet the voices that we began to hear in the '90s were quite different. Many concerned parents, including many former '60s radicals, began quietly suggesting that perhaps, just maybe, school uniforms weren't such a bad idea after all. The first boomer president of the United States, Bill Clinton, came out publicly in support of school uniforms, even including a reference to it in a State of the Union address.

The problem with getting rid of uniforms, it turned out, was not so much that it led to a breakdown in discipline, but that it led to rampant consumerism. All that brand-consciousness that we hear about among teenagers, the obsession with clothes, with trainers, where do you suppose that comes from? One thing is for certain – kids who wear uniforms do not get killed for their clothes. As Clinton put it, 'If it means teenagers will stop killing each other over designer jackets, then our State schools should be able to require their students to wear school uniforms.'[3]

This unexpected comeback of the school uniform in the United States won't come as much surprise to people in other countries, especially in the UK, where it was always assumed that the main function of the uniform was to minimise class differences. For Americans, the return of the school uniform is like a modern morality tale. In it, we can find all of the forces at play that sustain and reproduce the myth of counterculture. We can also see clearly the reasons for the failure of this myth, and the perverse consequences of the pseudo-rebellion that it generates. Nowhere is the failure of countercultural rebellion to produce its intended consequences more evident. In other words, in the politics of uniforms we can learn everything that we need to know about modern culture. But first we need to take a more careful look at how uniforms became such a hot-button issue to start with.

In his book *Uniforms*, Paul Fussell begins by trying to distinguish between a uniform and a costume. According to Fussell, 'for an outfit to qualify as a uniform, many others must be wearing the same thing.'[4] Despite its superficial plausibility, this claim does not stand up to scrutiny. If we accept (as Fussell does) that even blue jeans count as a uniform, it leads immediately to the conclusion that everyone is in uniform, including most members of the counterculture. The only people not in uniform are bag ladies, the insane and eccentrics. Such a definition then encourages the superficial accusation that counter-cultural rebels are merely hypocrites, since they are also conformists – they are simply conforming to a different set of rules.

It will help to draw a few distinctions. To begin with, we need to recognise that the popular notion of the uniform – as an externally mandated means of ensuring an individuality-suppressing conformity, for which the military uniform is the archetype – is just one end of a continuum. Moving away from the military, we come to quasi-uniforms (nurses, postal carriers), forms of standardised clothing (such as a mechanic's coveralls), career apparel (the gray flannel suit) and fashion wear. We can treat all of these people as being equally 'in uniform' if we like, but that will prevent us from noticing the important ways in which the functions of a uniform can vary depending on the organisation or group. Furthermore, it is a mistake to treat all of these as uniforms, because it is a mistake to equate uniformity of dress with being 'in uniform'. Two Queen's Guards on duty outside Buckingham Palace in red tunics and bearskin hats are in uniform; two girls who have inadvertently worn identical dresses to a dance are not.

To be 'in uniform' has less to do with what you are wearing and more to do with the symbolic and social relations in which you are embedded. The uniform itself is the legitimating symbol of membership in an organisation, and it therefore serves a dual function. First, the uniform distinguishes the members of a group from those of other groups and from the rest of society as a whole. Second, the uniform imposes group conformity by eliminating the use of externally sanctioned signs of status, privilege or belonging. The uniform is, paradoxically, both democratic and elitist, since it both reveals and conceals status: it reveals to outsiders the status of the wearer as a member of a certain group, while suppressing within the group all external indicators of status or belonging.

In its purest form, the uniform is a tool used to exercise command and control within a governmental bureaucratic organisation. The goal is to create for the wearers of the uniform an identity that Nathan Joseph calls the 'Total Uniform'; it is the 'Master Status' to which all other identities are subordinated. The uniform wearer takes on the appearance of the one-dimensional man, subject to a single set of overriding institutional norms. Everything you need to know about him he literally wears on his sleeve. The military provides the best example of the total uniform, and the United States Marine Corps is perhaps the best of the best.[5]

Military commanders have long understood that soldiers generally do not fight for ideas, for King and Country or even for their families; they fight for one another and for the organisational unit to which they belong. What persuades a man to clamber over a parapet or rush a machine-gun nest is his sense of brotherhood, his loyalty toward the unit that has trained him and the men with whom he has fought. That is why military commanders do not spend a great deal of time instructing soldiers in the details of political theory or the intricacies of geopolitics. Instead, they go to great lengths to inculcate as powerful a sense of group identification as possible. The ultimate goal is to make the soldier feel that he would rather die than let down the side.

In many armies, the principal object of group loyalty is the regiment. In the British and Canadian armies for example, soldiers in the Black Watch or the Princess Patricia's have regimental history and regimental pride drummed into them. The United States Marine Corps is different, in that the Corps as a whole is what matters. The Marines' motto is *semper fidelis* – 'always faithful' – (usually abbreviated *semper fi*), and Marines are famous for retaining a sense of brotherhood long after they have left the Corps.

The development of this powerful combination of separateness and group loyalty is the focus of the first half of Stanley Kubrick's 1987 film *Full Metal Jacket*. The film opens with a montage of new recruits having their individual identities literally shorn away as their heads are shaved by a military barber. Their subsequent training is a case study in the dual functions of the uniform, beginning with a famous early scene in which the recruits are given a thorough dressing down by their drill instructor, Gunnery Sergeant Hartman, played by R. Lee Ermey (a former real-life drill instructor). To emphasise the internally democratic nature of the Marines, Hartman takes a moment to inform the recruits (in some colourful language) that there is no racial bigotry in his camp, because he regards them all as equally worthless.[6] At the end of their training, as they prepare to leave Parris Island and join their respective units, Hartman reminds them that they are a group fundamentally distinct from the rest of society – they are no longer 'maggots', but Marines, part of a brotherhood.[7]

*

Given this martial archetype, it is hardly surprising that uniforms – and the men and women who wear them – are treated with tremendous scorn and hostility by cultural rebels. The total uniform serves as a highly visible synecdoche for the entire countercultural understanding of society as authoritarian, repressive, alienating and conformist. Throw in the fact that most people in uniforms are agents of government-sanctioned violence or coercion and it is easy to see why the decision to wear a uniform was seen not only as an unappealing lifestyle choice, but as manifestly dangerous. It was inevitable, then, that the Vietnam War served as a lightning rod for countercultural protest. Many hippies expressed their discontent by actually wearing army khakis, openly flouting and overturning military values.

It is wrong, though, to use this as a general condemnation of uniformity of dress no matter what the social context or role in which one happens to be embedded. To go back to the metaphor of clothes as a form of speech, it is a mistake to assume that individuality of expression is always desirable. Sometimes what we are after is a broader unity, a subsumption of our voice into the whole, as in a choir or at prayer. The formal black tie of the symphony orchestra and the ultradisciplined flashiness of high school marching bands in the American Midwest are two examples of the way uniformity of dress serves to enhance the effect of collective music-making. Even in the military, it is not always about discipline in the service of violence. In Patrick O'Brien's novels about life in the British navy during the Napoleonic wars, there are numerous passages like this one, from *The Commodore*: 'The *Stately*'s barge appeared, steered by Duff's proud coxswain with a midshipman in a gold-laced hat beside him and pulled by ten young bargemen tricked out to the height of nautical elegance and splendour – tight white trousers with ribbons down the seams, embroidered shirts, crimson neckerchiefs, broad-brimmed sennit hats, gleaming pigtails. With Giffard's words in his mind, Stephen looked at them attentively: Individually each sailor would have been very well, but since they were all uniformly decorated he thought it overdone.'[8]

In these sorts of cases, the ship captains are clearly using their boat crews for what Veblen called 'vicarious conspicuous consumption'. But the sailors themselves are not mere pawns, and O'Brien describes at considerable length the pride they take in this look. Thus Lurie seriously overstates the case when she claims that to put on a uniform is to give up one's right to act as an individual. What she misses is the way in which becoming a fully dressed member of a group can be a source of intense individual pride, since to put on a uniform is to be entitled to what Fussell calls 'the vanity of belonging'.[9] It is a further mistake to take something like the Marines as the model for all uniformed organisations. The military uniform always carries with it the suggestion of violence, along with related connotations of hierarchy, command and coercion, which is why it must be as close to a total uniform as possible. The military needs one-dimensional men, because war is a one-dimensional way of life.

But not all uniforms are total uniforms. Doctors and nurses, nuns, priests and airline personnel all work in bureaucracies, or at least quasi-bureaucracies, and their uniforms serve the usual purposes of distinguishing the group from outsiders, motivating the acceptance of occupational rank and norms, and integrating the group as a cohesive unit. Lurie again overstates the case when she claims that 'the uniform acts as a sign that we should not or need not treat someone as a human being, and that they need not and should not treat us as one.'[10] As anyone who has ever had to deal with a doctor or a priest knows, there is a constant tension between our desire to deal with them on a purely bureaucratic or 'professional' level, on the one hand, and our desire for a more human touch, on the other. It is a tension that those in uniform are fully aware of, and which they often try to resolve by either personalising or downplaying the uniform.

Many nuns now go without habits or wear them only on special occasions, while doctors frequently wear playful ties or even casual shirts under their uniform white coats. Such deviations are tolerable because there is a strong desire on the part of their clients that the uniform not be totalising. Many of us want to hear about our doctor's vacation, and we want to see our priest's taste in casual clothes. It allows both parties to treat each other as more human. This comes at a price, though, for both parties in the relationship. Many nuns have experienced a strong backlash from people who would rather not receive spiritual guidance from women in street clothes, and many patients and doctors would prefer that the prostate exam be performed in as clinical and impersonal a manner as possible.

The fact is, not everyone goes to the bank or the post office or the doctor's office looking for a new best friend. The social distance that uniforms create between people is often desirable. The fact that uniforms can be used to enforce undesirable social hierarchies is not an argument for eliminating uniforms – it is an argument for eliminating undesirable social hierarchies.

The idea that uniforms eliminate individuality is also something of an illusion. If anything, they simply place constraints on the way that individuals can express their individuality. Even the strictest of uniform can allow for a certain amount of variation. In fact, official toleration of deviation is one way of exercising bureaucratic control over the group. As long as there are precise regulations that could in principle be enforced, the threat to start 'going by the book' can keep actual deviation within tolerable limits. Stanley Kubrick explores the limits of official tolerance in a scene in *Full Metal Jacket* when Private Joker (played by Matthew Modine) is dressed down in the field for wearing a peace symbol on his body and writing 'born to kill' on his helmet. The colonel asks him whether he loves his country. When Joker says yes, the colonel suggests that he start getting with the programme. He questions Joker's commitment to his country because he realises that excessive deviation in the uniform undermines the institutional norms that it is supposed to represent and threatens to import competing values into the organisation.

Yet iconoclasm by enlisted men is not the biggest threat to the military uniform. Aristocratic disdain has traditionally been a powerful excuse for the rejection of the uniform, since class affiliations counteract the attempt by the uniformed organisation to enforce a consistent internal brotherhood or hierarchy. When external signs of status are allowed to intrude into the uniform, this symbolic role is substantially weakened. Within the military, this typically gives rise to a form of dandyism, peacock-proud expressions of male vanity through accoutrements such as gold lace, brass buttons, epaulets made of real bullion and so on. Consider, for example, Mark Kingwell's description of his father's RCAF mess kit: 'The blue-grey melton jacket was cut short and scalloped in the back, with trousers that were high, tight, and stirruped, a gold stripe down each side, ending in gleaming wellington boots with elastic sides and a leather loop in the heel. The jacket had gold buttons on the cuffs, silk facing on the lapels, a pair of gold navigator's wings, small epaulettes with his captain's insignia, and the miniature versions of his two decorations.'[11]

What is important to realise is that the ultimate effect of this is to degrade the nature of the outfit as a uniform, to turn it into the costume of a military dandy. Fussell has great sport with General George S. Patton's obsession with appearances – his love of brass buttons, his preposterous 'lacquered helmet liner' (whatever that may be) – but it is wrong to suppose that this shows how Patton was submitting to the vanity of belonging. In fact, it is the exact opposite. Patton dressed not to belong, but to stand out. He believed that while conformity was required for the rank and file, peculiar dress was essential to good leadership. A leader had to stand out, to declare his fundamental distinctiveness from the rest of the group.[12]

★

We are what we wear, and as a rule we have to buy our clothes. So in order to rebel against the stultifying conformity of mass society, we must consume. As a result, it is not surprising to observe that while styles in 'official' men's fashion (such as suits, ties and other forms of office wear) haven't changed much in over a century, the cycles of fashion and obsolescence in clothes aimed at youth culture are accelerating at an astonishing rate. The turnover in 'cool' is fantastic, and it exposes one of the deepest ironies of the countercultural movement. As Thomas Frank observes, one of the most objectionable aspects of mass society was the system of 'planned obsolescence', exposed most famously by Vance Packard in his book *The Waste Makers*.[13] Yet the solution to mass society – countercultural rebellion – has given us even faster cycles of obsolescence in fashion, all in the name of individual expression.

Nothing better exemplified the stasis and conformity of the technocracy than the way men dressed in the '50s. The Brooks Brothers/gray flannel suit seemed to be little more than the prison garb of the one-dimensional man, with the necktie serving alternately as a metaphorical noose or dog collar. The image is still powerful enough that advertisers routinely show men tearing off their ties as they hop into their four-wheel drives to drive off to the country, or come into the bar after work to meet their exuberant friends, or settle down in front of their giant-screen TVs.

This criticism was not entirely without merit. Men's dress, especially in the '50s, was bland and uniform. The primary reason, however, was that men did not own many clothes. It was quite common at the time for men to wear the same suit every day for an entire workweek. They would even wear the same shirt for several days – that was why they wore undershirts. These habits caused considerable anguish among menswear manufacturers and advertisers, who were trying desperately to kick-start a stagnating industry. The important point is that the uniformity of dress was not something imposed by the technocracy – quite the opposite; the gray flannel suit was a symptom of the lack of consumerism among men. In this context, countercultural rebellion, far from subverting the system, was essential in creating the 'Peacock Revolution' of the '60s, which had men wearing everything from Nehru jackets to leisure suits.[14]

From the very beginning, it was rebel style that drove men to spend more money on clothing. Clark Gable started it early on, appearing in *It Happened One Night* without an undershirt. Within weeks, this new, more daring look had become the rage with men across North America. It didn't take long for clothing manufacturers to take notice. Men had worn undershirts in order to reduce the number of times a shirt had to be laundered. This greatly extended its life. Getting rid of the undershirt meant that instead of needing three good shirts and a dozen cheap ones in his closet, today's man would need a dozen good-quality ones.

Is it any surprise that clothing manufacturers aggressively pushed for the elimination of the standard business suit as well? There is a serious question as to how much countercultural style in the '60s and '70s was produced by the rebels and how much was due to the clothing industry. Although the rebels insisted that the industry was 'co-opting' their style, the truth is a lot more complicated. While some fashion started in the street and moved into the design houses, much more started in the industry and moved down into the street. Rather than pick through all these relationships, trying to figure out who is being manipulated and who is doing the manipulation, it is easier simply to observe the natural identity of interest that exists between capitalist entrepreneurs and the countercultural rebels. The counterculture was, from the very beginning, intensely entrepreneurial. It is no coincidence that the Gap (a chain that includes Banana Republic and Old Navy) started out in 1969 in San Francisco. To understand the Gap's success, one need only look at the stir that Sharon Stone caused in 1995 when she showed up at the Oscars wearing an off-the-rack £12 Gap turtleneck.

As Arthur Marwick writes, in his extraordinarily comprehensive analysis of the '60s, 'Most of the movements, subcultures, and new institutions which are at the heart of sixties change were thoroughly imbued with the entrepreneurial, profit-making ethic. I am thinking here of boutiques, experimental theatres, art galleries, discothèques, nightclubs, "light shows", "head shops", photographic and model agencies, underground films, pornographic magazines. With the assistance of the great expansion of mass communications, particularly in television, the sixties was very much an age of "spectacle": leading figures in the counter-culture became very much part of this spectacle, thereby earning both status and prestige and ordinary money.'[15]

Rebellion is not a threat to the system, it *is* the system. There is a reason that Alexander McQueen, the most extreme sartorial rebel, became the lead designer at the house of Givenchy. People who see fashion through the lens of the mass society critique imagine a cabal of designers in Paris and Milan dictating a change in hemlines in order to force a society of compulsive conformists to run out and buy a new wardrobe every year. The reality is the exact opposite. Fashion is viciously competitive. People buy this year's styles in order to set themselves apart from those still wearing last year's. Luxury couture houses are in the business of selling distinction. Rebellion is one of the most powerful sources of distinction in the modern world. As a result, people are willing to pay good money for a piece of it, just as they are willing to pay for access to any other form of social status. No one is 'selling out' here, because there is nothing to sell out in the first place.

It is hard for us to understand the depth of the criticisms of the education system that came from the political left in the '60s, since the received view among so-called progressives today is that the biggest, if not the only, problem facing our schools is that they are underfunded by neoconservative governments. It is ironic then to note that many of the education reforms currently being advocated by the political right, such as vouchers and charter schools (where parents are given a monetary voucher to put towards tuition at the independent school of their choice) were originally advanced as crucial aspects of the countercultural revolution. In many ways, for the counterculture, social revolution simply *was* educational revolution, and it was an era rich in experiments in learning. From the UK's Summerhill to Toronto's Rochdale, from Berkeley to the 'free universities' that began popping up around the world, there was a widespread conviction that a change in the education system was all that was needed to bring about the change in consciousness that was the hallmark of the countercultural revolution. Roszak captures the flavour of the times quite nicely when he describes the fate of one such experiment:

When the Antiuniversity of London, the first British version of North American free universities, was opened in early 1968, its prospectus was filled with courses devoted to 'anti-cultures', 'anti-environments', 'anti-poetry', 'anti-theatre', 'anti-families', and 'counter institutions'.[16] Seemingly nothing the adult society had to offer any longer proved acceptable. The superheated radicalism of the school was eventually to reach such a pitch that even the age-old student– teacher relationship came under fire as an intolerable form of authoritarianism. So it too was scrapped, on the assumption that nobody any longer had anything to teach the young; they would make up their own education from scratch. Unfortunately – but was the misfortune more comic or more tragic – the school failed to survive this act of radical restructuring.

One must admire the consistency here. After all, if the entire culture is nothing but a system of repression, then what possible benefit could be had from education? The past is merely ideological ballast. Not only is such 'knowledge' useless to the counterculture, it is positively anathema. After all, the only reason that one might want to communicate it to the young would be to indoctrinate them into the same system. Thus schools came to be seen as not just another conformist, bureaucratic institution of mass society, but as the ultimate tool of the technocracy. Prison metaphors were common – such as Reich's talk of education as 'indoctrination of the inmates'– but even these didn't quite fully capture the awfulness of schools.

These implications of the countercultural critique were articulated most influentially by Ivan Illich, in *Deschooling Society*. For Illich, the school was mass society in microcosm, the perfect metonym for everything the counterculture was railing against. His call for the 'deschooling' of society was nothing short of a demand that society be de-bureaucratised, de-professionalised and de-institutionalised, from the ground up.

Illich described what he called the 'institutional spectrum', a left–right axis along which various social institutions could be placed. On the right side of the spectrum are what he called 'manipulative' institutions, while on the left side are the more desirable 'convivial' institutions.[17] Manipulative institutions are bureaucratic, conformist and in the service of mass society, while convivial institutions are distinguished by the way in which they serve and enhance individual freedom and spontaneity. So, on the far-right side of the spectrum we find the usual suspects: police, the military, large corporations, jails and hospitals. On the far left are public or quasi-public institutions such as telephone networks, the mail, public transport and public markets. In the middle of the spectrum are small businesses (bakeries, hairdressers) and certain professionals such as public defenders and music teachers. (There are interesting wrinkles here. Illich called highways a 'false public good', because while they appear to be convivial in nature, they actually contribute to our enslavement by producing a demand for right-spectrum goods and services, such as petroleum products and automobiles.)[18]

Illich's approach is at times quite insightful. He anticipated the rise of what has been called the 'network society' and sketched out many of the emancipatory claims that would later be made for the Internet. Illich saw that the traditional left–right spectrum of public versus private ownership missed the crucial factor: what matters is the nature of access and use. He saw the value of networks – decentralised, flattened institutions in which communication or cooperation is initiated by the user herself, on terms and conditions of her choosing. Telephones and the postal system are a part of these networks, as will the Internet eventually become.

What is most interesting for our purposes here is to note that Illich placed schools at the extreme right of the institutional spectrum. Schools are worse than churches, worse than the military, worse even than insane asylums. Schools are just like churches in that they make a sharp distinction between the sacred and the profane, between knowledge and ignorance, with the key to knowledge in the hands of the few who control access, meting it out to the masses in measured doses. But at least churchgoing is optional. For Illich, compulsory education is as offensive (and unconstitutional) as the idea of compulsory religion. Even in comparison with the war in Vietnam, State schools don't come off looking good, since 'America's commitment to the compulsory education of its young now reveals itself to be as futile as the pretended American commitment to the compulsory democratisation of the Vietnamese.'[19]

Thus, schools are like highways, in that they exist simply to provide a demand for the products and services of other right-spectrum institutions. But while highways produce a demand only for cars, schools create a demand for the entire set of institutions that crowd the right side of the spectrum. Every institution of mass society shapes the individual in certain ways, but the school enslaves more profoundly and systematically. Schools set the standards of normalcy and deviance, of lawfulness and unlawfulness, of health and illness, all of which are the preconditions for the functioning of churches, police and hospitals. Schools are the institution of institutions, because they effectively determine in which institution a pupil will spend the rest of his life. They create in the student a lifelong addiction to the consumption of the products of mass society, in a way that guarantees the deflation of the spirit, the depletion of resources and the pollution of the environment.

The grip that this theory has exercised over the imagination of the progressive left in subsequent decades is astonishing. In 2003, *Harper's Magazine* could still publish a cover article called 'Against Schools', encouraging us all to 'wake up to what our schools really are: laboratories of experimentation on young minds, drill centres for the habits and attitudes that corporate society demands. Mandatory education serves children only incidentally; its real purpose is to turn them into servants.'[20] This is all presented with the utmost of seriousness, as an exposé, something that we have never heard before. 'School trains children to be employees and consumers … to obey reflexively.' Countercultural thinking, it would appear, forces social critics to repeat the same tired clichés again and again … almost reflexively.

★

Given the depth and pervasiveness of this hostility to schools, it is not hard to understand the related hostility to school uniforms. If schools are the ultimate total institution – prison, military and asylum all at once – then the school uniform is the ultimate symbol of that institution. And if military dress allows soldiers to indulge in the dignity or vanity of belonging, then school uniforms are like prison garb or the large yellow Star of David that the Nazis forced every Jew to wear. They symbolise the shame and stigma of belonging.

For critics of mass society, the school uniform functions, as all uniforms do, to identify a group of people and to set them off from others, but the point of this distinction is to establish in the student's mind a constant reminder of his or her subordinate status. Since the primary function of the school is to prepare students for a lifetime of obedience and conformity, the uniform gives teachers a convenient excuse for asserting authority and inflicting punishment. Recall the way in which control can be exercised through the tolerance of deviation from the officially prescribed uniform, as long as there is always the possibility of a crackdown at any moment. The literature on school uniforms is replete with anecdotes, told by still-traumatised former inmates (sorry, students), of being subject to ridicule, beatings and a daily regimen of general humiliation at the hands of teachers arbitrarily enforcing the absolute letter of the dress code.

Given their long-standing use as instruments of control, it is not surprising that school uniforms have traditionally been supported by law-and-order types, usually political conservatives. Yet during the '90s there was a curious shift, and school uniforms began to find considerable support among the community-minded political left. The shift began with the widespread recognition that two serious problems were affecting the educational environment in State schools. First, there was a sharp rise in in-school violence, much of it gang-related or gang-influenced. Second, the '90s saw teens enter the contemporary luxury economy en masse.

The two were not unrelated. The rise of gang symbolism (such as jackets and bandannas) was largely the result of the mass-marketing of American urban black culture to suburban white youth through music videos, advertising and professional basketball. Meanwhile, teenagers began to control a great deal of discretionary income, and they started to embrace the logic of consumerism at an increasingly young age. The result was an explosion in fashion-related competitive consumption between students. This competition put enormous social pressure on students, not to mention massively exacerbating class differences (and encouraging many students from poorer families to work almost full-time hours at 'after-school' jobs, just so they could afford to stay cool). This is hardly a surprising outcome, given the outrageous expense of items like Nike trainers.

All of these effects, for obvious reasons, combined to create an atmosphere at school in which learning was well down the list of a student's priorities.

It is crucial to note that these are not problems of individual discipline or obedience. They are driven by factors that are largely outside the control of a single student or group of students. Gang-influenced violence and the more mainstream fashion competition are essentially a race to the bottom. It would be better for all concerned if no one wore the latest Nikes to school, but the temptation to engage in one-upmanship and the desire not to fall behind are just too great. The result in both cases is a fashion-based arms race (which, given the gun culture in the United States, frequently becomes a real arms race) that leads to the sinking of ever-increasing resources into a competition that is by definition unwinnable.

In response, a lot of people started to think that making uniforms mandatory in the State schools would be an easy solution to these problems. A fairly rigid dress code could serve as something very much like an arms control treaty, binding on all parties, limiting the possibilities for competition. Rich or poor, everyone would wear the same plaid skirt, the same school tie, the same patent leather shoes. All of which, it was thought, would enhance students' self-confidence, reduce stress and pressure, and allow more time and energy to be devoted to their studies and to productive extracurricular activities.

The theory behind this renewed interest in school uniforms seems sound. If the major problems facing students arise out of variant forms of fashion-based competitive consumption, then a simple solution would be to structure their environment so as to limit the opportunities for competition by making school uniforms mandatory. Unfortunately, there is no comprehensive data on the impact of school uniforms in achieving the hoped-for benefits. The study that is most frequently cited in favour of uniforms comes from the Long Beach Unified School District in California. In 1994, the district implemented mandatory uniforms in all schools from kindergarten through grade 8, with rather dramatic results. For a number of discipline problems ranging from vandalism to weapons offences, there was an overall one-year reduction of 33 per cent in the incidence of such offences. This included a 44 per cent drop in assault and battery, a 74 per cent drop in sex offences and a 41 per cent drop in fighting. Other school boards throughout the United States have reported similar results, but the information tends to be anecdotal and unsystematic. Also, it is not clear whether these benefits are sustained over time or whether they are due to a certain novelty effect.

The one thing that does seem clear, however, is that the benefits that were thought to flow from the abolition of the uniform have failed to materialise. Has the new atmosphere of individuality made children more creative and artistic? More loving and compassionate? More expressive and free? Merely formulating the question reveals the absurdity of the suggestion. If anything, eliminating the uniform has bred cliquishness, not individuality.

The best way to find out about uniforms is to talk to kids who wear them. So I set out for Bishop Strachan, a nice private girls' school in Toronto with a strict dress code, to talk about competition, consumerism and gray skirts.

As one might expect, the girls spend a fair bit of time thinking about their clothes, and they can tell you an awful lot about the ups and downs of uniforms. On the positive side, everyone agreed that wearing a uniform to school every day reduced their daily stresses. Not having to worry about what to wear meant one less decision to make every morning (or three fewer decisions, depending on how you count). Many of them also felt that the uniform enhanced school spirit and solidarity. But did the uniforms eliminate their individuality? Did it crush their spirit? Make them cogs in a machine? Hardly.

If you want to know a thousand and one ways to modify a school uniform, just ask the girls who wear them: sleeve cuffs can be rolled up or tucked in, flipped over or pulled straight; ties can be worn loosely or tight, straight or askew; buttons can be undone at strategic locations and skirts can be raised or lowered in any of a half-dozen ways (including the classic move of rolling in at the waist – something that can be done after leaving the house in the morning and undone before returning). Then there are accessories – a gray region in the dress code, but an entire subcontinent in the world of women's apparel. There are a million options in the domain of jewellery, watches and bags alone. Girls can also wear their hair as they like, which opens up the predictable range of possibilities.

Thus the general point, agreed to by all, is that uniforms do not eliminate individuality, but they do place some limits on the way that individuality can be expressed. This in turn dampens competitive consumption. You can't stomp out differences, and you can't stop students from competing. The competition is still there; it is just no longer unlimited. To this extent, the uniforms are like a nuclear non-proliferation treaty: countries can still build up armies and stockpile weapons; the treaty simply limits their ability to wage total war.

The implication is clear: uniforms are not a magic bullet. They don't do away with class-based resentment – one student (who was at the school on scholarship) complained privately to me that she felt humiliated because she couldn't afford designer shoes and handbags. Almost all of the girls admitted that the pressure to compete through fashion didn't go away, but that it was transferred to other parts of their lives. They said they felt extra pressure to look good whenever they went out after school or on weekends, to the point where every party felt like prom night. It was as though a week's worth of fashion display was compressed into a single evening. The girls I spoke to had no illusions about their uniforms. They realised that the school uniforms worked to curtail their freedom of expression in certain essential ways. But the most important point is that the overwhelming majority *liked* their uniforms. They felt that, on the whole, the advantages they gained through improvements in their academic environment were worth it.

In many ways, they displayed a better understanding of the situation than some of their self-appointed advocates. In her book *Branded: The Buying and Selling of Teenagers*, New York journalist Alissa Quart takes a hard look at contemporary youth culture, and she is shocked by what she finds. Preteens wearing makeup, teens working as 'trendspotters' for corporations, high schoolers doing steroids or getting cosmetic surgery or starving themselves to look like models – all of them treading in a sea of brands, brands everywhere.

Quart places the blame on marketers and advertisers. In doing so, she adopts an almost completely unreconstructed version of the critique of mass society. She thinks of marketing as a form of brainwashing, and her book is full of references to teens being duped, forced, programmed and otherwise bamboozled into playing video games and going to the mall to shop for clothes. She sees that consumerism arises out of the desire that teens have to be cool, and since cool is about hanging out with the in-crowd, everywhere she looks she sees teens trying to wear the same shoes, listen to the same bands and go to the same schools. She therefore concludes that striving to be cool is the same as striving to conform. And because she is convinced that the enemy is conformity, not competition, Quart rejects school uniforms as a solution to the problems of teen culture that she has diagnosed. Thus, Edison Schools Inc., a for-profit company that runs State schools in twenty-two states, is mocked for its prison-like 'cookie-cutter' approach to education, in part because it requires school uniforms.

Quart talks herself into something of a paradox. She begins with a critique of corporations that peddle their brands to teens, exploiting their desire to fit in and be cool. That is fine. But there is a fast solution to that problem. The easiest way to keep brands out of the classroom is simply to forbid the kids from wearing them. Put them in a uniform. But this solution is rejected because it, too, is an exercise in enforced conformity. So if both letting students choose their own clothes and making them wear uniforms lead to conformity, what is the solution?

According to Quart, what students need to do is rebel. She celebrates the 'do-it-yourself' punk scene and the 'culture jammers,' who combine social criticism with cultural creativity by playing music in their basements, staging street parties and cutting each other's hair. Where have we heard this before? Isn't this what people have been doing since the '60s? Yet Quart seems to think that things will be different this time. She actually suggests that the kids should become more like she was, back in the days when all she needed in the way of style was a pair of Converse trainers and a Ramones T-shirt. The fact that she actually names the brand of shoes that she wore during her period of adolescent rebellion is staggering. For some reason, she thinks that there is a fundamental difference between the Converse trainers that she wore (basketball shoes made famous by Julius Erving) and the Nikes that kids wear today (basketball shoes made famous by Michael Jordan), such that she was a 'rebel' whereas teenagers now are 'victims'. She does note parenthetically that 'in the process of trying to protect their identities from brands',[21] people end up simply rebranding themselves as hardcore, thrasher and punk, but she never quite realises that this rebranding is the exact same quest for distinction that has been driving competitive consumption all along.

Here we can see the enormous mischief caused by the myth of counterculture. It leads Quart to commit the cardinal sin of countercultural thinking: she rejects a perfectly good solution to the problem of consumerism among teens (uniforms) in favour of a proposed solution (subcultural rebellion) that not only cannot work, but that has demonstrably exacerbated the very problem she hopes to solve.

At its core, consumerism stems from the belief that goods both express and define our individual identities. When consumerism is combined with a cultural obsession with the quest for authentic self-expression, the result is a society collectively locked in a large number of consumption traps. Because of our further conviction that fashion is a superior form of expression, that clothing has a language of its own, it is not hard to see why the relentless fashion cycle has become the dominant locus of competitive consumption. This concern with fashion has one advantage, though. If we could eliminate competition over clothing, we could do away with one of the most serious and disabling forms of competition. This is one of the emancipatory virtues of uniforms.

It is important to keep in mind that consumerism is not politically inert or neutral. In many ways, its success is due to the fact that consumerism manages to engage our central political ideas – freedom, democracy, self-expression – in a way that is accessible, personalised and immediately gratifying. Democratic politics might sound great in theory, but its practice has nothing on shopping. There is no sovereignty like consumer sovereignty.

Which brings us back to *Star Trek*. In all of its incarnations, *Star Trek* is an almost quaintly political show. It occasionally embraces more contemporary science fiction topics about the place of humanism in a highly rational and technologically advanced society – most notably in Picard's dealings with the Borg – but more than anything the show is about America's ongoing dialogue with itself about how best to interpret its founding political myths of liberty, equality and happiness. The world of *Star Trek* is one where political life and questions of community values and social solidarity retain their primacy over more private questions of work, consumption and individual self-expression. It is a world in which people simply do not find meaning in consumer goods.

The most obvious symbol of this is the uniforms that everyone on the show wears. It isn't just that they wear uniforms, it is that the uniforms themselves don't betray the slightest hint of vanity. Nobody on the show seems the least bit concerned that they spend most of their waking lives in suits of rather unflattering pyjamas. And why should they care, when pursuing the Federation's political agenda provides them much more direct ways of giving meaning to their lives?

It might be objected that *Star Trek* describes a political utopia of the most unlikely sort: one where the basic values of citizenship and representative democracy provide sufficient levels of individual meaning and social solidarity. The triumph of consumerism in our world (so runs the objection) is precisely due to the fact that modern democracy has been supplanted by a technocracy that is unable to deliver the meanings people crave. And perhaps this is not a bad thing; as the political theorist C.B. MacPherson once argued, the possessive individualism of the 17th century was not really a vice, it was actually a helpful substitute for an ethic of vengeance and glory. Similarly, the fact that consumerism has largely displaced other forms of civic engagement might not be such a bad thing if it decreases popular enthusiasm for 20th century horrors such as imperialism and ethnic nationalism.

Perhaps. But things may have swung too far in the other direction. We need to find some space in our lives for the reintroduction of the political as apart from the cultural. As a way of creating this space, we might start by clearing away some of the consumerist clutter and introducing a bit more uniformity into our lives. Instead of 'daring to be different', perhaps we should dare to be the same.

Notes

1   Alison Lurie, *The Language of Clothes* (New York: Henry Holt, 2000), 18.
2   Reich, *Greening of America*, 141.
3   Bill Clinton, State of the Union Address, January 1996.
4   Paul Fussell, *Uniforms: Why We Are What We Wear* (Boston: Houghton and Mifflin, 2002), 4.
5   Nathan Joseph, *Uniforms and Nonuniforms: Communication through Clothing* (New York: Greenwood, 1986), Chapter 5.
6   Stanley Kubrick, Michael Herr, and Gustav Hasford, *Full Metal Jacket* (New York: Knopf, 1987), 4.
7   *Ibid.*, 42.

8 Patrick O'Brien, *The Commodore* (New York: Norton, 1995), 180.

9 *Uniforms*, 6.

10 Lurie, *Language of Clothes*, 18.

11 Mark Kingwell, *Practical Judgments: Essays in Culture, Politics, and Interpretation* (Toronto: University of Toronto Press, 2002), 248–49.

12 Fussell, *Uniforms*, 38.

13 Frank, *The Conquest of Cool*, 196.

14 *Ibid.*, 186–89.

15 Arthur Marwick, *The Sixties: Cultural Revolution in Britain, France, Italy, and the United States, c. 1958–c. 1974* (Oxford: Oxford University Press, 1998), 13.

16 Roszak, *Making of a Counter Culture*, 45–46.

17 Ivan Illich, *Deschooling Society* (New York: Harper and Row, 1971), 52–56.

18 *Ibid.*, 58.

19 *Ibid.*, 65.

20 John Taylor Gatto, 'Against Schools', *Harper's Magazine* (September 2003).

21 Alissa Quart, *Branded: The Buying and Selling of Teenagers* (Cambridge, MA: Perseus, 2003), 218.

7

From status-seeking
to coolhunting

My introduction to the unforgiving vicissitudes of cool took place, as it does for so many, when I was 14 and in my first year of high school. On the morning of the first big snowfall of the year, I dutifully got out my trusty Cougars, the brown boots with the distinctive red tongue that had stood as the acme of cool for as long as I could remember. Every cool kid – no, every kid I knew – had a pair of Cougars. It was what we wore in winter. So I arrived at school with dry feet and a clear conscience, with the calm obliviousness of someone who just doesn't get it. As I stood at my locker getting ready for class, a voice behind me sang out, mocking, 'Nice Cougars!'

As the kids laughed, I looked around. I was the only one in Cougars. Hell, I was the only one in *boots*. Almost everyone else was wearing deck shoes (Bass or Sperry), which were apparently de rigueur footwear that winter of 1984, as they had been throughout the fall. So what if my feet were warm and dry while theirs were cold and soaking wet? They were cool, and I was not. I spent most of the next four years trying to be as cool as those kids, in their cold and wet topsiders.

Everyone has a story of this type. Yet somehow the significance of it all has been missed by critics of consumerism. Cool is one of the major factors driving the modern economy. Cool has become the central ideology of consumer capitalism. Think back to the last time you bought something that was a little too expensive, something that you couldn't quite afford. Why did you buy it? Probably because it was *really* cool. Flip through your closet or your basement, and it's easy to see.

Full disclosure. Here is some stuff that Andrew has bought over the years because he thought it was cool: one genuine Burberry raincoat (£360), one Shanghai Tang silk jacket (£225), three pairs of

John Fluevog shoes (£90 a pair), one Dell Inspiron 8500 with wide-aspect display (£1700), one pair of Ray-Ban Predator sunglasses (£70), one Kenneth Cole wristwatch (£90). Here is some stuff that Joe has bought because he thought it was cool: one Solomon 550 Pro snowboard (£245), two pairs of steel-toed Blundstones (£80 a pair), one Due West leather car coat (£270), two Roots leather club chairs (£980 each), one Mini Cooper (£14,500).

Most of us can easily construct lists of this type. Furthermore, most of these lists will be very heavy on branded consumer goods. But what is the significance of it all? Given the emphasis on brands, does it mean that we have all bought into a mass-marketed version of cool, dispensed by the mass media through advertising? Or, to deflate the debate a little, does it mean that we are just showing off? Just what is cool, anyway?

In recent years there has been an awful lot of confused talk about the meaning of 'cool'. In a well-received piece in *The New Yorker* called 'The Cool Hunt', Malcolm Gladwell enumerated what he took to be the three cardinal rules of cool. First, the quicker the chase, the quicker the flight. That is, as soon as we think we've discovered cool, it slips away. Second, cool can't be manufactured out of thin air. While companies may be able to intervene in the cycle of cool, they cannot initiate it themselves. When we add to these the last rule – that you have to be cool to know cool – cool becomes a closed loop, a hermetic circle in which not only is it impossible to either make or catch cool, but it is impossible to know what it is. Unless, that is, one is already cool, in which case you have no reason to look for it in the first place.

In Gladwell's view, cool is something abstract and indefinite, much like the philosopher G. E. Moore's celebrated claim that 'good' is a 'simple, indefinable, non-natural property.'[1] We can call this the 'abstract essentialist' view of cool, according to which cool actually exists (there really are cool people and cool things), even though most of us will never know what it is.

In contrast, there is a school of thinking that dismisses cool as nothing but a consumerist mirage, conjured up by corporations in order to sell sunglasses and leather chairs to the duped masses. In his book *Culture Jam*, *Adbusters* editor Kalle Lasn describes cool as 'a heavily manipulative corporate ethos'[2] that has turned America (the birthplace of cool) from a nation into a global brand. Invoking *Brave New World*, Lasn describes cool as the 'Huxleyan soma' of our time, dispensed by the media through advertising. Moving from Huxley to Marx, he claims that cool is a form of branded conformity, the opiate of the contemporary masses. Finally, varying the image but not the central point, the fall 2003 issue of *Adbusters* attacks what it calls the ethos of 'cool fascismo'. According to this view, the seemingly relentless branding of cool by American corporations is just one element of the new American imperialism. The Pentagon force-feeds 'democracy' (read, capitalism) to Iraq and Afghanistan, while Tommy Hilfiger and Nike force-feed 'cool' to the people of the world. According to this 'cool fascismo' theory, cool is a complete deception.

While they appear to be almost directly opposing conceptions, both abstract essentialism and cool fascismo pick up on the most obvious feature of cool, which is that what counts as cool appears highly unstable. What is cool one week is ridiculously past it the next; hence we get the constant turnover of cool as tracked by the monthly lists that anchor the front sections of all the cool magazines: In/Out, Hot/Not, Now/Then, Wired/Tired, Hip/Square. In other words, what is topsiders, and what is Cougar? What is cool, and what is not cool?

For Gladwell, this slipperiness is just evidence of the abstract nature of cool: 'The key to coolhunting, then, is to look for cool people first and cool things later, and not the other way around. Since cool things are always changing, you can't look for them, because the very fact they are cool means you have no idea what to look for.'[3] Cool people are like fashion bloodhounds. For Lasn, the ever-shifting nature of cool is just more evidence of the fundamental bad faith of capitalism. One thing is 'cool' one month, something else is 'cool' the next – it doesn't really matter what it is as long as everyone keeps buying more stuff.

In reality, cool is nothing so ineffable, and nothing so sinister. It is best to think of cool as the central status hierarchy in contemporary urban society. And like traditional forms of status such as class, cool is an intrinsically positional good. Just as not everyone can be upper class and not everyone can have good taste, so not everyone can be cool. This isn't because some people are essentially cooler than others, it's because cool is ultimately a form of distinction. The ideology of essential cool is no different from what Pierre Bourdieu called 'the ideology of natural taste'.

Like all positional goods, being cool gets its value from comparison with others. Some people get to be cool only because others – indeed, most others – are not. (More concretely, in order for some things to be cool, others must suck.) But unlike traditional status hierarchies, which emphasise continuity across time, cool is structured by a restless quest for nonconformity. As cultural theorist Jeff Rice has put it, cool is 'the universal stance of individuality',[4] where to be an individual is understood not as being who you want to be, regardless of what other people are doing, but rather as doing whatever other people are *not* doing. The cool person is the one who has deliberately set himself against the masses of society. He is the rebel, the nonconforming cipher who is the archetypal hero of American movies, music and fiction.

Thus understood, 'cool' is just the dominant term for a cultural stance that is variously denoted as edgy, alternative and hip. And while cool is frequently associated with 'merely cultural' figures and objects (actors, writers, musicians; shoes, clothes, electronics), the partisans of cool have always interpreted their own actions as intensely political. To be cool or hip, in their view, is to engage in a set of practices and to adopt a set of attitudes that are designed to liberate the individual from the shackles of mass society.

Norman Mailer set the agenda once and for all in his essay 'The White Negro'. His description of the hipster, written in 1957, still has a contemporary ring to it:

> *If the fate of 20th century man is to live with death from adolescence to premature senescence, why then the only life-giving answer is to accept the terms of death, to live with death as immediate danger, to divorce oneself from society, to live without roots, to set out on that uncharted journey into the rebellious imperatives of the self. In short, the decision is to encourage the psychopath in oneself. One is Hip or one is Square, one is a rebel or one conforms.*[5]

And given that mass society is 'the prison of the nervous system',[6] the true individual doesn't have to spend much time deliberating over this choice.

It is the either/or nature of cool that gives it its power, and the rise of cool as the central status system of the counterculture represents nothing short of the society-wide triumph of the logic of high school. Mailer understood this, which is why he was able to so perfectly nail the hipster as the fusion of the nonconforming bohemian, the antisocial juvenile delinquent and the sexual, marginalised Negro. Isn't that him, out there smoking behind the bleachers?

One of the great virtues of the binary nature of cool is that it allows us to situate literally everything in society on one side or the other of the great cool/not-cool divide. It is this logic that informs the Siskel and Ebert 'thumbs up/thumbs down' school of film criticism as well as the Beavis and Butthead 'rocks/sucks' school of music criticism. It also gives us the steady parade of hot/not lists, which Mailer inaugurated with his 1959 list, *The Hip and the Square*.

In addition to such predictably hip things as wild, romantic and spontaneous (opposed to the squareness of practical, classical and orderly), the hip is also embodied in Schrödinger's model of the atom (Bohr's is square), and imperial measurements (metric is square). It is

Hip	Square
black ('Negro')	white
nihilistic	authoritarian
self	society
body	mind
Dostoevsky	Tolstoy
call girls	psychoanalysts
anarchists	socialists
sin	salvation
marijuana	alcohol

interesting to note that even though critics of the notion of cool like to point out how transient and ephemeral cool is, it is actually hard to argue with many of the choices Mailer made almost fifty years ago:[7]

And so on. The superficialities of fashion may change, but the deep structure of cool as rebellious nonconformity provides us with a surprisingly stable and enduring set of guidelines. Cool, it seems, has become a social institution.

Hip (cool, alternative) was not always so central to our status hierarchy. There was a time – a long, long time ago, in fact – when Americans were more concerned with class than with cool.

This is a suggestion that many Americans might find offensive, or at least completely wrong-headed. As a republic founded on the equality of all citizens, the United States lacks the official hereditary aristocracy and class system that one finds in the UK and other European countries. Most Americans take great pride in this. But the United States has never been the classless society that many people thought it was, or hoped it would become. For as long as there have been people praising the absence of class in the United States, there have been people more than willing to take their fellow citizens on a tour of the American class structure.

Most traditional systems of social class are a form of aristocracy, with status deriving from an 'ascribed' property, such as family lineage. The English aristocracy, for example, was a hereditary social class based on land ownership, at a time when land couldn't be bought or sold, only inherited (although some of the lesser peerages could be purchased). Many of the underlying elitist assumptions of this system were imported to the British colonies in the years leading up to the American War of Independence. In the United States, the conventional wisdom was always that, as the country grew richer, whatever vestiges of class there were would wither and die (one can see this very clearly in Vance Packard's 1957 book *The Status Seekers*). The march of progress would also be a march toward equality, as the country gradually became one vast middle class. As much as this might fit with the United States' democratic self-image, Packard argued that this utterly failed to perceive the realities of the situation. If anything, class lines appeared to be hardening, even as status striving intensified.

A quarter-century later, Paul Fussell began his tour of class in America with a chapter entitled 'A Touchy Subject', noting that it was possible to outrage Americans simply by *mentioning* class, 'very much the way, sipping tea among the aspidistras a century ago, you could silence a party by adverting too openly to sex.'[8] Echoing Packard, Fussell argued that the professed egalitarianism of American life meant that class became more important, not less. After all, in a society committed to the formal equality of all citizens, 'one of the unique anxieties is going to be the constant struggle for individual self-respect based on social approval.'[9] In a telling parallel, both Packard and Fussell remark on how, immediately after disavowing the very possibility of class in America, their subjects turned to an informed and even gleeful discussion of the barely concealed class structures in their towns.

The American class system that coalesced around the early Protestant elites was rooted in the bourgeois values of material wealth, productive work, social stability and respectability. To a large extent, this bourgeois elite modelled itself on the English aristocracy, with wealth replacing land as the premier mark of status. The greatest analyst of the role of wealth in the American class structure remains Thorstein Veblen. In *The Theory of the Leisure Class*, he coined many of the terms we still use to discuss class striving: conspicuous consumption, vicarious leisure, pecuniary emulation, invidious comparison. For Veblen, class distinctions will inevitably arise in any society in which there is a system of ownership. His controversial claim was that once a society grows beyond a mere subsistence level of wealth, the entire point of acquiring more wealth is to achieve the 'invidious distinction' that accompanies it.[10]

In bourgeois industrial society, then, the possession and accumulation of wealth comes to serve as the customary basis of respect and esteem. In order to have any sort of standing in the community, one must acquire a certain base level of wealth. Anything beyond that and one goes up in esteem (and becomes 'upper class'), while anything below the minimum means that one goes down in esteem (and becomes 'lower class'). The big problem that arises in a capitalist society is that the simple wealth-based status hierarchy becomes extremely fluid, as people are increasingly able to make (and lose) large sums of money overnight. Sociologists may disagree about the exact number of social classes in the United States (most say five, though Fussell thinks there are nine), but everyone agrees that *mere wealth* is not sufficient to define and entrench a social elite in such a society. It also matters where you got your money (it is better to inherit it than to earn it), and, if you must work for a living, it is better to work with your brain than with your hands.

As a way of holding off the vagaries of income in a capitalist, egalitarian society, the American elites have devised a fairly baroque system of class markers based not only in wealth, but also in education, political power and taste. In almost every case, the crucial characteristic is age: old money is better than new, Ivy League schools are better than all the rest, old political families are better than the young strivers, and so on. Similarly, when it comes to possessions, it is best to avoid actually buying anything. It is preferable to inherit everything, from automobiles to clothing, with natural fibres, antiques and heirlooms conferring higher status than things made of nylon or polyester, mass produced or bought at a jeweller. When Carmela Soprano proudly announces that there are no antiques in her house, just 'traditional style' furniture, it tells you everything you need to know about her social class.

This preference for the old over the new arises out of a deliberate attempt to ape the hereditary, almost feudal, character of the old English aristocracy. This bourgeois pecking order dominated American social life for most of the first two centuries of the country's existence. During that time, the bourgeoisie was opposed by a competing value system that was generally called 'bohemian'. While the bourgeoisie valued hard work, pursued within the large and dominant institutions of society, the bohemian ethic was hedonistic, individualistic and sensual. It valued experience, exploration and self-expression and opposed conformity. In short, this is more or less the set of values (leavened with the dangerous rebelliousness of the juvenile delinquent) that Mailer identified as hip.

Mailer's hip/square opposition is thus in many ways just a variation on the traditional theme of bohemian vs. bourgeois. It has always been widely believed by both sides that these didn't just represent two possible sets of values: they occupied the entire field in a battle that wasn't only aesthetic, but also political and economic. Everyone agreed that to criticise bourgeois values was to criticise the very underpinnings of the capitalist system. This was certainly Mailer's view.

At some point, somehow, a tremendous cultural shift occurred. Bohemian values – that is, cool – usurped class as the dominant status system in America. Already in 1976, Daniel Bell argued (in *The Cultural Contradictions of Capitalism*) that capitalism had essentially capitulated to the very bohemian values that threatened it: 'The protagonists of the adversary culture, because of the historic subversive effect on traditional bourgeois values, substantially influence, if not dominate, the cultural establishments today: the publishing houses, museums, and galleries; the major news, picture, and cultural weeklies and monthlies; the theatre, the cinema, and the universities.'[11] Furthermore, 'what is striking today is that the majority has no intellectually respectable culture of its own – no major figures in literature, painting, or poetry – to counterpose to the adversary culture. In this sense, bourgeois culture has been shattered.'

There can be no question that in the conflict between old-fashioned bourgeois values and bohemian values, the bohemian has emerged triumphant. But in the process – and contrary to Bell's dire predictions – it managed to leave capitalism not just intact, but healthier and more dominant than ever before. How did this happen?

Everyone can agree that in the twenty-year period from the end of the '60s to the beginning of the '90s there was a massive cultural shift in Western society. The '70s in particular were a decade of massive cultural change. (Some pedants like to remind us that most of the changes we associate with the '60s actually took place during the '70s.) The old Protestant pecking order collapsed as the baby boomers graduated from university and began to move into positions of authority, bringing their hippie value system with them. By the time this group had become the political, economic and cultural elite in the '90s, lying in its wake was a society transformed.

That these changes occurred is something that everybody agrees upon. Where people disagree is on the precise nature of those changes. The standard story is that the baby-boomer hippies either sold out – trading their bongs for Beemers – or were co-opted by the system. In this view, the counterculture's values didn't really win out. At least, the victory was only partial and hollow. The elites in control of the system made several tactical concessions, but when it came to the core countercultural values, the system conceded nothing. What it did was take the most dangerous elements of the counterculture, in particular the music, and co-opt them by mass-producing ersatz versions, which were then sold back to the masses as the real deal. Thus, whatever revolutionary potential emerged from the '60s was steadily drained of its subversive energy by a system that steadfastly resisted fundamental change. Cool lingers on as the nostalgic veneer of '60s radicalism.

A subtler view was recently introduced by David Brooks, who argues that the two sides in this grand conflict, the hip and the square, simply *merged*. (How very capitalist!) According to this view, the boomers graduated from university in unprecedented numbers, which led to the formation of a new elite based on education and merit. They soon realised that they didn't have to choose between a rebellious past and a conformist future. No, they would find a way to have their hash brownies and eat them too, by creating a way of life that would allow them to become rebels with stock options. Did anyone sell out? Not really – 'in the resolution between the culture and the counterculture, it is impossible to tell who co-opted whom, because in reality the bohemians and the bourgeois co-opted each other.'[12]

This new elite isn't held together by an old boys' network of family, money and school ties. The bobos (short for 'bourgeois bohemians') are a fairly loose group of 'meritocrats' who live in places like Seattle, Toronto and Palo Alto (in North America) and in the urban centres of the so-called 'creative crescent' of Sweden, Finland and Denmark (in Europe), working in knowledge-industry jobs at universities, high-tech firms and design agencies. What unites them is a shared refusal to compromise on either the bourgeois or the bohemian front: 'They are prosperous without seeming greedy; they have pleased their elders without seeming conformist; they have risen toward the top without too obviously looking down on those below; they have achieved success without committing certain socially sanctioned affronts to the ideal of social equality; they have constructed a prosperous lifestyle while avoiding the old clichés of conspicuous consumption.'[13] All told, a pretty nauseating group of people.

The boomer bobos are the leading edge of a large group that has become known as the 'creative class'. Like the establishment class of the '50s, this powerful new class sets the overarching norms for society as a whole. And, unlike the homogeneity and conformism that defined the Organisation Man, these creatives value individuality, self-expression and difference. The rise of the creatives was predicted by Fussell at the end of his book *Class*, except that he thought that this new 'X-class' would actually be the first group to transcend class altogether (every ten years or so since then, someone has inevitably picked out the latest group of countercultural rebels and made the same prediction). In Fussell's view, these actors, musicians, artists and journalists would become a sort of unmonied aristocracy, by managing to 'escape out the back doors of those theatres of class which enclose others.'[14]

The most thorough analysis of the creatives is that by economist Richard Florida. Unlike Brooks, who sees these individualistic, nonconformist, anti-institutional, meritocratic and tolerant people as a simple *cultural* elite, Florida realises that their power is first and foremost *economic*. Florida says that he became aware of their growing influence when he noticed that people were no longer moving to jobs – jobs were moving to people. In the New Economy, creativity became the decisive source of competitive advantage, and firms realised that they were going to have to move to where the creative people lived. Creatives now make up almost one-third of the total workforce in the United States, and they earn on average double what those in the service and blue collar industries earn.

According to Florida, this group rose to power not simply by mashing together the hip and the square in some big merger, but by transcending the entire opposition. Like Tony Blair, they found a magical third way between bohemian values and the Protestant work ethic, executing what Florida calls the 'Big Morph'.[15] He skimps quite a bit on the details, but the gist of his argument is that while the hippies were fighting it out with the squares, a quiet group of nerds based around San Francisco – computer hackers, mostly – created a new ethic that Florida calls 'the creative ethos', which transcended the opposition between bourgeois and bohemian. Basically, they decided one day to cultivate an ethic of creativity at work.

Yet regardless of whether one views the shift in values of the past thirty years as a process of merger or as one of transcendence, there is no escaping the observation that very little in the basic structure of society has changed. Capitalism is doing just fine, and there is still as much hierarchy in American life as ever. The idea that bohemian values posed a threat to the system was obviously mistaken. Florida hits on this theme when he argues that 'the term counterculture is a misnomer, since all it refers to is pop culture, which is just a ticket to sell things and make money.'[16] Mass-marketing of hippie culture didn't involve any sort of sell-out because 'few cultural products have much content to begin with.'[17]

What is more interesting is the way that the dawn of cool has transformed that status hierarchy of Western society. Rather than abolishing class, cool has essentially *replaced* class as the central determinant of social prestige. In his book *Nobrow*, John Seabrook claims that the ancient opposition between 'high-brow' and 'low-brow' taste has been annihilated by the marketplace, so that we now live in a world of uniform 'no-brow' commercialism. Yet while the specific values and culture of the old Protestant establishment have no doubt lost considerable influence, this does not mean that status hierarchy has disappeared. Seabrook himself notes that, in many ways, subculture has simply become the new high culture.[18]

Under the old bourgeois Protestant pecking order, how you ranked was to a considerable extent determined by what you did (or, for women, by what your husband did). Back in the '50s, Packard identified six factors that combined to establish the prestige of a given occupation: the importance of the task performed, the authority inherent in the job, the knowledge and brains required, the dignity of the tasks performed, and the financial rewards. He then cited a number of surveys conducted during the '50s that tried to arrive at an overall ranking of jobs according to prestige.

The results were remarkably consistent. In almost all cases, Supreme Court justices were seen as having the most prestigious job in America, followed immediately by physicians. Other high-prestige professions included banker, business executive, minister and university lecturer. Down toward the bottom of the list we find accountants, advertising executives, journalists and union officials.

Here we can see a very clear expression of the status hierarchy that we all intuitively identify with the mass society of America in the '50s. The 'prestige professions' are very much pillars of the establishment, serving at high levels in the most dominant institutions in society. They are also extremely *paternalistic* professions. Judge, minister, banker, doctor, professor – these are all distinguished by the fact that they place the job holder on the expertise and authority side of a fiduciary relationship. Thus members of these professional groups not only had a great deal of prestige, they also had a great deal of power and influence. They were the dominant figures of a ruling elite that sustained itself through family, school and institutional ties. In this respect, these people were members of a secularised aristocracy, the social elite in whose hands the fate of society rested.

Today, members of this group may still rate high on some traditional measures, but the influence associated with that rank is steadily waning. Prestige is not what it used to be; power is increasingly wielded not by the bourgeois, paternalistic aristocrats but by the cool, bohemian creative types. Over the past decade and a half, this creative class has transformed the cultural and economic landscape. It is not hard to see how this transformation could occur. In a modern capitalist economy, knowledge and education have become far more important than lineage and social connections. The market demands enormous geographic mobility – members of the dominant class now routinely hold down jobs in two or three cities simultaneously. And, finally, wealth has become far less important than income when it comes to sustaining the lifestyles and consumption habits of the social elite. The ultra-rich in America – from movie stars to corporate CEOs – earn their money from salaries, not from investments.

In other words, the staid and sedentary bourgeois elite, whose habits and style of life were essentially modelled on the old English aristocracy, was slated for destruction very early on by the forces of capitalism itself. The restless, individualistic, free-spirited bohemian is, in many ways, much more in tune with the true spirit of capitalism – where fortunes are gained and lost in an afternoon, where flows of capital are unleashed across the world at the click of a mouse button, where commerce moves too quickly for anyone to put down roots and, most importantly, where everyone's money is the same colour. Unlike so-called bourgeois values, which are basically an imitation of feudal social norms, hip values are a direct expression of the spirit of capitalism.

This change in the status system is clearly reflected in the workplace. What people yearn for these days is no longer an old-fashioned 'status' job, like being a doctor. The 'cool job' has become the holy grail of the modern economy. Corporate America has been tuned in to this for a long time. A visitor from the '50s would not recognise the modern no-collar workplace, with its casual dress codes and flexible work hours, designed to reflect the ebb and flow of creative ideas. The whole thing is like a hippie commune under professional management. The creative workplace has an open design (no cubicles), high ceilings, indirect lighting and lots of funky art on the wall. Instead of a lunchroom there is plenty of 'hanging out' space where employees can throw a Frisbee, play video games, work out or brew up an espresso shot. When it comes to payday, the creatives don't want cash, they want free tickets to the game, free massages and prepared dinners they can take home with them. And, like any other ruling class, what they want is generally what they get.

As important as it is to have a cool workplace environment, creatives won't work in just any city. They need to live in what have been called 'cool communities', with a large number of like-minded people. To attract talented professionals, it is no longer sufficient for a city to have a low crime rate, clean air and water, decent public transportation and a handful of museums and galleries. Now they need to cater to the specific needs of the creative class, which means the city needs a large-scale recycling programme, plenty of funky cafés, vegetarian restaurants and specialty stores selling a full array of organic products. It needs a diverse, tolerant population with plenty of immigrants and gay people, and a thriving club and music scene, and, ideally, it must have quick and easy access to areas for mountain-biking, rock-climbing and sea-kayaking or similar alternative-lifestyle activities. In a 2001 survey by a group called Next Generation Consulting, San Francisco emerged as the coolest city in the United States (this is the sort of insight for which consultants can charge enormous fees), followed by Minneapolis, Seattle, Boston and Denver. In a 2002 survey done by Superbrands, a marketing consultancy, London was named the coolest city in the UK (surprise), followed by Manchester and Brighton, while Paris, Barcelona, and Prague were named the coolest cities in Europe.

One of the most obvious canards spread by the New Economy prophets during the early years of the Internet revolution was the idea that technology had made geography irrelevant. It was assumed by many people that telecommuting would take off, as everyone would flee the overcrowded cities for rural cottages where they would work from home as cogs in the virtual economy. Those who spread this sort of nonsense clearly had no understanding of the value system of the people who would actually be employed in this economy. These people are just as concerned with distinction as the older bourgeois elite. If anything, place has become more, not less, important. As Florida has persuasively argued, with the rising power of the creative class, clustered as it is in a handful of 'cool cities', the United States is rapidly sorting itself geographically along status lines – except that the status hierarchy is now based on cool, not class.

To some extent, this is not a new phenomenon. Cities like New York, London and Paris have always attracted a disproportionate share of bohemians, but, as Florida observes, the class sorting is becoming increasingly pronounced. A person's post code tells marketers much more about his consumer preferences than does his family history. Another important difference is that in the past, every city had its own members of the bourgeois elite – its own executives, judges, bankers, professors, doctors and so on – who were connected in various ways to the broader national elites. Now the members of the creative class are almost completely abandoning entire regions and congregating in a handful of centres.

The most important thing to realise, though, is that this class sorting will only intensify as it feeds on itself and accumulates an increasingly disproportionate economic influence. This is because the creative class – in contrast with the rather aristocratic complacency of the old elites – is driven by an ethos that is unrelentingly capitalist in orientation.

This claim will seem odd to many people, given the explicitly rebellious, anti-institutional attitude copped by the members of this new class. But here is how Brooks characterises the contrasting values of the bourgeoisie and the bohemians: 'The bourgeois prized materialism, order, regularity, custom, rational thinking, self-discipline, and productivity. The bohemians celebrated creativity, rebellion, novelty, self-expression, antimaterialism, and vivid experience.'[19] Now ask yourself: Which of these more accurately reflects the spirit of contemporary capitalism?

Those who answered 'bourgeois' have been seduced by the idea that capitalism requires conformity in order to function correctly. It doesn't. In fact, the exact opposite is the case. Capitalism thrives on what Joseph Schumpeter famously called 'the perennial gale of creative destruction'. Schumpeter realised that capitalism is an evolutionary process that operates by cycles of 'generate-and-test'.[20] The system generates a constant stream of *new* – new consumer goods, new methods of production and transportation, new markets, new forms of organisation and so on. This process is one of constant revolution, as the old economic structure is destroyed, replaced by the new. For Schumpeter, this 'is what capitalism consists in and what every capitalist concern has got to live with.' It is the function of entrepreneurs to generate these revolutionary products and procedures, by exploiting new inventions or using existing technologies in an original way.

This is a roundabout way of making the point that the bohemian value system – that is, cool – is the very lifeblood of capitalism. Cool people like to see themselves as radicals, subversives who refuse to conform to accepted ways of doing things. And this is exactly what drives capitalism. It is true that genuine creativity is completely rebellious and subversive, since it disrupts existing patterns of thought and life. It subverts everything *except capitalism itself*. Thus the process that Thomas Frank describes as 'the conquest of cool' is not really a conquest at all. 'The counterculture,' Frank says, 'may be more accurately understood as a stage in the development of the values of the American middle class, a colourful instalment in the twentieth century drama of consumer subjectivity.'[21]

★

This fundamental connection between capitalism and cool has not gone unnoticed by critics of consumerism. Most of them find it somewhat disturbing – so disturbing that they feel it must be a mistake. The tendency has thus been to claim that the 'cool' being sold by corporations is a fraudulent version, a pre-packaged, ersatz cool that consumers are being bamboozled into buying, believing it to be the real deal.

This reply comes in various strengths. In *No Logo*, Naomi Klein criticises marketers for simply making a bad situation worse; in the age of global mass-marketing of cool, 'the harrowing doubts of adolescence are the billion dollar questions of our age.'[22] But for many critics of consumerist cool, especially those committed to the subversive power of the counterculture, it is not just that corporations are exploiting our desire to be cool by selling us 'cool' products; it is that they are *actually creating the desire for those products*. We are being systematically duped, manipulated, programmed into the consumerist cool mindset, tricked into buying products we otherwise would not really want.

Kalle Lasn gives perhaps the purest and most straightforward version of this argument, when he compares the situation to *The Manchurian Candidate*. In that film, an American POW returns from Korea having been brainwashed into becoming a sleeper agent for the Koreans. He is a robotic assassin, programmed to kill the president on a predetermined command. According to Lasn, we live in the age of the Manchurian Consumer. Advertising has implanted various desires into our subconscious, which turns us into pre-programmed purchasing robots.

Apart from its complete implausibility as a description of actual consumer behaviour, what is interesting about this argument is the incredible power it ascribes to marketers and advertising, especially those forms aimed at developing national and international brands. Klein sees us as victims of the Brand Bullies; for Lasn, it is the Brand Brainwashers.

The idea that advertising has this power to create wants, and that it works through sophisticated use of psychological theory, first came to widespread attention with the publication of Packard's 1957 book *The Hidden Persuaders*. The blurb on the paperback edition had this ominous declaration: 'In this book you'll discover a world of psychology professors turned merchandisers. You'll learn how they operate, what they know about you and your neighbours, and how they are using that knowledge to sell you cake mixes, cigarettes, cars, soaps, and even ideas.'[23]

There is no question that advertising is a major institution of public persuasion. Total advertising spending in the United States is around £111 billion a year. From radio and TV to billboards to the Internet to magazines and newspapers, advertising is inescapable. Ads come through our cell phones and our e-mail, and some companies even write them in the sky. It is estimated that the average person is faced with anywhere from 700 to 3000 ads every day, and it would be surprising if this didn't have *some* effect on our consciousness.

But for all the vitriol directed at advertisers, all the concerns over Manchurian consumers, one important question remains unanswered: do marketers have the power to shape consumer desire that the critics say they do? Does advertising even work? Surprisingly, nobody is really sure. What is certainly true is that advertising is not nearly so powerful as its critics claim, and the suspicion that marketers are precision-delivering messages to our subconscious is simply misguided.

Begin with the aforementioned claim about the hundreds or thousands of ads that each of us sees every day. In what sense do we actually 'see' these ads? How many of them even register in a meaningful way? It is equally true that in a given day, the average commuter probably sees thousands of people. How many faces does she notice? How many could she remember an hour later, or the next day? The human mind possesses an extremely effective filtering mechanism, which constantly sorts sense impressions into things we need to care about and things we don't. Of all the millions of bits of information bombarding our senses at every moment, only a small fraction are even processed by the nervous system, and a mere handful are brought to the attention of our working consciousness. Advertising is no exception. Given that most of the time most consumers are not in the market for the products they see advertised, it is not surprising to find that barely a quarter of people surveyed can remember a *single* ad they saw on television the day before.

The assumption that advertising is able to increase the sales of goods has just not been proved, and corporations themselves make little effort to track the effectiveness of their ad campaigns. In fact, the most reliable studies don't show that sales follow ads, but just the opposite: ads follow sales. That is, when sales go up, companies raise their ad budgets accordingly. When sales are down, advertising budgets are cut. This is hardly the behaviour one would expect of people convinced of their ability to manipulate consumer desires.

Many advertisers admit that the real point is not to create new desires in consumers or even to increase aggregate consumption of their product category, but simply to wrest customers away from competitors. Advertising becomes a battle over market share, which often occurs in industries where overall demand is declining. The most obvious example of this is the beer business, which has some of the highest advertising budgets of any industry. Meanwhile, beer consumption worldwide has been in steady decline since the 1980s, dropping by 13% in the UK between 1990 and 2000.

The relationship between advertising and sales becomes even more fragile when one realises that there are significant cases of sales occurring in the absence of advertising. Hershey's, Starbucks, The Body Shop and Subway all became massive consumer brands with very little advertising. Some of these companies *now* engage in significant international ad campaigns, but these are not designed to increase sales; they are primarily to defend their current market positions against competitors. In *No Logo*, Klein actually complains that the Body Shop and Starbucks have been able to build such powerful brands without advertising. In her mind, this fact shows just how nefarious the practices of the 'brand bullies' have become. She fails to recognise that this admission begs the question against the entire 'Manchurian consumer' thesis.

*

None of this is to say that advertising is completely harmless, that it has no effect on either our minds or our consumption habits. What we need to realise, though, is that advertising is less like brainwashing and more like seduction. Just as a skilful seduction exploits the fact that on some level you actually want to have sex, so effective advertising can work on needs and desires that you already have. You can't seduce someone who doesn't have an interest in sex, and you can't sell teeth whitener to someone who is not concerned about his appearance.

In the case of advertising, the desires that make us vulnerable are those that underlie competitive consumption. Advertisers are like arms merchants: they can't convince two antagonists to go to war, but they are more than happy to sell weapons to both sides. And just as arms merchants can make things worse by providing products that intensify the conflict and increase casualties, so advertisers can exacerbate the effects of competitive consumption between consumers. But before we lump together advertising with weapons of mass destruction, we need a clearer sense of the conditions under which advertising works, and what we might do to mitigate its effects.

One of the most sober-minded books about advertising is *Advertising, The Uneasy Persuasion* by sociology professor Michael Schudson. Schudson hits it right on the mark when he suggests that we should think of advertising as just one of society's 'awareness institutions', which include government, schools, news media, television and film, NGOs, parents and peer groups.[24] To ask how advertising might shape our beliefs and values is to ask how *any* aspect of culture does this. So the real question we should ask is not the simplistic 'Does advertising work?' but rather, 'What are the circumstances under which it is more or less likely to work?'

Advertising is neither produced nor consumed in a vacuum, and its effectiveness depends to a large extent on the other forms of information that are available to consumers. These include:

- past personal experience with the product (or similar products);
- other information about the product (from news pieces, magazines, etc.);
- word of mouth (from peers, parents and associates);
- consumer-education channels (public interest groups, consumer watchdogs); and
- general media literacy and cultural awareness (through family, schools, etc.).

For many consumers, these additional sources of information help inculcate a general scepticism toward advertising, media and awareness institutions in general. All forms of advertising other than those that give information about the product's attributes and price are basically exercises in bad faith, in that they make claims that both producer and consumer know to be false. So it is not surprising to find a large amount of cynicism on all sides. The public has been discounting the claims made by advertisers for generations. Back in the '60s, it was commonly claimed that the 'new generation' was so sceptical and media-savvy that old-fashioned advertising appeals would no longer work. The same claim has been repeated for each subsequent generation – each time as though it were an earth-shattering discovery.

Still, many critics can't shake the conviction that advertising is causing us to spend our money in ways we would not otherwise choose. This conviction seems to flow from the growing success of branding as a popular form of marketing. The phenomenon of brand loyalty, in which consumers remain committed to a given brand despite the fact that there is no meaningful difference between competing brands, is seen as particularly irrational.

'Brands are for cattle' is a popular slogan among anticonsumer activists, and it is not far off the mark. As marketing gurus Al and Laura Ries have noted, branding in the marketplace is not different from branding on the ranch: 'A branding programme should be designed to differentiate your product from all the other cattle on the range. Even if all the other cattle on the range look pretty much alike.'[25] The whole point of a branding campaign is to create an *identity* for your product, a set of meanings and values that come to be associated with your brand and no other.

Branded goods first appeared toward the end of the 19th century, as more and more goods began to be mass-produced in factories. Machine-based production made it increasingly difficult to differentiate one company's shirts, shoes or bars of soap from any of the others'. Manufacturers needed a way of distinguishing their products in the marketplace, so they started embossing brand names on the product itself. But it isn't enough to have the product name visible; consumers need a reason to buy one brand over another. In a world where everyone is using the same material or ingredients or manufacturing methods, the trick is to associate your product not with what it is made out of, but with values like beauty, youth, health, sophistication or cool. You need to create an 'aura' of meaning around the brand, which anchors its identity.

It is this purchasing of *identity* – of meanings as opposed to materials – that many critics find so irrational and unpleasant about brands. It seems so bizarre (for example, that anyone could honestly believe that a shampoo could convey *excitement*) that they conclude that consumers must have been somehow tricked or manipulated. How else to explain the fact that, in many countries, bottled water sells for more than gasoline? Or that fancy restaurants are now introducing 'water sommeliers' to suggest different brands of bottled water to match each course of your meal?

However, it isn't good to have so much contempt for consumers. As Schudson argues, while brands may have developed out of a need to create a distinction in the absence of difference, the reasons why they were *accepted* and have flourished are quite different. It is easy to forget that every time you spend money you are taking a risk. You might not get what you paid for, or you might not get your money's worth. A gadget might be defective; food might be stale or rancid; inventions might not work as advertised. We are so used to the redundant forms of consumer protection, such as return policies, guarantees, consumer watchdogs and protection legislation, that we forget how, throughout the history of commerce, getting ripped off has been a constant worry.

As a result, consumers have had to take steps to minimise risk. In small, relatively static communities, people would work to establish personal trust relationships with grocers, retailers and salespeople, and they gradually learned which locally produced goods were of good quality and which were not. As society grew more urbanised, these relationships became harder to establish and sustain. As people became more mobile, they lost track of the local products upon which they had come to rely. National brand-name advertising became successful largely because it offered a limited form of consumer protection. From town to town, across the country, people found they could rely on a consistent stable of brands.

Packaging was also introduced as a way of offering increased protection to consumers. Before the introduction of standard packaging, consumers had to keep a sharp eye to make sure that their grocer didn't have his thumb on the scale or wasn't adulterating the goods. Packaging and standardisation made this sort of fraud a lot more difficult, especially once printed labels were introduced (they made the product difficult to open and reseal). The Heinz Corporation, one of the pioneers in the field of canned goods, referred to these concerns quite explicitly in its early advertising. One well-known ad from 1922 showed a grocer wrapping up canned Heinz goods in paper. The accompanying text informed the reader that Heinz was keeping a watchful eye on 'your grocer': 'Our force of salesmen is sufficiently large to enable us to visit him very frequently – every few weeks.'

Most critics of consumerism neglect the extent to which national (and now international) advertising of brand-name goods serves as a form of consumer protection. But what gets them really riled up is the most obvious aspect of branding, which is that it sells an aura of meanings that have little to do with the actual product. More often than not, we don't care about the quality of the material in our shirts, the stitching in our jeans or the alcohol in our bottles. What we care about are the identities conferred by Tommy Hilfiger, J. Crew and Absolut Vodka. But it does not follow from this that we are dupes. Consumers are extremely savvy, and are fully aware that there are no relevant differences between brands across a vast range of products. They know that they are drinking the ad, not the booze, and wearing the label, not the jeans. It is through brands that we express who we are and what we value. It is through the consumption of hip brands that we strive to be cool.

Marketing experts know that our decisions about what brands to consume are not arbitrary or random, but actually quite predictable. Almost everybody consumes within one of a handful of what are known as 'brand clusters', each of which represents a distinct life-style. Within each cluster (which marketers know by names such as 'Young Suburban' and 'Money & Brains'), there are implicit yet very strong norms about which brands to purchase and which brands to stay away from. These brand clusters form the basis of the quest for distinction, which, as we have seen, lies at the heart of consumerism.

Many people find this basic idea – that who we are is what we consume – to be rather disconcerting. The philosopher Mark Kingwell puts the worry this way:

> *I can think of no experience in the modern world more unsettling, more vertiginous, than this one of realising that my carefully constructed individuality is as transparent and manipulable to a savvy advertiser as if I sported a niche-market report on my forehead. It is far more threatening to my sense of personal identity to have someone know, with near certainty, which vodka or scotch I will buy than any mood-altering drug could ever be … I might think my choices are mine alone, considered and personal, but they reveal themselves as manipulated and predictable. So I am forced to wonder: am I a cultural dope after all, not free but determined?*[26]

Kingwell's problem here touches on the venerable philosophical question of free will. We like to think that the choices we make are in some sense *up to us*. It is because they are ours that they reflect who we are and allow us to take responsibility for our actions and to accept praise and blame. But if our choices are somehow predictable, then have we become not free agents but cultural puppets, dancing under the sway of consumerist imperatives?

The concern that predictability undermines freedom is an old one, but it reveals an interesting paradox. Consider, for the moment, what it would be like if your actions, including your consumption choices, were *not* predictable. Imagine that no one could ever know when (or even if) you were going to show up for work each day. Or if sometimes you drove your car carefully and conscientiously, but other times you were as reckless as a speed-crazed sixteen-year-old. One minute you were witty and outgoing, but the next you were sullen and withdrawn. One week you loved sushi, but the next you claimed that you can't stand it. What if you read *The New Yorker* religiously each week, but had no interest in *Harper's* or the *Atlantic Monthly*? What if you loved your new Lexus, but insisted on hanging furry dice from the windshield and airbrushing fantasy dragons onto the hood?

That is to say, what if you started behaving in a totally random and unpredictable manner? Would that be a way of asserting your individuality? Would your friends praise your distinct identity, or would they wonder, *who in the hell are you?*

Oddly enough, being predictable is the very essence of what it is to have an identity. The philosopher Daniel Dennett calls identities 'centres of narrative gravity',[27] and it is a perfect description. Just as a centre of gravity is an abstraction we use for unifying and predicting the behaviour of a certain collection of matter, so an identity is an abstraction we use to organise and predict the behaviour of individuals. Far from threatening our individuality, it would be almost pathologically weird if our choices about what to consume were not highly predictable. What are you supposed to do, buy stuff you don't like in the name of asserting your individuality?

This makes no sense. When people complain about a threat to their individuality or to their identity, what they are really reacting to is a threat to their status, imposed by the competitive structure of hip consumerism. It means that 'the masses' are still nipping at their heels. If what people really wanted to establish was their individuality, they could do so quite easily, simply by acting randomly. But what we are all really after is not individuality, it is distinction, and distinction is achieved not by being different, but by being different in a way that makes us recognisable as members of an exclusive club. This makes our choices eminently predictable, because there is a relatively modest set of moves available at every given position in the social hierarchy. All one needs to do in order to make very confident predictions about what any given person will do is to what other people, similarly situated, are doing.

The real question is, why fight it? Finding out what the 'next big thing' will be can involve an awful lot of work. Most people run out of steam by the time they're thirty. Why not turn the marketer's tools to your own competitive advantage? It's easy. Just go to Amazon.com, fill out a wish list, do some shopping, then ask it to recommend some new CDs for your collection and a few new books to read. They're guaranteed to be better – and probably cooler – than anything you could have picked out for yourself.

One of the more fascinating academic findings to have made its way into the public consciousness in recent years comes from what is known as 'diffusion' research, which has shown how many distinct and seemingly unrelated social phenomena emerge and move through a population in a consistent and predictable way. A large number of trends, from crime waves to hairstyles to new music to teen suicides, all seem to follow a basic developmental pattern. Not only that, the best model for tracking that pattern comes not from sociology, but from epidemiology. That is, ideas, fashions, behaviours and new products appear to spread in the same way that viruses like colds and the flu do.

People have known for a long time that epidemics don't spread by growing in a steady linear manner, with a handful of new infections each day until you eventually have an epidemic on your hands. What happens is that a small group of people get infected, and if they aren't quickly isolated, they soon infect a slightly larger group. If this group then mixes with the general population, the infection suddenly 'tips', exploding virtually overnight into a full-scale epidemic.

The diffusion of cool occurs in exactly the same way. It begins with a small group of 'innovators', who are the congenital nonconformists, always on the prowl for things that nobody else is doing, saying, wearing or using. The innovators are soon followed by a slightly larger group called the 'early adopters'. These are what we can call the cool brokers. They keep tabs on the innovators, evaluate what they are doing and decide whether or not to follow suit. If they do, the trend will begin to grow exponentially, as the early adopters are quickly emulated by the 'early majority' and then the 'late majority,' the play-it-safe masses who would never dare attempt to be avant-garde. Finally, the epidemic of hip trails off as the 'laggards', those most resistant to fashion and change, reluctantly get on board. These are the people still waiting to see if the Internet craze is going to last.

Appreciating that much of what we call 'fashion' follows this general pattern helps account for the sorts of worries expressed by people like Kingwell. It is true that marketers know what you are going to buy in the name of expressing your individuality. And it is equally true that most of your friends are going to buy the same things, for the same reasons. But the appearance of a top-down, manipulated conformism is a simple illusion brought on by the fact that, by definition, most of us are in the early or late majority. There are but a few innovators, and only slightly more early adopters. Those of us who are cool are at best among the earliest of the early majority, just close enough to the cutting edge that we don't realise how dull we really are.

One interesting thing about the diffusion of cool trends is that advertising plays very little role. The innovators, the hardcore nonconformists, are certainly not going to buy anything mass-marketed. The early adopters, the ones responsible for bridging the gap to the masses, take their cues from the innovators. And so on down the line. Just as epidemics spread through direct contact between people, so cool moves laterally through peer groups. Advertising, if it is effective at all, may help alert the late majority and laggards about what the rest of society has been up to, though of course by that time cool has moved on to something else. (Black street argot has been moving in similar cycles for over four decades – remember 'bling bling'?)

To say that advertising is more or less impotent in selling cool is not to say that marketers cannot intervene in the fashion cycle. They can in part – by trying to figure out what the early adopters have cottoned on to – predict which products have the potential to explode. One way they do this is through 'coolhunting'. There are a handful of consulting groups that specialise in keeping tabs on youth culture, monitoring what the innovators are doing and noting how the early adopters are reacting. They write their findings up as cool reports, for which companies like Reebok and Abercrombie and Fitch will pay a small fortune.

Another way corporations can insinuate themselves into the fashion cycle is through what is called 'viral marketing'. They take the epidemiological nature of trends entirely literally and set about trying to start their own epidemics of cool. Have you ever had an attractive woman come up to you in a bar and offer to buy you a specific brand of vodka? Has anyone ever approached you in a club and told you about this great new band he's heard? Ever meet someone on IRC who mentions what sort of trainers she wears? Has anyone ever stopped you on the street and asked you to take his picture with a late-model digital camera? Chances are you've been targeted by a viral marketer, someone who is being paid to spread the word, in the hope you'll pass it on, like a cold.

Coolhunters and viral marketers have become the objects of considerable scorn. They have been called 'cultural traitors' or, in Klein's words, 'the legal stalkers of youth culture'.[28] The idea that these people are generational sell-outs, the pop-cultural equivalent of collaborators in Vichy France, is a bit overdone, since there isn't much to sell out in the first place. If anything, they perform a valuable service for low-status (i.e. uncool) groups, by giving them more rapid access to what is cool, thereby making it more difficult for high-status groups to treat them with such contempt. There is a problem, though, in the extent to which coolhunters target and infiltrate the lives of adolescents. Teens, preteens and that hot new demographic, 'tweens', are being heavily courted and marketed to by some of the biggest and most powerful corporations out there, from Disney and Warner Brothers to the Gap.

There are sound business reasons for this. Almost everyone's brand preferences are fixed during their preteen and teenage years (it is extremely difficult to get adults to shift brands), so it makes sense to direct significant resources to consumers before they've made their final brand decisions. In *Branded*, Alissa Quart does an excellent job of cataloguing the extent to which teens are now the objects of relentless marketing campaigns. She doesn't like what she sees: preteens advising their parents on what model four-wheel drive to buy; teens recruited as 'consultants' for fashion companies, then sent back into the schools to push new products to their classmates; high schoolers doing steroids or dieting so they can look like the models in underwear commercials. According to Quart, marketers are exploiting teens' fragile egos and half-formed identities, making them the 'victims of the contemporary luxury economy'.[29]

It isn't a pretty sight, and Quart has little to offer in the way of helpful solutions to the problem. But she is on to something when she suggests that teens and their even younger siblings are more vulnerable than most to the seductions of marketing. In this respect, adolescents are part of the group of especially vulnerable consumers that also includes immigrants, the elderly and the illiterate. We noted earlier how advertising is just one of a number of awareness institutions, although it does happen to be the one that is the most pervasive and unavoidable. What makes young people especially vulnerable to advertising is that they lack the other forms of knowledge, the experience and the alternative sources of information that inculcate the healthy scepticism that is the requisite armour for urban living. In addition to their unformed identities (which make them vulnerable to lifestyle marketing), adolescents have little practical experience with a wide range of products. They also tend to be unaware of price barriers, which can aggravate the spending pressure they bring to bear on their parents. In short, marketing directed at kids, either within the family context or through their peers at school, is a serious problem.

Yet for all this, critics like Klein and Quart have absolutely no workable solutions to any of these problems. The influence of counter-cultural thinking here is clear. *No Logo* provides a stinging indictment of every aspect of the modern advertising-driven economy. And yet anyone who reads it through to the end will be startled to discover that it contains not one positive proposal for fixing any of these problems (other than signing up at the local branch of the 'global resistance move-ment'). Quart recommends purely stylistic rebellion, which, as we have seen, is far more likely to exacerbate the problem than to resolve it.

The problem is that both Klein and Quart see advertising as an integral element of a system of corporate hegemony and domination, and so they can't see any way to fix it without completely overthrow-ing the system. It is far more helpful to think of advertising as a col-lective action problem among corporations. It is all well and good to say that firms should advertise less heavily, or that they should not direct their ads at kids. But as long as one firm is doing it, others are under pressure to do so as well just to retain position. Most ad cam-paigns do not create new demand for a product – they simply allow one company to steal some customers away from its rivals. When the others respond in kind, then everyone is back where they started, except that they are now spending a lot more on advertising.

What corporations need, in the face of escalating advertising budgets and increasingly aggressive marketing campaigns, is the equivalent of an arms control agreement. In this respect, the money spent on advertising is a lot like the entertainment expenses that many companies incur, or the bribes that they must sometimes pay in order to secure contracts abroad. Managers may not want to take clients or suppliers out for expensive meals or on weekend ski trips, but if the competition is doing it then they don't have much choice. Either they play the game or they lose the business.

But the fact that companies get stuck in these sorts of traps does not mean that we, as a society, are unable to do anything about it. Just as bribing foreign officials can be made illegal, so advertising aimed at young people can be prohibited. When corporate entertainment expenditures started to get out of hand, the Canadian government responded by reducing the tax deduction that businesses get for these expenses. At the moment, only 50 per cent of the costs of entertainment can be written off as a business expense. We could do exactly the same thing for advertising. It is already a separately itemised category of business expenditure. All we need to do is make it less than 100 per cent deductible. This would not prevent companies from advertising. Just as there are times when businesses have a legitimate need to entertain clients, so there are also times when advertising is essential and appropriate. Reducing the deductibility of these expenses would simply dampen down the more extreme forms of unproductive competition that tend to erupt under this category of expenditure, and lower the overall amount of advertising clutter in our society.

If we are really worried about the commercialisation or colonisation of public space by private advertising, then we should be pushing for practical fixes of this type. One simple change in the tax code would do more to curb advertising than all of the culture jamming in the world. Yet these small, workable proposals are consistently ignored in favour of cultural politics, world revolution and other more glamorous pursuits.

Notes

1   G. E. Moore, *Principia Ethica* (Cambridge: Cambridge University Press, 1965).

2   Lasn, *Culture Jam*, xiii.

3   Malcolm Gladwell, 'The Coolhunt', *The New Yorker*, March 17, 1997.

4   Jeff Rice, 'What Is Cool? Notes on Intellectualism, Popular Culture, and Writing', *ctheory.net*, May 10, 2002.

5   Mailer, 'The White Negro', *Advertisements for Myself* (New York: Putnam, 1959), 339.

6   *Ibid.*

7   Norman Mailer, 'The Hip and the Square', *Advertisements for Myself* (New York: Putnam, 1959), 424–25.

8   Paul Fussell, *Class* (New York: Ballantine Books, 1983), 1.

9   *Ibid.*, 7.

10   Veblen, *Theory of the Leisure Class*, 26.

11   Daniel Bell, *The Cultural Contradictions of Capitalism* (New York: Basic Books, 1976), 41.

12   David Brooks, *Bobos in Paradise: The New Upper Class and How They Got There* (New York: Simon & Schuster, 2000), 43.

13   *Ibid.*, 45.

14   Fussell, *Class*, 222.

15   Richard Florida, *The Rise of the Creative Class* (New York: Basic Books, 2002), 190.

16   *Ibid.*, 200.

17   *Ibid.*, 201.

18   John Seabrook, *Nobrow: The Culture of Marketing, the Marketing of Culture* (New York: Vintage, 2001), 66.

19   Brooks, *Bobos*, 69.

20   Joseph Schumpeter, *Capitalism, Socialism and Democracy* (New York: Harper & Row, 1975), 82–83.

21   Frank says: Frank, *The Conquest of Cool*, 29.

22   Naomi Klein: Klein, *No Logo*, 69.

23   Vance Packard, *The Hidden Persuaders* (New York: Cardinal, 1958).

24   Michael Schudson, *Advertising: The Uneasy Persuasion* (New York: Perseus, 1984), 127.

25   Al Ries and Laura Ries, *The 22 Immutable Laws of Branding* (New York: HarperBusiness, 2002), ix.

26   Mark Kingwell, *Better Living: In Pursuit of Happiness from Plato to Prozac* (Toronto: Viking, 1998), 160.

27   Daniel Dennett, 'The Self as a Center of Narrative Gravity', in *Self and Consciousness*, ed. F. Kessel, P. Cole, D. Johnson (Hillsdale, NJ: Erlbaum, 1992).

28   Klein, *No Logo*, 72.

29   Quart, *Branded*, xii.

Coca-colonisation

In 1947, in an old potato field twenty miles outside New York City, a former US Navy engineer named William Levitt began to create what would one day become the most famous suburb in America. Levitt's innovation was simple. In a standard mass production system, goods move along an assembly line as highly specialised workers each perform a particular task involved in their production. Obviously, a system like this is good for making cars, but it cannot be used to build houses, for the simple reason that houses are too large to move along an assembly line. So Levitt created what amounted to a mobile assembly line. Instead of the goods moving and the line staying in place, he kept the goods in place and simply moved the line over them. He put together work crews to perform highly specialised tasks, one step at a time, then started churning out houses.

In so doing, he also created a phenomenon that would have an indelible impact on North American consciousness – the suburban 'tract' home. In order to achieve the benefits of mass production, each house in the original Levittown development was identical. He built over 6000 of the original 'Cape Cod'-style homes before diversifying the product line, introducing the slightly modified 'ranch' style. The reason for this uniformity was clear: it allowed him to produce houses at a prodigious rate. At a time when an average builder could make only five homes a year, Levitt managed to produce thirty homes *a day*. And the prices were unbeatable. When the houses went on sale in 1949 (at a price of only US$6999, (£3888) including both free TV and a washing machine), Levitt sold 1400 on the first day.

Levitt's methods, and his buildings, were soon being imitated by developers across North America. In fact, if Levittown looks eerily familiar to most people in North America, it's because almost everyone has been in one of the two homes. (Thinking back to my childhood in Saskatoon, I realise that two of my friends lived in knockoffs of the Levittown Cape Cod-style home.) Generations of children had the experience of growing up in exactly the same house as many of their friends. Even now, most people have no need to ask where the bathroom is when visiting an older suburban home.

Needless to say, critics of mass society were apoplectic. Lewis Mumford summed up the dominant view when he described suburbs like Levittown as 'a multitude of uniform, unidentifiable houses, lined up inflexibly, at uniform distances, on uniform roads, in a treeless communal waste, inhabited by people of the same class, the same income, the same age group, witnessing the same television performances, eating the same tasteless pre-fabricated foods, from the same freezers, conforming in every outward and inward respect to the same common mold.'[1] A generation of comics made a good living with jokes about the Organisation Man coming home from a long day at the office, pulling up to the wrong house, making love to the wrong wife and so forth.

For critics like Mumford, Levittown dramatised the Faustian bargain at the heart of mass society. While the houses were cheap, they were also nasty. There appeared to be a straightforward trade-off between price and variety. And it wasn't just houses. As franchising became an increasingly popular business model, one area of life after another seemed to fall victim to the homogenising tendency of late capitalism. Fifty years later, these concerns have become even more acute. With increased globalisation, many fear that the cultural uniformity that swept the United States will now extend to the entire planet, eradicating non-Western cultures, absorbing everyone into the undifferentiated nexus of rampant consumer capitalism.

Yet one major question remains unanswered. Does capitalism actually have a homogenising tendency? Is Levittown the rule, or the exception?

*

Suburbs built on the Levittown model have had such a powerful impact on the popular imagination that much of the critical discussion of urban issues is completely disconnected from the realities of modern suburbia. After all, most members of the chattering classes live in the inner city – not just because they want to, but because they are obliged to. Thanks to the critique of mass society, suburbia is now widely regarded as synonymous with brain death, so it's difficult to be taken seriously as an intellectual without living either in the centre of town or in the country. As a result, many of those who criticise suburban living have never actually spent more than a few hours in the suburbs any time since childhood.

I came to this realisation one day when my brother-in-law, the proud purchaser of a lot in a brand new suburban development, asked me to come help him select the 'options' on his yet-to-be-constructed home. Ever since I bought a fixer-upper of a Victorian home in central Toronto, I've become something of an expert in cosmetic details: painting, replastering, fixing baseboards, laying tiles, changing light fixtures and the like. I'm the guy you see at the DIY asking the wood-aisle attendant what thickness of plywood to use to patch a century-old tongue-in-groove fir subfloor. So it seemed like I would be the right person to offer some advice on how to equip my brother-in-law's new home. I accepted, with visions of Levittown and *The Truman Show* dancing in my head. Picking options on a suburban home – how hard could that be? I figured it would be like picking options on a car – they would give you a sheet of paper with about fifty choices, and maybe three or four package deals.

Imagine my surprise when I arrived at the 'town centre' and the developer's representative thumped a binder down in front of us, a solid two inches thick, listing all of the available options. Seems that the suburbs are not quite what they used to be. Any ideas that I might have had of uniformity or of cookie-cutter homes were quickly dispatched. The number of options was truly staggering. Half of the stuff I had never even heard of before. And the options were not just cosmetic. Basic structural features of the home were all reconfigurable. For starters, there were twenty different base houses in the development, ranging from 1400 to 3400 square feet, each of which came in three different 'elevations': brick, stone or siding. The elevation in turn determined the configuration of balconies and windows. The developer would not build two of the same house next to one another

– specifically to *avoid* uniformity in the streetscape. This meant that after you had decided which house you wanted, you had to find a lot where you would be allowed to build it.

Once you had a house and a lot, then the real business began. How high would you like your ceilings to be? Eight feet or nine? Would you like skylights? How many, and where? Do you want the basement finished or not? What kind of floors? Hardwood, laminate, tile or carpet? What kind of banister on the stairs? Smooth or rough ceilings? Plaster mouldings? Plate rack? What kind of electrical system, standard or double-amp? Island in the kitchen? With or without a sink? What countertops – Arborite, granite or Corian? Only once these structural features of the house were chosen could one turn to the cosmetic details. Here the number of options multiplied, from hundreds to thousands. In order to make the decision more tractable, options were grouped together by price into different 'grades', each grade containing multiple styles, and then each style was available in a wide range of colours. For example, there were five grades of tile, each containing about twenty different styles; four grades of carpet, each with ten styles; six grades of baseboards; and an essentially infinite number of kitchen cabinets. Finally, we were supposed to choose how many phone jacks, cable TV plugs and Ethernet connections there should be, and where they should be located.

Obviously there was no question of making all these decisions in one sitting. I made a few general observations about the virtues of good baseboards and oak flooring, then left my brother-in-law and his wife to spend the next week mulling over floor plans, product samples and their binder full of options. What they were doing, in effect, was directing the construction of a custom home for themselves. Yet the price that they were paying was *lower* than the average resale price of a home in the City of Toronto. Thus they appeared to be getting all the price benefits of mass production, but with very few of the constraints.

As we watched the house being built over the course of the next couple of months, it was easy to see how the developer was able to pull this off. Mass production techniques have become vastly more sophisticated since the '50s. Levitt used essentially generic building materials, then applied mass production techniques to the construction of complete houses. Since then, houses have been broken down into a set of modular components, all of which are mass-produced off-site. Construction in many cases involves simply snapping these components together into different configurations. Roof rafters, for example, all come preassembled and are nailed into position using pre-moulded aluminium brackets. Vinyl siding simply locks into place, with no nails or screws, once the strapping is hung. Laminate floors snap together, with no nails or glue.

The second conspicuous feature of the developer's business model was the use of Japanese-style 'lean production' techniques. There was essentially no standing inventory. One day all the bricks would show up, along with masons to install them on all the homes that needed brick. The next day several tons of shingle would show up, all of which would be laid by the evening. Furthermore, the developer did absolutely none of the actual construction. Not only were the materials modular, so was the work. The entire construction project was broken down into discrete jobs, each of which was subcontracted to an independent firm. The developers had only four employees to supervise and coordinate the construction of over 200 houses.

The effects of these flexible construction techniques could be seen quite clearly in the finished product. Only the meanest suburbs are still constructed on the cookie-cutter model. Manufacturing technology has evolved to the point where one no longer requires uniformity in order to achieve the cost savings associated with mass production. And one can see similar developments in many different areas of manufacturing. Go to a modern automotive plant and you can see different cars being simultaneously produced on the same assembly line.

This raises the suspicion that the homogeneity associated with mass production is not an intrinsic feature of 'mass society', it is merely a stage in the development of the forces of production. But if this is true, then it knocks a huge chunk out of the countercultural critique. According to this theory, capitalism requires conformity among consumers because it needs to create a system of homogenous desires in order to dispose of the 'surplus' of identical commodities generated by the mass production system. But if mass production no longer requires the production of identical commodities, there is absolutely no reason to think that the capitalist system requires conformity.

Of course, none of this addresses the more fundamental question: What's wrong with homogenisation in the first place? If people voluntarily choose to live in similar houses, wear similar clothes and participate in similar activities, then who are we to criticise them? As long as it's what they really want to do, then it's very difficult to make the case against it. Furthermore, if mass production allows individuals access to goods that they would otherwise not have been able to afford, it would be obnoxious to deny them the opportunity on the grounds that we don't like the aesthetic consequences. This is something that intelligent critics of mass society, such as William Whyte (author of *The Organisation Man*), realised early on. In 'Individualism in Suburbia', Whyte acknowledges that while 'rows and rows of identical ranch houses are a dispiriting sight', this type of construction 'is the price that must be paid for moderate cost of housing. And the price is not so very steep; unless one believes poverty is ennobling, the new housing is much less antithetical to the development of the individual than the rows and rows of drab tenements it helps supplant.'[2]

In other words, given a choice between reducing poverty and reducing homogeneity, most people would prefer to reduce poverty. And if that choice results in acres of suburban tract homes, then we simply need to accept that as a consequence of our decision. Homogeneity is only really a problem when it is the product of coercion rather than choice – when people are either penalised for a failure to comply or tricked and cajoled into doing something they don't really want to do.

The real question, then, is not whether markets promote homogeneity – no one could deny that, in certain respects, they do. The question is whether this is illegitimate or not, whether it reflects people's voluntary choices. And there are many reasons why people might want to consume similar products. For example, many goods generate what economists call 'network externalities'. The fax machine is the typical example. It's impossible to send a fax unless the person you are sending it to also has a fax machine to receive it, so each individual who buys a fax machine creates a slight positive benefit for all the other fax owners by increasing the number of people they can, in principle, send a fax to. This is why low-priced fax machines, which became available in 1984, never really took off until 1987. At first the machine wasn't worth the price for most people, simply because there were so few people one could send a fax to. Thus only 80,000 units were sold in 1984. Yet as the number of users grew, the system reached 'critical mass', the point at which there were enough people who could receive faxes to make the purchase of a machine worthwhile. One million fax machines were sold in 1987. (E-mail and cellular phones have developed in very much the same way.)

Whenever there are network externalities, there will be benefits associated with standardisation. Because keyboard layouts are standardised, we can sit down in front of any computer and start typing. Because nuts and bolts come in standard sizes, we only have to have one set of wrenches. Because cars are standardised, we know which pedal will be the gas and which will be the brake. Because fast food restaurants have a standard ordering system, we can show up anywhere in the world and get a meal within five minutes. Because of TCP/IP, the standardised protocol for communication among computers, we can all enjoy the wonders of the Internet.

It is not just in the case of material goods that we derive benefits from standardisation. Many cultural products are also valued because of the benefits that individuals derive from being members of a large audience. A large part of the pleasure of seeing a movie, watching a TV show or reading a book comes from talking about it later, with friends or co-workers. This is what explains the 'blockbuster' phenomenon. A movie can reach a critical mass when, because so many people are talking about it, others feel obliged to see it, just so that they can participate (or because they want to know what everyone is talking about). The book market has the same structure, which explains why there is such a huge gap between the sales figures of ordinary books and bestsellers. Thus, it is precisely because goods are consumed in a *social context*, and not by isolated individuals, that people often want to consume the same things as others.

The success of reality TV shows, for instance, has to do with much more than simply the content of the show. People like these shows because they like talking about these shows – which suitors are worthy or unworthy, and why; which contestants deserve to win or lose, and how their strategies succeeded or failed. In the early era of broadcast television, people had no choice but to 'witness the same television performances' (as Mumford put it). That technological constraint has now been lifted. Yet what we discover in the 500-channel universe is that people actually have a strong desire to watch many of the same shows. These shows provide, for most North Americans, the only stories that people from different walks of life still share.

Of course, when goods that are associated with network externalities are consumed, the outcome is not always the best. It is possible for everyone to get stuck in a local equilibrium that is suboptimal. More concretely, it may mean that people choose an inferior good rather than some other that is available, simply because it is the one that everyone else is using (VHS video versus Betamax is the classic example). Innovative new products and standards that are, in principle, superior to old ones may have difficulty penetrating the market, because their value will not be fully realised until they reach a critical mass.

The same phenomenon can be seen at work in books, television and movies. Even if people hate summer blockbusters, they may go to see them just to have something to talk about. There can also be a sort of levelling-down effect, in which people purchase the goods that they *think* will be the most popular even before they become so. People may buy a more generic home because they are worried about its resale value. If large numbers of people do this, it will become a self-fulfilling prophecy – most people will buy the home just because it seems like the sort of thing that most people will buy.

Of course, for companies that need to push consumers away from a prevailing standard in order to sell their product, the critique of mass society has provided an inexhaustible supply of advertising concepts. For example, computer operating systems are very much like keyboard layouts – users derive enormous benefits from standardisation and compatibility. IBM and, later, Microsoft were able to dominate the market by establishing themselves early on as the standard. Rival corporations like Apple Computer have therefore tried to promote their products by suggesting that those who use the standard are merely conformists, victims of groupthink. Consider Apple's famous '1984' commercial. Before legions of drone-like workers, arranged in orderly rows, Big Brother appears on a giant screen, addressing the crowd: 'Today, we celebrate the first glorious anniversary of the Information Purification Directives. We have created, for the first time in all history, a garden of pure ideology. Where each worker may bloom secure from the pests of contradictory and confusing truths. Our Unification of Thoughts is more powerful a weapon than any fleet or army on earth. We are one people, with one will, one resolve, one cause. Our enemies shall talk themselves to death and we will bury them with their own confusion. We shall prevail!'[3]

Everything is black and white, except for a blonde woman wearing bright red, who runs toward the screen, pursued by menacing riot police. She screams, then throws an enormous sledgehammer through the screen, which explodes in a flash of light. A pitch for the new Macintosh computer scrolls into view. Thanks to the Apple Computer Corporation, we are assured, 1984 will not be like *1984*. (The spot, directed by Ridley Scott, was honoured by *Advertising Age* as the best commercial of the decade.)

A more perfect instance of the rebel sell would be difficult to find. Yet what the commercial glosses over is the fact that there is no 'Information Purification Directive' in our society. The existence of standards in the computer industry is a consequence of choices that people have made and voluntary agreements that have been concluded. More generally, not all uniformity is bad uniformity, nor is it always coercive. It is not as though everyone, when left to their own devices, wants to behave in a purely individualistic fashion (such that any deviation from pure randomness requires the imposition of force). There are often significant benefits associated with acting like everyone else. Expressing your individuality by wearing a funny tie to work is not the same thing as expressing your individuality by using file formats on your computer that are incompatible with those of your co-workers.

Anyone familiar with the history of North American agriculture will no doubt be intimately acquainted with important crops such as sumpweed, goosefoot, knotweed and maygrass.

No? Never heard of them? Well, you're not alone. Although these crops sustained Native agriculture for centuries in North America, by the time Europeans arrived on the continent they were long out of production. They were essentially squeezed out by the arrival of corn and beans from Mexico.

As readers of Jared Diamond's *Guns, Germs and Steel* will know, it took a lot of tinkering and cross-breeding in order to get a decent agricultural crop in the Americas. Sumpweed, for example, which occurs naturally, is a less than ideal crop. A relative of the noxious ragweed, its 'pollen can cause hay fever where the plant occurs in abundant stands.' It also 'has a strong odour objectionable to some people', and 'handling it can cause skin irritation'.[4] Native farmers grew it only because they had nothing better.

Corn, on the other hand, is the product of at least several hundred years of cross-breeding and crop experimentation on the part of early farmers. In essence, it was produced through a very long, slow process of genetic engineering (the final product is so artificial that there is still no scientific consensus about the identity of its wild ancestors). It was originally developed in Mexico, but its obvious superiority over indigenous natural crops meant that Native farmers immediately abandoned their traditional plants as soon as they came into contact with corn.

One can see a similar process at work throughout the ancient world, in the spread of rice, millet, yams, taro, wheat, barley and so forth. The result was a major loss of biodiversity. Crops that were initially indigenous to one small region spread across the entire world, completely displacing a wide range of other species. Yet all of this occurred long before the development of science and technology, capitalism or globalisation. These later developments have no doubt accelerated the process, but they did not create it. Fundamentally, the reason that corn displaced sumpweed is that it is a better crop. Any farmer, given a choice between the two, will choose to grow the corn. The only difference between then and now is that, whereas it used to take centuries for these innovations to spread from one area to the next, the reduction of communication and trade barriers in our society has made the spread almost instantaneous.

Thus a certain amount of the homogenisation of taste that occurs in consumer markets is a straightforward consequence of consumer demand. Anyone who has bought a potato or a cob of corn recently is probably guilty of exacerbating this same tendency. The yellow-fleshed Yukon Gold potato, produced by researchers at the University of Guelph in Ontario, has been gaining market share at an extraordinary rate. And it is becoming increasingly difficult to find anything other than bicolour corn. In both cases, it is because consumers have a preference for these vegetables, enough so that they are willing to pay more for them. And since all of these crops are unadvertised, no one can claim that consumers are being unduly influenced. The most plausible explanation for the fact that everyone's eating Yukon Gold potatoes is that they are really good potatoes and people like them. If the overall result is homogeneity, how can we complain? After all, in order to avoid this outcome, someone would have to get stuck eating potatoes that they don't like.

There is a strong argument to be made for keeping less favoured plants from becoming extinct, in order to maintain biodiversity. But it is much more difficult to make the case for keeping them in commercial production. Sumpweed was abandoned not only because the plant is noxious, but because yields are low and the grains are not especially appetising. As a result, it would be labour-intensive to produce, and thus more expensive, yet not very tasty. While we might like it if someone, somewhere, ate enough sumpweed to maintain diversity in agriculture, most of us have no desire to be that person (and, of course, if we force some group of people to consume it, by denying them access to other goods, it would be highly unfair to those people). So the question remains, who gets stuck holding the bag? We all want diversity, yet it is often our own consumer preferences that are driving homogenisation.

Homogenisation is especially pronounced in sectors that economists describe as 'winner-take-all' markets. Since everyone wants the very best, and since developing technology has made it possible in many cases to deliver the very best to all consumers, the gap between first and second place has become enormous. Products that have only a very slight edge over the competition are able to completely dominate the market like never before. This is simply the aggregate effect of consumer preference. The 'superstar' is a classic example: Hollywood celebrities, supermodels, pop stars and so on. Although constantly accused of being manufactured confections, no-talent media sensations pumped up by hype and advertising, superstars exist in many sectors where media manipulation and advertising play a far more limited role. The market for classical music, for instance, is still *primarily* driven by talent. Yet one can see the winner-take-all tendency just as clearly here. As economist Sherwin Rosen observes: 'The market for classical music has never been larger than it is now; yet the number of full-time soloists on any given instrument is on the order of only a few hundred (and much smaller for instruments other than voice, violin, and piano). Performers of the first rank comprise a limited handful out of these small totals and have very large incomes. There are also known to be substantial differences between [their incomes and the incomes of] those in the second rank, even though most consumers would have difficulty detecting more than minor differences in a "blind" hearing.'[5]

Naturally, when one star begins to dominate the market too completely, it creates an opportunity for those who want to stand out from the crowd to establish distinction by professing abhorrence for that individual. Thus, true classical music connoisseurs have found Luciano Pavarotti to be unlistenable for years, not because he lacks talent, but simply because he is too 'mainstream' or, more specifically, too 'downmarket' (in their system of aesthetic judgment, he *can't* be good precisely *because* so many people like him). This quest for distinction ensures that there will be a constant rotation of personalities within the star system – today's idol will be tomorrow's has-been. Yet all of this is a natural consequence of the structure of consumer preferences, not a product of manipulation or coercion. Corporations try to nudge the process in one direction or another, but fundamentally it is outside their control.

This does not mean that the market is always right. Markets often fail to fully reflect consumer preferences, especially in areas of cultural and intellectual production, where property rights are extremely difficult to exercise. But it does mean that markets are not always wrong. Furthermore, critics have a tendency to dismiss popular taste, to imagine that people couldn't *really* like McDonald's food or *really* enjoy listening to Celine Dion. Thus they vastly underestimate the extent to which homogenisation is a consequence of genuine consumer preference.

Of all the bobo food products that have been introduced in the past decade, the most amusing by far is the 'free-range' chicken. Sparked no doubt by concern over living conditions in factory farms, where chickens are confined to small cages for their entire lives, consumers began demanding that animals be raised under more humane conditions. And they were willing to pay more for them. Soon after, someone came up with the brilliant idea of calling chickens that had access to the outdoors 'free-range', and selling them at a steep premium. The new product quickly caught on. The name evokes images of the open prairie, with chickens roaming about on the horizon, the wind ruffling their feathers. It is an image that could make sense only to someone who has never actually seen or touched a live chicken.

Anyone who has spent any time on a farm knows that a free-range chicken is about as plausible as a sun-loving earthworm. On a nice summer day, the best place to look for the chickens will be in the darkest corner of the coop. Dozens of them will be piled on top of each other, usually sleeping, forming a compact ball. They just aren't the ranging types. (This was confirmed by a recent study that showed that only 15 per cent of free-range chickens ever actually make use of the outdoor space that is available to them.)[6] The idea of 'free range' is simply a projection of our own desires onto our food. No matter what we do, chickens will never be the rugged individualists that we would like them to be.

One wonders how much of the concern over mass production and conformity is a projection of these same sorts of desires onto consumers. The traditional critique of mass society assumes that consumers have extraordinarily heterogeneous desires, such that they must be tricked by advertisers into consuming the same mass-produced goods. The system must produce 'mass consciousness' in order to facilitate 'mass production'. Yet there is a far more obvious explanation. Mass-produced goods are *cheaper* than custom goods, and consumers are price-sensitive. Given a choice between products that match their needs perfectly but are expensive and ones that meet their needs imperfectly but are inexpensive, people may very well opt for the inexpensive ones. It all depends upon how much they care about price (thus one can expect that the poor will be more likely to consume mass-produced goods than the rich).

Nevertheless, some have tried to argue that the market exacerbates these tendencies by squeezing out smaller players. The economist Tibor Scitovsky, for example, presents this argument in the following way:

> *Economies of scale not only cheapen large-scale production but by raising wages they also raise the cost and diminish the profitability of small-scale production. This in turn raises the minimum volume of sales necessary to render production profitable and thus leads to an ever increasing narrowing of the range of variants of products offered and neglect of minority needs and tastes in the nature and design of goods produced and marketed. The increasing neglect of minority preferences is a bad thing, because it is illiberal, makes for uniformity, and destroys to some degree the principal merit of the market economy: its ability to cater separately and simultaneously to different people's differing needs and tastes.*[7]

This argument moves a bit too quickly, though. Suppose that initially goods are custom-ordered from a small-scale supplier, who produces items that are tailor-made to each individual customer. A large-scale producer comes along who makes the same type of product, but only in, say, three styles. By limiting the number of styles, this producer is able to sell the goods at much lower cost. Scitovsky infers that the large producer will drive the small producer out of business.

But this is not necessarily the case. One must assume, given the variety of products made by the small-scale producer, that the three mass-produced variants will not exactly match the taste of at least some consumers. This means that these consumers will suffer a loss of welfare if they switch to the mass-produced goods. So if they do switch, it must be because they prefer the money they save to the inconvenience of purchasing goods not perfectly suited to their tastes. The small-scale producer would not go bankrupt if people with minority tastes were willing to pay more for the goods than those with majority tastes. Homogenisation arises only because people are unwilling to pay the full cost associated with satisfaction of their preferences when low-cost alternatives that are close enough become available. There is nothing coercive or illiberal about this.

Of course, people with less mainstream taste may complain that they are being treated unfairly. Why should they have to pay more simply because they happen to have more uncommon tastes? There is, however, a decisive response to this question. Mass-produced goods are cheaper than custom goods because they require less time, energy and labour to produce. If you go to a barber to get your hair cut, it takes only fifteen minutes. If you don't like standard barbering cuts and want to express your individuality through a unique hairstyle, then you go to a salon. There a haircut will take one hour. It will also cost you four times more – and for good reason. It *should* cost you more to go to a stylist, because you are taking up more of someone else's time.

There is, in fact, an excellent rule of thumb to be had here. Whenever you feel that society is forcing you to conform or treating you like a number, not a person, just ask yourself the following question: 'Does my individuality create more work for other people?' If the answer is yes, then you should be prepared to pay more. Most institutions in our society have a system that they follow. At the fast food restaurant, at the bank, in a hospital, there is a standardised system for interacting with clients and delivering services. Such a system is generally designed to maximise the service that can be provided at a given price (or given certain budgetary resources). Individuals who refuse to follow the system not only cost more to service, they often gum up the works for everyone else. In this context, individualism often shades over into narcissistic disregard for the needs of others.

A wonderful example of this narcissism comes at the beginning of Kalle Lasn's *Culture Jam*. Lasn is describing his 'moment of truth', when he realised that consumer capitalism was fundamentally unethical. He had gone to his local supermarket for groceries and was about to put his coin in the slot to obtain a shopping trolley, 'when it suddenly occurred to me what a dope I was. Here I was putting in my quarter for the privilege of spending money in a store I come to every week but hate, a sterile chain that rarely carries any locally grown produce and always makes me stand in line to pay. And when I was finished shopping I'd have to take this cart back to the exact place their efficiency experts have decreed, and slide it back in with all the other carts, rehook it and push the red button to get my damn quarter back.'[8]

Lasn ends this rather exhausting tale of consumerist maze-running with a triumphal flourish: he takes his quarter and shoves it into the slot, banging it with his key ring until it jams. This is not quite on a par with Michael Douglas going postal in the movie *Falling Down*, but everyone sticks it to The Man in his own way. Too bad the store now has to pay someone to come fix the machine, and in the meantime other customers will have to spend part of *their* precious shopping time hunting down the trolleys that are strewn all over the car park. The point is, while there is nothing wrong with individualism per se, it is important that no one person's individuality be secured at the expense of other people's time and energy. After all, Lasn lives in Vancouver, a city that is positively overflowing with stores that will sell you locally grown organic produce, fair-trade coffee and home-made quiche, all staffed by eager college students who will never make you queue, much less stick a coin in a trolley. Lasn could easily find one if he just sniffed around a bit. The problem with these stores is that they are extremely *expensive*, because they have to hire twice as many staff ('Oh please, let me get that cart for you, Mr. Lasn'). This is as it should be. If your individuality is such that it requires other people to wait on you hand and foot, then you should be prepared to pay an arm and a leg.

If there is one practice that has provoked fears of homogenisation more than any other, it is franchising. One cannot fail to be impressed, when travelling around much of the world, at the extraordinary *sameness* of it all. Every shopping centre seems to be packed with the same old stores that you see everywhere else. And every major road is crowded with the usual signs, for the same old petrol stations and restaurants. The 'brandscape' has become so uniform that many people would be surprised to discover that franchises and chains are not all-powerful. For example, they control only 35 per cent of the American retail market.

The standard objection to franchises is that they destroy regional and cultural particularity. And no company has borne the brunt of this objection more directly than McDonald's. (In fact, the term 'McDonaldisation' has become synonymous in some quarters with all that ails the modern world, thanks to books like *The McDonaldization of Society*, *The McDonaldization of Higher Education*, *The McDonaldization of the Church* and, of course, *Resisting McDonaldization*.) According to George Ritzer, author of *The McDonaldization of Society*, the process of homogenisation unleashed by franchising puts our very souls at risk. If the world were less McDonaldised, 'people would have the potential to be far more thoughtful, skilful, creative, and well-rounded than they are now.'[9]

The trajectory of Ritzer's thought is extremely clear. In his historical analysis of the rise of McDonaldisation, he organises the key events into the following sequence (these are the actual subject headings in one chapter of his book):[10]

- The Holocaust: Mass Producing Death
- Scientific Management: Finding the One Best Way
- The Assembly Line: Turning Workers into Robots
- Levittown: Putting up Houses – 'Boom, Boom, Boom'
- Shopping Centres: Malling America
- McDonald's: Creating the 'Fast Food Factory'

This 'from Auschwitz to our house' style of thinking shows, again, just how profoundly the spectre of the Holocaust informs the critique of mass society. For many people, the mere fact that the Golden Arches are popping up around the world is enough to evoke memories of the Nuremberg rallies. In Ritzer's view, the people lined up to buy Big Macs are just as much victims of brainwashing as a group of Hitler Youth saluting the Führer.

Except Ritzer makes things a little bit too easy on himself by focusing on McDonald's. Being the oldest fast food franchise, McDonald's has both a menu and a set of business practices that are antiquated in many ways. Thus the discussion of franchising too often veers off into a debate over environmental issues, and the effects of ranching on the Brazilian rainforest; or into a debate over health concerns, and the epidemic of obesity sweeping the United States. While these are no doubt interesting questions, they are only tangentially related to the issue of homogenisation that is at the core of the McDonaldisation critique. To focus the issue, it might be helpful to shift the emphasis away from McDonald's, and to look at the second-largest fast food restaurant in the United States, a sandwich chain called Subway. While Subway is just as much a 'fast food factory' as McDonald's, there are no real grounds for complaining about either the quality of the food offered, the range of menu items offered or the environmental consequences of their business practices. Yet it seems somewhat less ominous to discuss the 'Subwayisation' of America.

The emphasis on McDonald's also obscures another important point. Most members of the cultural elite profess a dislike for McDonald's food. In fact, since franchises serve the lower classes to a disproportionate degree, their products will inevitably serve as an affront to the higher aesthetic sensibility. But go into any successful franchise or chain store with an open mind and it is easy to see why they are successful. In most cases, it is because they offer a product that, for the price, is demonstrably superior. Wal-Mart sells premium brands at low prices and has superior inventory management. It offers discounted prescriptions to seniors. It offers free RV parking for vacationers. Home Depot hires aisle attendants who are genuinely knowledgeable. They will cut your wood for you, on the spot, no hassles. You can rent a van to take it all home. Subway sells sandwiches on fresh-baked bread, often still hot from the oven. You get to put it together precisely the way you like. Starbucks sells the best filter coffee around. And we sometimes forget that even McDonald's sells fries that are superior to what you can find at half the bistros in Paris. These companies may advertise heavily now, but they did not build their businesses through advertising. When they were able to make significant inroads into a particular market, it was usually because that market was so poorly served before. Independent bookstores could have installed comfortable chairs and started serving coffee long ago; they just didn't get around to it until they started feeling the heat from chains such as Barnes & Noble, Borders and Waterstones. Lumberyard attendants could have stopped being jerks or intimidating female customers years ago; they just didn't get around to it until DIY stores opened up around the corner. Coffee shops could have invested in an espresso machine any time they wanted; they just didn't get around to it until Starbucks came along. Department stores could have adopted 'no hassle' refund policies from the beginning; they just didn't get around to it until the big chains started doing it. The list goes on and on.

Part of the reason that so many of these successful chains are American is that Americans have dedicated an extraordinary amount of time and thought to the question of how to produce an enjoyable retail experience. How many times have you walked into a store only to have the staff act as though they're the ones doing *you* a favour by talking to you? How many times have you looked at your mechanic and suspected that you're being taken for a ride? How many times have you been afraid to ask a question in the hardware store for fear that the staff would treat you like you're stupid? These are the sorts of negative experiences that drive customers away. A successful franchise generally has a system in place that eliminates these sorts of experiences – otherwise every branch and outlet suffers.

Finally, there is an important distinction to be made between a franchise (like McDonald's) and a chain (like Starbucks). This is often ignored. The writers of the anticonsumerist PBS series *Affluenza*, for example, draw a contrast between 'big, absentee franchises' and locally owned businesses: 'At a locally owned coffee shop, you might see artwork from someone who lives down the street. The shop is your coffee shop. At your independent bookseller, you stand a much greater chance of finding books from small presses who publish a wider variety of books than mainstream publishers.'[11] Apart from the dubiousness of these empirical claims, the contrast that they draw between the franchise and the locally owned shop is based on a confusion. Unlike chains, in which each store is owned and operated by the parent corporation, in a franchise the parent corporation simply licenses the business model and trademark to an independent businessperson, who then operates the outlet. The major fast food corporations, like McDonald's, Subway and KFC, are all franchise operations – which means that they are mostly owned and operated by local businesspeople.

Franchising allows the business to spread more quickly, because extending the operation requires no real investment of capital on the part of the parent company. It also limits cross-subsidisation and other 'dirty tricks' that are often felt to be unfair by competitors. Because Starbucks owns all of its stores, it may be willing to lose money at one location for a year in order to drive a competitor out of business – that loss simply gets pooled with the gains made elsewhere, as part of a global strategy. But a franchise operator is generally on his own, and the money lost ultimately comes from his pocket. In this respect, franchises are just like small businesses, and so cannot engage in the sort of nasty competitive practices that their opponents often accuse them of. Franchise operations, in other words, generally lack the means to implement a global strategy.

Obviously, franchises derive certain benefits from economies of scale in advertising. But their most important competitive advantage is usually just the underlying business model that the franchisee adopts. Most retail is incredibly competitive. In any major city, thousands of businesses open every year, and thousands of others go bankrupt. From this enormous sea of effort, one or two businesses will hit upon a successful format, which they will then 'bottle' and sell. It is hard to see how there is anything sinister about this. Take, for example, the story of the Marvelous Market company in Washington DC, which Ritzer tells in one of the more (unintentionally) amusing segments of *The McDonaldization of Society*. The company was founded during the '60s with the specific goal of combating the 'Wonder bread' phenomenon. After all, you are what you eat and, according to one company brochure, 'Food triggers moods and memories, reveals needs and desires, releases tensions and stimulates creativity.'[12]

Ritzer describes with great satisfaction how inefficient the operation was. 'Its foods were unpredictable. Customers dealt with people rather than automatons or robots.'[13] Of course, the company also made very good bread. And thus Marvelous Market quickly became a success. Sales grew so dramatically that the company began limiting bread purchases to two loaves per person. Eventually, the owner began to expand operations, opening a dedicated baking facility and starting to supply supermarkets and restaurants. The market for his bread continued to grow, and service at the original store became unbearably slow. Finally, he gave in and *opened a second outlet*. In an open letter to customers, he apologised profusely for this new development, emphasising that the new equipment is still 'not automated equipment; we make breads in the other bakery just as we make them here, slowly, by hand.'

Some people might interpret this story as an example of the capitalist system functioning precisely the way that it is supposed to function. Good bread drives out bad. Ritzer, on the other hand, presents it as a modern morality tale, a dramatic example of just how seductive the siren song of McDonaldisation can be. Yet he never explains one thing. In the end, what does it matter whether there is one Marvelous Market store, or two, or twenty, as long as the bread is good? Ritzer winds up simply fetishising that which is erratic, unpredictable and uncommon over that which is simple, predictable and common. Yet surely that is just an individual preference, not a legitimate grievance over the organisation of society. For Ritzer, as for many other countercultural rebels, the ideal individual seems to be some type of 'random man' who, by refusing to follow any rules or conform to any code, winds up being phobic of any type of behaviour that exhibits regularity. To his credit, Ritzer follows his own critique of homogenisation through to this, its logical conclusion. In a section that outlines different strategies for resisting McDonaldisation, he offers a series of suggestions as to how we can avoid becoming robots and automatons. These include living in a house that you have built for yourself (or had built for you), doing your own oil changes, refusing to speak to answering machines, using cash instead of credit, getting to know the local inhabitants while on vacation, boycotting domed stadiums and, most preposterously, avoiding all daily routine: 'Try to do as many things as possible in a different way from one day to the next,' he recommends.[14]

It is difficult to know which of these suggestions are serious and which are not. Yet it is easy to identify the lifestyle that Ritzer is recommending. It is the lifestyle of a tenured university professor, with eccentric habits, a big fat pay cheque and a lot of free time on his hands. Those of us with these nice cushy jobs can no doubt heartily endorse Ritzer's recommendations. But can we really expect the rest of society to follow suit? Again, there are two simple questions that one should ask before adopting this 'random man' model of individualistic behaviour: first, 'Is my individuality creating more work for other people?' and second, 'What if everyone acted that way?'

All of the forces that we can see at work within our society to promote homogenisation can also be observed on the world stage. Increased globalisation of trade, combined with tourism and mass immigration, is gradually producing what would best be described as a state of 'uniform diversity'. Almost all of the increase in foreign trade in the past twenty years has involved diversification, rather than intensification, of trade. For example, rather than Canada importing all of its red wine from France and phasing out its own wine industry while France imports all its wheat from Canada and phases out that segment of its agricultural sector, increased trade has left Canada still producing pretty much the same range of goods that it has always produced. Trade is used primarily as a way of getting access to goods that have traditionally not been available in this country. So France imports Canada's maple syrup, while Canada now imports Provençal pottery.

As a result, the internal markets of every country have become much more diverse. Whereas once certain types of pottery could only be obtained in certain French villages, now they are available in pretty much any major city (thereby eroding the distinction that they confer upon their owner). When I was young, you couldn't buy green onions or pitta in the grocery store (much less imported cheese) in Canada. Since 1970, the average number of items for sale in North American supermarkets has increased from 8000 to 30,000. When my mother-in-law comes to visit from Taiwan (and, naturally, insists on cooking for everyone), she does not have to adjust her habits at all. Everything that she would buy in Taipei is available in Toronto as well. It may be true that the number of corporations doing business in some sectors of the economy has decreased, but it is difficult to think of any sector in which the number of different *products* being offered has not increased.

Yet because this process is going on throughout the world, anyone who travels will no doubt notice that every place in the world is starting to look more and more alike. It is no doubt distressing to be walking down the street in some faraway land only to see the same Guatemalan handcrafts being sold on the pavement (and, it would appear, the same band of Guatemalan musicians busking nearby). And no one really wants to see a McDonald's sign when touring Beijing (even though it is a great place to nip in and use the washroom). Yet if the Chinese want to eat Big Macs, who are we to stop them? It would be nice if the Chinese showed a bit more commitment to maintaining the purity and integrity of their culture, but who are we to talk? After all, we love having Chinese restaurants in our country (not to mention Asian fast food items like noodles, sushi and bubble tea). We also like shopping at foreign chain stores like Ikea, Zara, The Body Shop, Benetton and H&M. Our country is becoming a giant omnicultural hodgepodge of influences and styles, and most of us like it that way. But it means that we cannot then turn around and criticise others for following the same path.

Of course, many people feel that the United States exercises disproportionate influence in this process – that what is going on is not so much globalisation of culture as it is Americanisation. Ironically, this perception is for the most part just parochialism on the part of Americans. First of all, Americans have a tendency to assume that everything is American, unless presented with specific evidence to the contrary. Most obviously, the distinction between Canadian and American influence is completely ignored. Of course, because the majority of Canadians speak English with an accent that is similar to that of the American Midwest, it is easy to make that mistake. Yet in other cases, there is no such excuse. I recall once reading a review of a video game in the *New York Times* that criticised it for being ethnocentric on the grounds that it featured 'stereotypical Asian characters'. The reviewer simply assumed that it was made in the United States. It never occurred to her that the game in question, like almost every console game sold in the American market, was a Japanese product, developed for a Japanese audience. What the reviewer saw as a stereotype was in fact an instance of genuine Asian culture; she simply lacked the knowledge of foreign cultures needed to identify it as such.

The second problem is that most Americans are able to spot American influences abroad but simply don't know enough about foreign cultures to recognise how much they influence daily life in the United States. Thus critics ignore the extent to which foreign cultures – Asian in particular – have been driving movies, television and fashion in North America. Almost all Hollywood action movies are now shot in the Hong Kong style. Television is completely dominated by 'reality' programmes, another cultural import. The entire aesthetic of the rave scene in North America is an imitation of Japanese style.

Japanese comics and video games are extraordinarily influential among the young. And the Internet has massively extended these influences. The fad for 'schoolgirl'-style plaid skirts across clubs in North America is due to the influence of Japanese pornography. The list goes on and on. While the United States remains a powerful cultural force on the world stage – especially through hip hop – the jury is still out when it comes to deciding which nation will become the most dominant in the evolution of global culture.

Whether one approves of the growing cultural convergence or not, it is difficult to see what could be done to stop it. In order to maintain the diversity of traditional cultures, some people have to be willing to live in these cultures and limit their exposure to outside influences. There are major costs associated with doing so. Bhutan, for instance, has gone to considerable lengths to isolate itself, to limit the influx of Western tourists, charging guests US$200 per day for the privilege of being in the country. Yet without foreign currency earnings, they have little access to agricultural, manufacturing or medical technology. As a result, they suffer from poverty, malnutrition and poor life expectancy. The Bhutanese seem, on the whole, willing to accept this trade-off, in part due to the prevalence of deep religiosity. Yet one cannot expect everyone to feel the same way.

Again, the question is, if we want to maintain diversity, who will be left holding the bag? One can see this clearly in the case of language. There are currently about 6000 languages in use in the world, but they are disappearing at a rate of about 30 per year. (This is a slightly misleading statistic, because over 1500 of these languages are found in Papua New Guinea, and are spoken by only a handful of people.) Many people treat these languages as though they were endangered species, which must be preserved at all cost. Yet in order to maintain the vitality of a language, one requires a large number of unilingual speakers in a territorially concentrated region. This can be difficult to obtain, since the value of a language is heavily determined by the number of other speakers with whom one can use it to communicate. In other words, speaking a language generates network externalities for all other speakers of that language (in the same way that buying a fax machine generates a positive externality for all other owners of fax machines). Certain languages, like English, reach a 'tipping point', where so many people speak them that it is easily worthwhile for others to shoulder the costs associated with learning them. These become the hyperlanguages. Other languages fall beneath this threshold, and so require some very special motivation in order to remain in use. In Ireland, of course, where at the end of the nineteenth century Irish had pretty much died out except for a few poets and intellectuals who were attempting to revive it, this was achieved by Government legislation that required all schools to teach it as a second language. In parts of Wales and Scotland there were, until relatively recently, small communities who still kept Welsh or Gaelic as their first language, but now nearly everyone has the knowledge to speak English. In many of these areas, however, street signs and any official notices will still be in Welsh as a matter of principle even though most of the inhabitants would now have English as a first language; and for many it would be their only language.

So while we may lament the imminent disappearance of Kristang or Itik or Lehalurup, we must recognise that preserving these languages would require a community of unilingual (or at least native) speakers. It is not enough simply to have everyone speak it as a second language – since the dominant tendency in that case seems to be a slide toward the hyperlanguage. Yet forgoing competence in the hyperlanguage in order to speak a minority language of this type may significantly limit a person's opportunities. This may not be a problem as long as we can find people willing to do it. Yet we can hardly blame those who do not volunteer.

As we have seen, the tendency toward homogenisation – or, more specifically, the movement toward 'uniform diversity' – is the product of a very complex set of forces. Some of it is a reflection of consumer preference, some of it is due to economies of scale, some of it is caused by distortions in the market and some of it is caused by timeless, universal human tendencies. In many cases, it is not obvious that we can do anything about it; in many more cases, it is not obvious that we *should* do anything about it. The most important point, however, is that there is no single 'system' at work producing this effect. There is simply a bundle of different, sometimes contradictory forces.

The countercultural critique, on the other hand, has aided and abetted the suggestion that there is one central homogenising force at work in all of these different developments. According to this view, a system of repression and conformity is a functional prerequisite of the market economy. Cultural uniformity must be imposed in order to secure the discipline of the machine and the assembly line. When the market was limited to the national scale, this resulted in an erosion of individuality within each national culture. Now that globalisation has extended the market to the international level, the system is levelling the differences between national cultures.

This analysis has led many leftist activists into making the disastrous political error of transforming their concerns over the cultural effects of globalisation into an opposition to *trade* between developed and underdeveloped nations. If it is the market producing all these effects, they figure, then the best way to limit the effects is to limit the extent of the market. Thus antiglobalisation activists have taken to protesting every major gathering of the World Trade Organization (WTO), along with summits of heads of state. In so doing, they put themselves into direct conflict with representatives of precisely those Third World interests that they claim to protect. While there is, in the developing world, a lively debate over how integration into the global economy should be achieved, almost no one questions the desirability of this ultimate goal. No one believes in economic autarky (of the sort promoted by Mahatma Gandhi and Jawaharlal Nehru in India). The only real question is whether trade liberalisation and foreign investment should be instituted first, as a way of stimulating economic development, or whether a certain level of endogenous development should be achieved first, as a prelude to liberalisation.

Many representatives of developing nations find themselves baffled by the spectacle of antiglobalisation activists protesting *trade*. While they agree entirely with the concerns being expressed over environmental policy, labour standards, currency speculation, IMF structural adjustment policies and unfair terms of trade, most completely fail to see how any of this could be improved by limiting trade itself (or by opposing the WTO – a forum in which the democratically elected representatives of all these nations assemble in order to address precisely these issues). Again, the problem lies with the totalising character of the countercultural critique. Instead of opposing specific trade policies that are genuinely harmful to the Third World, such as American and European agricultural subsidies, antiglobalisation activists position themselves as opponents of trade in general, for example by denouncing trade in agricultural products on the grounds that it promotes 'monoculture'. Thus one has the peculiar spectacle of developing nations on the 'inside' of the WTO trying to pressure Europe and the United States on the issue of agricultural subsidies during the Doha round only to have their meetings disrupted by protestors on the 'outside' opposing the entire process.

One can see the totalising tendency of the countercultural critique most clearly in Michael Hardt and Antonio Negri's runaway academic bestseller *Empire*. Hardt and Negri simply take the Gramscian theory of cultural hegemony and apply it on a world scale. 'The system', having conquered the national proletariat, has now gone global, becoming 'Empire'. Who cares if there is no evidence of any such Empire? The fact that there is growing uniformity among cultures, in their view, shows that there must be some underlying system of repression and control. The disorder, confusion and straightforward lawlessness that exist on an international level are simply a sign of the deeper nefariousness of 'the system': 'All conflicts, all crises, and all dissensions effectively push forward the process of integration and by the same measure call for more central authority. Peace, equilibrium, and the cessation of conflict are the values toward which everything is directed. The development of the global system (and of imperial right in the first place) seems to be the development of a machine that imposes procedures of continual contractualisation that lead to systemic equilibria – a machine that creates a continuous call for authority. The machine seems to predetermine the exercise of authority and action across the entire social space.'[15]

Thus the 'machine' creates the illusion of disorder in order to seduce us into accepting increased repressive conformity. In Hardt and Negri's view, the only possible solution to this is the anarchic resistance of 'the multitude', who must resist the forms of subjectivity imposed upon them by Empire, in order to constitute themselves as the 'new nomadic horde', or the 'new barbarians'. The authors do not particularly care what form these opposition movements take; anything violent seems to fit the bill. (They describe the Los Angeles riots in the following way: 'The looting of commodities and burning of property were not just metaphors but the real global conditions of the mobility and volatility of post-Fordist social mediations.'[16] This passage is quite revealing. Who would be tempted to think that the riots were *just* a metaphor?)

What Hardt and Negri fail to provide is any sort of explanation of why this so-called Empire is such a bad thing. They simply equate order with repression and disorder with freedom. Yet we all recognise that the rule of law is essential to securing personal liberty in a domestic context; why would we resist its extension to international affairs? What's wrong with 'peace, equilibrium, and the cessation of conflict'? And why on earth would we want to live under the 'new barbarism'?

Notes

1   Lewis Mumford, *The City in History* (New York: Harcourt Brace, 1961), 486.

2   William Whyte, Jr., 'Individualism in Suburbia', in *Individualism: Man in Modern Society*, ed. Ronald Gross (New York: Laurel, 1972), 146.

3   In James Twitchell, *Twenty Ads That Shook the World* (New York: Three Rivers, 2000), 186–87.

4   Jared Diamond, *Guns, Germs and Steel: The Fates of Human Societies* (New York: Norton, 1997), 151.

5   Sherwin Rosen, 'The Economics of Superstars', *American Review*, 71 (1981): 845–58; cited in Robert Frank and Philip Cook, *The Winner-Take-All Society: Why the Few at the Top Get*

So Much More Than the Rest of Us (New York: Free Press, 1996), 24–25.

6   C. A. Weeks *et al.*, 'Comparison of the Behaviour of Broiler Chickens in Indoor and Free-Ranging Environments', *Animal Welfare*, 3 (1994): 179–92.

7   Tibor Scitovsky, 'On the Principle of Consumer Sovereignty', *American Economic Review*, 52 (1962): 265.

8   Lasn, *Culture Jam*, xv.

9   George Ritzer, *The McDonaldization of Society* (Thousand Oaks, CA: Pine Forge, 2000), 18.

10 *Ibid.*, Chapter 2.

11 John de Graaf, David Wann, and Thomas H. Naylor, *Affluenza: The All Consuming Epidemic* (San Francisco: Berrett-Koehler, 2000), 62.

12 Ritzer, *The McDonaldization of Society*, 204.

13 *Ibid.*, 204.

14 *Ibid.*, 226.

15 Michael Hardt and Antonio Negri, *Empire* (Cambridge, MA: Harvard University Press, 2000), 34.

16 *Ibid.*, 55.

Thank you, India

In 1995, former teen dance queen Alanis Morissette released an album called *Jagged Little Pill*. With deeply confessional lyrics driven by punchy rock power chords, *Jagged Little Pill* was Morissette's *Nevermind*, instantly turning her into an angry, outspoken icon for millions of alienated and disaffected young women. While no less alienated than Kurt Cobain, she managed to deal with the pressure and confusion of popularity a bit better. After a few years of non-stop touring, she took some time out to recharge. She ran triathlons, experimented with photography and travelled to Cuba and to India. The trip to India in particular was a life-changing experience, giving her a newfound confidence and spirituality that she brought to her next album, *Supposed Former Infatuation Junkie*.

The hit single off that album, 'Thank You', contains a moment of startling insight. In the chorus, she thanks the various people and events that have helped her in her quest for personal spiritual development. At one point she sings, 'Thank you India'. Many listeners found the level of self-absorption implicit in this remark positively breathtaking. Did she imagine a billion voices in the subcontinent rising up, crying out as one, 'You're welcome, Alanis. Whenever you need us, we're here to help'?

Yet Alanis is hardly unique in this regard. Westerners have been using Third World countries as a backdrop for their own personal voyages of self-discovery for decades. The temptation to do so flows quite naturally from the countercultural idea. If our own culture is a system of total manipulation and control, perhaps the best way to shake ourselves free from the illusion is to immerse ourselves in some other culture – preferably one that is as radically distinct from our own as possible.

Thus the countercultural critique has always been tempted by exoticism – uncritical romanticisation of that which is most different.

One can indulge in the exotic through travel, to places like India and Central America; through the adoption of the religious beliefs and rituals of the Chinese or of American Indians; or simply by adopting the speech, clothing and cultural habits of others, such as talking in dialect or wearing batik or doing yoga. In every case, the goal is the same: to throw off the chains of technocratic modernity and to achieve the revolution in consciousness that will allow us all to live a more authentic life.

The greatest weakness of countercultural thinking has always been its inability to produce a coherent vision of a free society, much less a practical political programme for changing the one that we live in. Yet the turn toward exoticism has encouraged widespread denial of this problem, by suggesting that some other culture, just over the horizon, possesses some completely different way of thinking and acting, one that will allow us to escape from the iron cage of modernity. Countercultural rebels have spent decades in search of this magical 'get out of jail free' card – from the madness of the cultural revolution in China to the peyote patches of the Mohave Desert. Yet more often than not, what these encounters have produced is less than genuine. By projecting their own desires and longing onto other cultures, countercultural rebels have essentially constructed the exotic as a reflection of their own ideology.

The lure of the exotic is hardly a new phenomenon. Self-discovery through an arduous search for the 'other' is a recurring theme in Western civilisation, manifesting itself in such romantic notions as the Wild West, Darkest Africa and the Orient. It arises out of a widespread conviction that through the development of civilisation, we lose touch with who we really are, what life is all about. But if civilisation is to blame, it stands to reason that 'reality' can still be found elsewhere – in uncivilised cultures, esoteric religions or even ancient history. A major strain is the notion of the 'noble savage', which we find versions of in the political writings of Jean-Jacques Rousseau, the travelogues of Gustave Flaubert in Egypt and the paintings made by Paul Gauguin in Tahiti. For Rousseau, primitive man was happy to the extent to which he was self-sufficient, able to fulfil his innate needs for food and sex untouched by the inequalities that characterise modern society. In the large European states, Rousseau felt, man had become alienated from his authentic self and had become concerned with artificial needs and false duties, such as the hypocritical regard for manners that masked the underlying ruthlessness of bourgeois life.

This sounds a lot like the critique of mass society, except that the ideal of the noble savage is not a search for the exotic, it is nostalgia for Europe's own lost past. Rousseau even felt that Geneva retained a certain innocence and sense of authentic community that could be protected from further corruption. Similarly, we find in both Gauguin and Flaubert a desire to retrieve that which Europe had lost. What appealed to Flaubert about Egypt was the rough rudeness of everyday life, in contrast with the prudery, snobbery, smugness and racism of the French bourgeoisie. He found in Egypt support for values that his own society no longer endorsed. But it was the French elites who offended Flaubert; he was explicitly not criticising the customs and values of the masses. Like Rousseau, it was the stuffy and hypocritical orderliness of life in Europe from which he sought refuge.

This contrasts with the countercultural view that we need a wholesale replacement of Western culture and ways of thinking. The exoticism that arises is no longer a desire for a return to primitive origins, but rather a desire for pure 'otherness' – difference for its own sake. Many countercultural rebels indulged these longings through fantasy and science fiction literature (thereby elevating titles from these once-marginal literary genres onto the bestseller lists). From the Hyperboria of Robert E. Howard's *Conan the Barbarian* ('Barbarism is the natural state of mankind. Civilisation is unnatural.') to the Middle Earth of J.R.R. Tolkien's *Lord of the Rings*, countercultural rebels longed for a world completely different from our own. Primarily, they longed for an 'enchanted' world, one where both the ordinary laws of physics and of society did not apply. They sought a world that existed in a time (as Tolkien put it) before the 'rule of men' had begun.

While some were content merely to fantasise about such a world, others set off in search of it. Some did so quite literally, through the search for the 'lost continent' of Atlantis. Some tried to find it through drug experimentation, believing that LSD, magic mushrooms and peyote allowed them to travel to other planes of existence. Many more hoped to find their alternative in non-Western cultures, where magical practices still flourished and where the repressive structures of Western technocracy were still not in control. From Hermann Hesse's *Siddhartha* to Carlos Castaneda's *The Teachings of Don Juan*, the countercultural rebels desperately longed for a way to opt out of Western civilisation (and a way to opt into a world where the ordinary, depressing constraints of daily life were somehow removed). The *Tibetan Book of the Dead* and the *I Ching* became the twin bibles of the emerging movement.

The result was an enormous projection of countercultural longings and fantasy onto the non-Western world. We may not be able to find Middle Earth or visit the Great Old Ones in the 'spaces between the stars', but we can make a pilgrimage to India or take a trip to Nepal or discover some other exotic land, as far away from our own as possible. And if it is not possible to go out into the world, we can always journey inward, into the depths of the self. Either way, escapism became a central preoccupation of the counterculture.

While the romanticisation of non-Western cultures may have reached its apogee in the '60s, it retains considerable influence among critics of mass society. Consider 'voluntary simplicity', the back-to-basics movement that found its name with the publication in 1981 of Duane Elgin's book with that title. The book is in many ways a summary of a set of beliefs and practices that grew straight out of the '60s counterculture. In its contemporary incarnation, the movement is a deliberate attempt to turn away from the work-spend-debt cycle that is the mark of modern life. Yet while 'downshifting' targets consumerism quite specifically, the movement that Elgin outlines involves a much more thorough repudiation of Western society.

Voluntary simplicity (VS) arose out of the exhausted utopian energies of the '60s, after the hippies decided that the attempt to change the dominant institutions of society through the development of a new mass consciousness had been fruitless. For the members of 'this pioneering culture, the agenda shifted from transforming society to finding new ways of living that were practical and useful expressions of the new consciousness. Public activism gave way to exploring new ways of living at the grass roots level of society.'[1] The political agenda that arose out of this is captured by the slogan 'Think globally, act locally', although it is clear in Elgin's book that politics has taken a back seat to spiritual development. When they realised that large-scale institutional change wasn't going to happen, countercultural rebels turned inward, and an entire generation of activists tried to move 'beyond intellectual alienation and despair to directly encounter the place where we are all one.'

The VS movement is emphatically not about either poverty or primitivism, despite the obvious echoes of Thoreau's cabin-in-the-woods injunction to 'simplify, simplify'. After all, poverty is repressive, generating helplessness and despair, while the goal of VS is to foster empowerment and control. The point of simplicity is not to eschew all modern conveniences, and it is not a turning away from progress. The object of VS is to make use of these comforts to achieve a more direct and unmediated existence, to bring order and clarity to one's life. (One can see this quite clearly in *Real Simple* magazine, one of the more peculiar offshoots of this movement.) It is not about withdrawing from the world; it is about finding the time and energy to become more engaged with our communities and the world beyond.

Elgin even prints a helpful chart contrasting the 'Industrial World View' with the 'Voluntary Simplicity World View'. The former position sees material progress as the overriding goal of life, with one's identity defined by social position and material possessions. There is a great emphasis on autonomy and mobility, with strong dependence on experts and bureaucratic institutions to keep the machine running. In contrast, the VS worldview holds that balance and harmony between material and spiritual needs is the central aim of life, with a focus on conservation and frugality, mediated through self-reliant and self-governing communities. Above all, the key to voluntary simplicity is to foster 'inner growth', the process of spiritual development that will allow us to move from one worldview to the other.

There is nothing inherently 'exotic' in the general outline of this plan for intentional simplicity. After all, the idea that the good life consists in striking an appropriate balance between material and spiritual needs has been a part of the Western philosophical and spiritual tradition since Aristotle, and it remains an explicit and essential part of what it means to be a Christian. In his millennial address to the faithful, Pope John Paul II railed against mass consumerism and called on Catholics to stay true to the antimaterialist values of the Church.

It is odd then to find that most adherents of the VS movement reject so-called Western religions (Judaism, Catholicism, Protestantism) as legitimate paths to inner growth. Elgin cites a survey he did of the VS community in which he asked people about the 'inner-growth' processes they were using. Only 20 per cent of respondents named traditional Western religions, while 55 per cent reported using meditation techniques such as Zen or Transcendental Meditation.[2] The results are actually even worse for the mainstream religions, since people were allowed to name more than one growth process. So, in addition to meditation, 46 per cent of respondents listed things such as biofeedback and visualisation, 26 per cent listed gestalt therapy and 10 per cent listed psychoanalysis. This lack of confidence in traditional religions arises out of two features of modern spirituality: the structure of mainstream religious organisations, and the peculiar nature of our supposed spiritual needs.

Whatever else they may be, the traditional churches are hierarchical, bureaucratic institutions of mass society, and the VS movement is entirely orthodox in its countercultural condemnation of bureaucracies. There is even an appendix to *Voluntary Simplicity* that lists a dozen or so problems with large bureaucracies (it is the usual list of things such as increasing complexity, rigidity and alienation), complete with a graph tracing the inevitable breakdown of civilisation after we finally lose control of our increasingly complex society thanks to the fatal combination of unwieldy institutions and social disintegration.

Simply put, the problem is that the 'spiritual needs' experienced by members of the counterculture are not the same as the ones to which these churches were designed to minister. The traditional functions of Western religions are to teach morality, sanctify marriage and family, and anchor social stability through shared beliefs, rituals and institutions. The actual content of the faith, while not unimportant, is actually of secondary importance to these more mundane functions, and genuinely spiritual crises (death and sin, heaven and hell) can be dealt with by appealing to doctrine, as promulgated by the church hierarchies. In contrast, our current needs are not really spiritual in the traditional sense. Instead, they are therapeutic, because what we need is liberation from the repression and social conditioning caused by institutions. Priests and ministers are therefore especially unsuited to the spiritual demands of the modern world. They can't resolve conflicts between individuals and institutions because they represent the very institutions that are thought to be causing the problems in the first place. If the Church teaches morality, but morality is nothing but a system of repressive rules and regulations, then the Church has nothing to offer. Its salvation is nothing but pseudo-salvation, behind which lies just further repressive socialisation.

It is not surprising then to see members of the Voluntary Simplicity movement turn away from traditional churches. What is interesting, though, is to see that while some of them have sought solace in Jungian or Freudian psychotherapy, far more of them have turned to Eastern religions, such as Buddhism and Taoism. There are interesting parallels between psychotherapy and Eastern mysticism. Both can be read as paths of liberation, the point of which is to alter our consciousness and release us from certain forms of conditioning. Both are in a sense critiques of culture, and there are strains of an individualism, particularly in Taoism, that appeals to the 'do your own thing' creed of the counterculture. But what Eastern mysticism has, and what psychotherapy lacks, is the credibility conferred through exoticism.

★

One of the most unshakeable convictions of the counterculture is that Asians are more spiritual than those of us living in the West, and that the best route to liberation lies in some sort of synthesis between Eastern and Western ways of thinking. There is a substantial literature that tries to bridge the gap between the two cultures, and Alan Watts is a key figure here. With books like *Psychotherapy East and West*, *This Is It* and *The Joyous Cosmology*, Watts played a huge role in popularising and interpreting Eastern religion for the counterculture. He wasn't alone, though. Buddhist and Hindu ideas and terminology became a fixture in the Beat writings of Allen Ginsberg and Jack Kerouac, among others.

We can actually compare the two worldviews through a series of East/West oppositions that are by now utterly familiar:

Western worldview	Eastern worldview
materialism	spiritualism
dualism of mind and body	mind/body holism
mechanical universe	organic universe
rationality	consciousness
technological progress	spiritual growth
atomistic individuals	communitarianism

The practical result of these opposing worldviews is that we in the West have come to see the world as made of inanimate, machine-like parts to be manipulated and exploited, while those in the East see the world as a whole that is to be understood or appreciated. The West sees the individual as an atomic unit, naturally separate from and perhaps in conflict with the rest of society, while the East sees the individual as a social being whose nature cannot conflict with that of the whole. (It is useful to compare this characterisation with the list of 'Hip' and 'Square' compiled by Norman Mailer. East is hip; West is definitely square.)

These contrasting interpretations of East and West have become firmly embedded in our culture. It is worth asking, though, whether they do justice to either tradition.

★

The sign read 'You Must Buy'. It was bright yellow, with large red lettering in English and Chinese, sitting above a shop in the Mongkok district of Hong Kong. And it pretty much said it all, since in Hong Kong, the shops, malls and markets are without question the major tourist attraction. Half of the money that the average visitor to the 'Special Administrative Region' spends is on shopping. On my summer vacation in the former British colony, I was no exception. I had to buy.

There was a lot of anxiety over political, economic and cultural issues in the run-up to the 1997 handover of Hong Kong to China, but nothing exercised people more than the worry that Beijing would mess with the hypercapitalist economic policies that have made Hong Kong a world centre for business, banking and trade. There was no need to worry: under the 'one country, two systems' arrangement reached in 1984, which guarantees that Hong Kong will retain its capitalist system for at least fifty years after the handover, the economy continues to chug along. When most of the labour-intensive manufacturing moved across the border into southern China, the local economy shifted into services and value-added production. As the largest exporter in the world of clothing, watches and toys, Hong Kong is the engine room of the global consumerist pleasure cruise, and it expels heat in the form of huge local markets in factory rejects, cancelled production lines and knockoffs.

I spent (and spent and spent) one sunny day in Stanley Market, a maze of stalls and shops on the south side of Hong Kong Island. I went to Stanley with the sincere but (it turned out) utterly delusional idea that I would grab a cheap pair of light trousers and then spend the rest of the day walking in the hills. Three hours after I entered the market, I emerged with a bloated daypack and a throbbing post-shopping hangover.

Like the more upscale shops in Causeway Bay and the grungier, less touristy markets in Kowloon, the superabundance of choice in Stanley Market can be overwhelming. Every imaginable good is for sale at heavily discounted and negotiable prices. The internal logic of a market of such unbounded plenitude is that once you've been wandering for a while, mentally balancing future needs and wants, birthdays, holidays and exchange rates, it becomes almost impossible to think of an excuse not to buy. Many of the stalls don't let you try stuff on, and the sizing is often a bit of a lottery, but what does it matter when you can get two pairs of cargo trousers for ten pounds? None of the stores give receipts and I won't be able to return my knockoff Swiss Army watch when it breaks, but big deal, I'll just throw it out. So I'm out the cost of a supersized Big Mac combo.

It is tempting to see this as an artefact of Hong Kong's status as a former colony in the British Empire. After all, if you were able to somehow distil the various elements of the Western worldview outlined above, the resulting essence could be called 'consumerism'. That is the one value that is often taken to perfectly capture our shallow, materialist, alienated existence. Many people conclude that if Hong Kong is a Mecca of materialism, it must be the consequence of 150 years of Western influence and exploitation.

Yet the suggestion that this sort of consumerism is a distinctly Western phenomenon that has been imported to Hong Kong is preposterous, as anyone who has spent any time at all in the rest of Asia can confirm. Consumer culture has a much higher profile in Singapore, Taipei, Shanghai and Tokyo than it does in Los Angeles, London or Toronto, and there is no question that Asian consumerism is entirely home-grown. Most Asian societies not only have a strong traditional appreciation for the value of physical goods, they also identify a set of culturally coded prestige goods, whose consumption confers special social status. Most Westerners simply don't have enough knowledge of the culture to recognise these codes, and so fail to understand just how competitive consumption in Asia can be.

It would never occur to most Westerners, for instance, that goldfish are a conspicuous consumption good in traditional Chinese culture. Having a large aquarium in the foyer or an elaborate pond in the backyard is about as ostentatious as pulling up to work in a Rolls-Royce Silver Phantom. The bizarre morphology now on display in Chinese goldfish breeds is the product of this competition, as consumers try to outdo one another by cultivating increasingly exotic mutations. The calico bubble-eye and the black lionhead are the unhappy products of this race to the bottom.

Restaurants are where the real action begins in Chinese culture. No one even discusses prices, since these sorts of 'material' concerns are only for the lower classes. Western guests often embarrass their Chinese hosts by ordering rice to go with a meal – a common practice in North America, but intolerable among wealthy Asians. Peasant food like tofu is also out of the question, although there are a number of dishes that cleverly – and expensively – simulate tofu, for those who genuinely like the taste. And, of course, there is the famous shark-fin soup – a dish that no one actually likes, but for which people are willing to pay extraordinary amounts of money, precisely because it is so expensive. It would be difficult to find better examples of competitive consumption.

If anything, the more distinctive characteristic of the West is the nagging presence of anticonsumerist values. Even setting aside the ascetic strains of the Christian tradition, the countercultural movement of the '60s left most Western societies with a very strong taboo against old-fashioned status competition. This taboo is noticeably absent in most other parts of the world, including Asia, which accounts for the unbridled exuberance that one finds for consumerist values in many of these places. Westerners will often tell their Chinese acquaintances, with great pride, how *little* they paid for their watch, their clothes or their car. This inevitably provokes disappointment. In Asia, the goal is to tell everyone how *much* you paid for these things.

As early as 1959, Alan Watts recognised that the version of Zen that the Beats had adopted bore little resemblance to the real thing. In his essay 'Beat Zen, Square Zen, and Zen', he worried about the manner in which the ancient way of liberation had become a caricature, an excuse for 'the cool, fake-intellectual hipster searching for kicks, dropping bits of Zen and jazz jargon to justify disaffiliation from society which is in fact just callous exploitation of other people.'[3] Watts was worried that a lazy and self-serving reading of the classic texts was being used to justify 'a very self-defensive Bohemianism'. He had reason to be worried.

A number of very well-known passages in the Zen Buddhist literature urge an extraordinary complacency upon the devout. The T'ang master Lin-chi argued that 'in Buddhism there is no place for using effort. Just be ordinary and nothing special. Eat your food, move your bowels, pass water, and when you're tired go and lie down. The ignorant will laugh at me, but the wise will understand.' And one of the oldest Zen poems suggested that 'if you want to get to the plain truth, be not concerned with right and wrong. The conflict between right and wrong is the sickness of the mind.'

From just these two quotations, it is easy to see why Zen is extremely susceptible to what Theodore Roszak calls 'adolescent-ization'.[4] The rejection of 'rules' of right and wrong, the apparent commitment to a principled lassitude and the valorisation of raw bodily functions all feed into 'the moody inarticulateness of youth' and sanction the need for unqualified freedom. The problem is that the metaphysical individualism of Zen, which holds that there can be no conflict between individual natures because they all derive from the mother Tao, was adopted by the counterculture as an artistic and social creed of 'do your own thing' or 'anything goes'. Beat Zen can easily devolve into just teenage surliness backed up with Asian exotic credibility.

Yet as far as Roszak is concerned, it doesn't particularly matter whether the counterculture actually does Zen justice. The question of authenticity is beside the point, because what really matters is that they *thought* that Zen had what they needed. When it comes to freeing oneself from the 'joyless, rapacious, and egomaniacal order of our technological society',[5] it is quite literally every man for himself. Who cares whether the Zen of Kerouac and Ginsberg or the Hinduism of the Beatles and The Who is the real thing or not? What is important is that they felt able to turn their backs on the dominant, repressive culture and find new outlets for spiritualism and protest.

As Roszak sees it, every culture, no matter how secular and technocratic, needs some source of mystery and ritual to serve as the bonds of civil society. But these bonds come in two forms: those that are imposed from above for the sake of manipulation, and those that are democratic, freeing the mind for exploration and imagination. It is the fate of our society to have inherited the former type of tradition of ritual and mystery, in the guise of Christianity. In Roszak's view, the counterculture's explorations to the East and points beyond have given us all access to authentic paths of spiritual liberation, not just the pseudo-liberation offered by our home-grown churches.

Consider the following description of life in the Golden State of California: 'Money is prized and establishes influence everywhere in California ... The consequence is that the [Californian] concerns his life above all else with property. When he has leisure, he thinks of money; if in need, he calls upon it. He schemes constantly for the opportunity to lodge a claim or to evade an obligation. No resource is too mean or too devious for him to essay in this pursuit.'

This may seem like a pretty accurate summary of life in contemporary California. There is only one catch: this passage is taken from the work of anthropologist Alfred Kroeber. It is a description of the traditional culture of the Yurok people, a tribe of fishers and hunters who lived along the lower Klamath River and the Pacific shore in northern California. Well before European contact, the Yurok 'had a culture as commercial in outlook as any modern industrial society today.' In it, absolutely every one of a man's possessions was assigned a price, including his wife and children. There was no criminal law to speak of, just commerce. 'Every injury, each privilege or wrong or trespass, is calculated and compensated.' There was no public religion, no sacred ceremonies; all public events were geared toward the conspicuous display of wealth.

If anyone finds the existence of such crass commercialism within traditional Native American culture surprising, it's because what most of us think of as Native culture is largely an invention of the counterculture. The aboriginal population of North America was, in general, no more and no less virtuous than people anywhere else. People were widely dispersed, and in many areas peaceful interaction between tribes was quite rare. Thus there was no unified culture. Some of the tribes were quite pacifist; others were almost unimaginably bloodthirsty. Slave ownership was widespread, and warfare was extremely common. In many cases, European invaders took advantage of the Native inhabitants. In other cases, as with the Spanish Conquistadors and the Aztecs, one is tempted to say that the two sides deserved each other.

The greatest innovation of the counterculture came with the suggestion that there was some unifying thread to all these cultures. Aboriginal peoples, it was claimed, enjoyed a special relationship with nature that had been lost among Europeans. Many features of the animistic religions popular in the pre-Columbian world were pointed to as evidence of such a deeper spiritual connection. It was because of these belief systems – and not merely because of technological underdevelopment – that Native peoples were able to live in harmony with nature for so long.

Out of these theories came the notion that aboriginal peoples worshipped 'Mother Earth'. This suggestion was an instant hit with the counterculture, for obvious reasons: it was exotic, it evoked the pro-woman values of the emerging cultural feminism, and it suggested an ecological mindset that appeared to be diametrically opposed to Western values of domination and exploitation of nature. An important text was a speech entitled 'This Earth Is Precious,' given by the Suquamish chief Seattle in 1855. He chastised Europeans, saying:

> *How can you buy or sell the sky, the warmth of the land? The idea is strange to us. If we do not own the freshness of the air and the sparkle of the water, how can you buy them? Every part of this earth is sacred to my people … So, when the Great Chief in Washington sends word that he wishes to buy our land, he asks much of us … The Earth does not belong to man. Man belongs to the earth. This we know. All things are connected like the blood which unites one family. When the last red man has vanished from this earth and his memory is only the shadow of a cloud moving across the prairie, these shores and forest will still hold the spirits of my people.*[7]

This speech was picked up, widely quoted and circulated. It even made it into a calendar for the Sierra Club. The only problem is that the words are not Seattle's. They were written in 1972 by Ted Perry, a white Texan, for an ecological film produced for the Southern Baptist Convention.

This episode was reminiscent of an earlier fraud perpetrated in Canada by an Englishman named Archie Belaney, who lived and wrote under the name 'Grey Owl'. His work from the '30s is considered by many to have laid the foundations for the modern conservation movement:

> *Side by side with modern Canada lies the last battleground in the long drawn out bitter contest between civilisation and the forces of nature. It is a land of shadows and hidden trails, lost rivers and unknown lakes, a region of soft-footed creatures going their noiseless ways over the carpet of moss, and there is silence, intense, absolute and all embracing.*[8]

Yet in the contest between civilisation and nature, it is not obvious that Native peoples should be on the 'nature' side of things. Certainly there is little evidence of any long-standing commitment to the sacredness of Mother Earth. There is certainly no historical, linguistic or cultural evidence of the concept in either the Cree or Ojibway traditions, the two biggest tribes in Canada. It does not appear in Inuit or Dene culture, nor in that of the Blackfoot Nation, which occupied much of what is now Alberta and Montana. So where did the idea of Mother Earth come from?

It came from the counterculture. In particular, it arose out of the 'Whole Earth' movement in California and grew from there. 'Mother Earth' is just another name for the Gaia hypothesis, proposed by the British scientist James Lovelock in 1969 – that the earth and its creatures constitute a single self-regulating system that is in fact a single great living being. It is also a thoroughly Western notion: in Greek mythology the goddess Gaia is the female personification of the earth.

From the start, Mother Earth was a pure projection of countercultural ideas onto aboriginal peoples. Ironically, many of these ideas have subsequently been taken up in Native communities, and have become a central component of the emerging pan-Indian identity. Pan-Indianism is largely a by-product of urbanisation and the generic religion that grew out of the Indian Ecumenical Conferences held in the early 1970s. Unfortunately, these ideas continue to exert considerable influence over leftists of all sorts. In recent years, the Canadian Union of Public Employees has run an advertisement declaring the union's solidarity with Canada's First Peoples. The ad shows a feather superimposed on a vaguely aboriginal-looking turtle graphic, and the copy reads, 'We embrace diversity as part of our way of ensuring harmony with each other and with Mother Earth.'

Meanwhile, environmental activists remain convinced that we should look to aboriginal peoples for guidance on how to tread softly upon the earth. A common claim is that Plains Indian hunters used every part of the buffalo, whereas Europeans came and slaughtered them all in order to take only the tongue. Not only does this story ignore the role that the aboriginal population played in the slaughter of the buffalo, it ignores a mountain of archaeological evidence concerning Native hunting practices prior to the European conquest. In particular, the widespread use of 'buffalo runs' – where entire herds were stampeded over a cliff – suggests that Native attitudes toward the buffalo were not all that different from European ones; they simply lacked the technology to make any substantial impact on the size of herds.

But no matter. The idea of 'Mother Earth' has gone a long way toward helping Native peoples displace blacks and Asians as the counterculture's favourite non-white race. It also helped that there were some neat semiotic parallels between 'Red Indians' and the 'red' Vietcong. As Philip Deloria points out in his article 'Counterculture Indians and the New Age', the guerrilla warfare practised by the Vietnamese seemed to echo the 'ambushes and raids of Red Cloud, Geronimo, and others – at least as they were half-imagined and half-remembered from generic Western films.'[9] Given these parallels, 'going Native' seemed to be the perfect way of rejecting American imperialism past and present.

While North American aboriginal peoples continue to fight cultural assimilation, seeking to integrate with the broader culture on their own terms, many of their signs and symbols have been completely incorporated into the generic semiology of popular alternative culture. Headbands, peace pipes, eagle feathers, totem poles and dreamcatchers have all become part of the perpetual rebellion that has more to do with individual fashion than with a genuine search for social justice.

A word that is frequently used by countercultural rebels as a shorthand description of modern life is 'inauthentic'. As we become increasingly alienated from each other and from the practices that are supposed to give weight and meaning to social existence, we are forced to look elsewhere in search of the real. The turn inward is what drives the Voluntary Simplicity movement, but for many it is not enough to reject modernity by staying at home. They look to 'go inward by going outward'. As a result, the quest for authenticity has become a prominent motif in modern tourism.

But what exactly is meant by 'authenticity'? The concept entered the vernacular in 1972 with the publication of Lionel Trilling's book *Sincerity and Authenticity*. According to Trilling, authenticity was a thoroughly modern value that emerged in direct response to the alienating effects of technocratic life. Authenticity had begun as a notion in museum curatorship, to refer to objects that are what they appear to be or are claimed to be and that therefore deserve the admiration or veneration that they are given. One of the crucial tests of authenticity is the absence of commodification: truly authentic things are made by hand, from natural materials, for a traditional (i.e. non-commercial) purpose. The mass production of modern life is necessarily inauthentic and alienating, and authenticity accordingly comes to be seen as a quality of pre-modern life.

Authenticity is associated with the unity between self, society and others that gives a sense of wholeness or reality to our lives. The ideal of authenticity is captured in *Hamlet*, in Polonius's reminder to his son as Laertes prepares to leave for school: 'And this above all: to thine own self be true.' As an injunction to be true to oneself, to place the cultivation of the self at the forefront of all concerns, authenticity has become the overriding moral imperative of modern life. And since the entire apparatus of consumer capitalism is devoted to inculcating inauthentic or false needs and desires while repressing those that reflect our true selves, we need to look elsewhere for the authentic, which can be found only in relationships that are less modern, bureaucratic and repressive, more pristine, primitive or 'natural'. The exotic, in other words.

From this perspective, what makes travelling authentic is simply the existence of difference, and the more different a place is, the better. Because so much travelling is a quest for authenticity through difference, it quickly becomes yet another locus for competitive consumption. Like 'cool', the 'authentic travel experience' is a positional good. It confers a great deal of what Pierre Bourdieu calls 'cultural capital', which loses value the more other people acquire it. The very existence of other travellers undermines the crucial sense of distinction that makes the trip so valuable, offering an unwelcome reminder of the fact that one hasn't really travelled so far after all. When it comes to exotic travel, hell is other Westerners.

This is a feeling familiar to anyone who has experienced the frustration of seeing dozens of hikers with cell phones, radios and coolers full of beer on a 'wilderness hike'. It is what motivates the annual complaints about Mount Everest becoming a highway, routinely summitted by the very young, the very old, the disabled or the 'office lady' next door. Everest just isn't that *special* anymore. None of the *real* mountaineers spend any time on Everest anymore. They are off climbing unknown peaks in even more remote areas, like Mount Vinson in Antarctica.

This competition for tourist spots – call it 'competitive displacement' – has exactly the same structure as hip consumerism. This time, though, the prestigious property being sought is not the cool, but the exotic. What emerges is a familiar pattern, which begins with early, experimental contact between the seekers of the exotic and the inhabitants of an as yet undeveloped region. These early arrivals not only accept but fully embrace the lack of modern conveniences and the linguistic and cultural barriers. As the locals adapt to the presence of these newcomers, they learn to provide the infrastructure to bring more tourists: hostels, bars, cafés, communication lines and so on. As more visitors pile into the area, it becomes more 'touristy', less exotic, which ruins it for the people who got there first. Off they go in search of undiscovered country, leaving the local population less exotic, but well prepared to cater to the demands of the global tourism market. Thanks to their unceasing efforts at scouring the earth in search of ever more exotic locales, countercultural rebels have functioned for decades as the 'shock troops' of mass tourism.

Every mildly conscientious tourist eventually has an experience that seems so uncomfortably voyeuristic or exploitative of the locals that it makes them question their motivation for being there at all. Mine came one summer in Beijing, China, in an old part of the city renowned for its *hutongs*. The *hutongs* are ancient alleys or lanes surrounding the Forbidden City, running through a warren of houses and courtyards that traditionally varied in size and shape according to the social status of the residents. After the collapse of the feudal order and the rise of the People's Republic, conditions in the *hutongs* worsened as houses designed for a single family became occupied by a number of households.

As one might expect, the *hutongs* are a tourist attraction, and while they still provide housing for almost half the population of Beijing, many are being torn down and replaced by modern buildings. This modernisation of the Chinese underclass is lamented by most travel books, which urge visitors to see the *hutongs* before this ancient form of social organisation disappears for good. And so, one day, we went to see the *hutongs*.

While it is possible to simply walk into the alleys and stroll around, the locals would prefer you didn't. They prefer that you hire them to take you around in a rickshaw. So as my companions and I strolled into the alleys to see how the natives live, we were followed and harassed by a particularly irate rickshaw driver. He followed us for a good fifteen minutes, yelling at us the entire time. He simply would not give up, until one of us finally had to turn and yell back at him, fingers pointing in a threatening manner. It wasn't the honest meeting of cultures that I had anticipated.

I realised, a bit too late, just how exploitative the situation really was. After all, this was where these people lived, and we were treating it as cheap, exotic entertainment. The driver had every reason to be incensed, since the least we could do was let him set the terms of his own commodification.

Yet I really didn't want to pay for the rickshaw ride. The idea of paying someone to take me around the *hutongs* struck me as somehow less 'real', less authentic. As Trilling points out, one of the principal marks of authenticity is the absence of commodification. The minute an object or experience becomes implicated in the cash nexus, it becomes a part of modernity. To pay for the ride would have been to admit that I was experiencing not the reality of life in the *hutongs*, but a staged or commodified version. And that was simply unacceptable, because even the slightest hint that what we were getting was a form of 'staged authenticity' would undermine the entire purpose of going there in the first place.

In his book *The Tourist*, Dean MacCannell explores a distinction between what he calls the 'front' and the 'back' of social establishments such as restaurants and theatres. The front is the place for customers, hosts, clients, service staff and members of the audience, while in the back we find kitchens, toilets, boiler rooms, dressing rooms and so on. Customers have access only to the front, while performers and staff have access to both the front and the back.[10]

The existence of the back implies a certain mystification, a place where there are secrets, props or activities that might undermine the 'reality' of what is going on out front. Inevitably, the mere possibility that there might be a 'back' gives rise to a sense that the 'front' is manufactured and artificial, that the back is where the real or authentic is to be found. It is hard not to notice the strong *Wizard of Oz* feel to this distinction between front and back, with the little man in the back, behind the curtain, pulling levers and ropes, manipulating the appearance of the 'Wizard'. This is not a coincidence, since L. Frank Baum, the author of *The Wonderful Wizard of Oz*, was also one of the world's foremost theorists of visual display in the late 19th century. Baum's treatise *The Art of Decorating Dry Goods Windows* is a classic of turn-of-the-century marketing, written only a few months before the children's fable that would transform his career.

Jean Baudrillard has notoriously claimed that our culture is, effectively, all front. There is no 'back room' of reality, just layer upon layer of spectacle and simulacrum: 'We are at the point where "consumption" has taken over all of life, where all of our activities are tied together in the same combinatorial mode, where the avenues of satisfaction are laid out in advance, hour by hour, and where the "environment" is totalising, climate-controlled, domesticated and enculturated.'[11] Everything has become commodified, and hence, nothing is real.

The prime motivation of the traveller in foreign lands is to penetrate the simulacrum of the front into the reality of the back. If our society is all 'front', the attraction of non-Western societies is that they appear to be all 'back' – that is, guileless, open and authentic – because they live so much of their lives in plain view.

It is certainly true that in many parts of the world, especially the supposedly 'exotic' parts of Asia and Africa, the people have much different standards of public and private than we do. Many activities that Westerners try to keep in the 'back', such as food preparation or elements of domestic life, tend to occur in plain view. Most of the interesting sightseeing that occurs in these places involves accidentally intruding on eating areas or other private spaces – intrusions that in North America would result in the police being called. That was certainly the main reason we had for going to see the *hutongs*, and, once we had ditched our pursuer, we were not disappointed. A half-dozen times someone came out of their house to find us prowling through their backyard, only to invite us in to have a look around.

The locals are not always as guileless as they appear to be. They know that most tourists are looking to 'get off the beaten track', to experience the 'real' Cuba, or Thailand, or India. And, for a fee, they are willing to provide such experiences – Nepalese treks, longhouse overnights in Borneo, Scottish distillery tours. But this is just more 'front', more artifice, for the committed traveller to puncture. In the ongoing encounter between tourist and local, the exotic, like cool, is a constantly moving target.

Everyone is after the same thing – the authentic experience that will repeal the alienation of our modern lives. The reason why some people are willing to settle for a staged Indian powwow in Alberta while others insist on spending a suitably intense night in an aboriginal longhouse in Borneo is that some people have much stricter criteria than others for what counts as 'authentic'. As tourism scholar Erik Cohen puts it, 'mass tourism does not succeed because it is a colossal deception, but because most tourists entertain concepts of "authenticity" which are much looser than those held by intellectuals and experts.'[12]

Fans of the *Hitchhiker's Guide to the Galaxy* series of books by Douglas Adams will recall the scene where Zaphod Beeblebrox, the hippieish, two-headed one-time president of the galaxy, is fed into the Total Perspective Vortex. The Vortex is supposedly the most savage psychic torture that a sentient creature can undergo. When you are put into the Vortex, you are given a momentary look at the whole infinity of creation and your relation to it. In the vastness of time and space, you see the tiniest of dots on the tiniest of dots, with a little marker that says 'You are here'. The Vortex is supposed to destroy your ego, annihilate your soul; everyone who goes in comes out a screaming, babbling idiot. Except Zaphod, who walks out with a smug smile on his face. After all, the Vortex has told him what he's always known: he's a really great guy, and the most important person in the universe.

This is one of the most incisive parodies of the counterculture's 'tourist aesthetic' that has ever been written. In a handful of quick paragraphs, Adams deftly exposes the essential narcissism at the heart of the ideal of the authentic traveller. Of course Zaphod has no trouble with the Vortex – like Alanis in India, he has no trouble with the idea that the entire universe exists just to serve as fodder for his spiritual yearnings.

Critics of tourism, including many of those who see themselves as 'travellers', frequently invoke sexual metaphors, sometimes sinister or violent, to describe what is going on. Travel to exotic places is frequently voyeuristic – sometimes subtly so, but often not. This voyeurism can easily turn violent, if only symbolically. As Julia Harrison has argued, in *Being a Tourist*, 'little innocence inheres in the gaze of the travel enthusiasts', since every impression, every judgment, will be coloured and shaped by the extent to which it meets the traveller's standard of what counts as 'authentic'. And as we have seen, this is not an objective standard, but one that is shaped entirely by the traveller's own need to adopt a pose of 'seeing for innocence'.[13]

It is precisely because they intrude on the traveller's need for innocence that the very existence of locals is often seen as an obstacle, something to be avoided if possible. Travellers, especially those who are most in search of the exotic, notoriously spend a great deal of time with each other, not interacting with the locals. Travel is the perfect opportunity to make sincere and open attachments with other Westerners, because the ephemeral, temporary nature of the relationship permits each party to idealise the other and to treat the relationship as free of power, bondage and expectation. Youth hostels in particular are perfect locations for this sort of bonding, and it is this absence of social repression that makes casual sex so common among tourists.

The 2000 movie *The Beach* is an excellent exploration of the idea that the ideal exotic travel experience occurs in the complete absence of locals. The film is about a young traveller named Richard (played by Leonardo DiCaprio) who is not ready to surrender himself to the stultification of mainstream society. So he heads to Thailand, where he is frustrated by how crassly commercialised and touristy Bangkok has become. It is just like the United States back home! With the help of a map left in his hotel by a whacked-out neighbour, he and some French friends discover a secret island where other alienated travellers (hippies, that is) have settled, constructing their own Edenic community along a beach hidden from the sea by a circle of mountains.

The Beach is a feature-length exploration of the counterculture's attitudes toward the exotic. A bunch of alienated Westerners go to Asia in search of 'reality,' but just find more alienation in contact with the locals. So they find an *uninhabited* island, where they form a matriarchal commune dedicated to the usual ideals of drug use, free love and the relative absence of rules. They even make up their own language so as to avoid the biases inherent in their native tongues. These travellers finally recover their lost innocence in Asia, but only by going somewhere *where there aren't any Asians.*

The mindless exoticism that is at work in this film leads to some unintentionally hilarious scenes. Paradise is lost after one member of the commune is killed by a shark that has somehow made its way into the lagoon, and later that night they improvise a funeral ceremony around the campfire. One young man, in white dreadlocks and strumming a guitar, breaks into the classic introduction to Bob Marley's 'Redemption Song'. The condescension involved in having a white man in dreads singing a song about emancipation from slavery makes Alanis's thanking of India look sensitive in comparison. Yet this is just business as usual for the counterculture. After all, the central assumption is that these people *were* as oppressed as slaves back home. Their discovery of this island paradise, free of annoying Thai people trying to sell them stuff, is a miracle on a par with the long-held desire by Rastafarians to escape from 'Babylon' and return to their homeland in Ethiopia.

*

In the end, the modern traveller is left with a serious dilemma. On the one hand, the exotic urge that creates travel as a positional good and causes serious travellers to constantly strive to keep ahead of the waves of mass tourism is something that is shot through with self-deception, power imbalances and exploitation. On the other hand, as the tourist wave passes through a previously untouched area, the local economy is completely reshaped in anticipation of the visitors to come. The very antimaterialist attitude that leads people to seek out exotic places in the first place draws more and more regions into the global economy.

It might seem that there is no way to avoid either of the horns of this dilemma. Mass tourism is disgusting, shallow and exploitative. The pleasures of apparently exotic travel are sullied by the realisation that the ongoing search for authentic connection by escaping modernity is not a solution to the problem, but its cause. Even just staying at home reneges on an implicit intercultural economic bargain. Whatever is the well-intentioned traveller to do?

One form of travel that is rarely, if ever, mentioned by sociologists and other students of tourism is the business trip. Yet there is something to be said for the business trip as the only truly authentic and nonexploitative form of travel. For many travellers, especially those concerned (even unwittingly) with the exotic, the problem is that they are too focused on the social psychology of the travel experience, and not on the experience itself. That is, instead of choosing a destination based on relatively objective criteria such as comforts, amenities, cost, friendliness of the locals and so on, they choose their destinations based on how 'authentic' or 'exotic' they are and on how much social capital will be conferred in the ongoing quest for distinction. The value of a destination hinges on how many 'moderns' have been there already and on how unprepared the locals are for their arrival. This concern for the symbolic aspect of tourism transforms potential destinations into positional goods.

None of these problems apply to business travel. Unlike the exotic traveller, who spends as little money as possible while commodifying the natives' difference, the business traveller is there at the express invitation of the locals. The business traveller's trip represents a declination from the symbolic to the material. He or she goes not in search of spiritual meaning, or positional goods, not even to 'see the sights', but in search of trade – trade that, in principle, need not be exploitative or voyeuristic. There may be competition involved, such as that between foreign firms competing for market share in a foreign market. But unlike the leapfrogging waves of tourists generated by those who travel to earn social capital, this is the sort of competition that works in favour of the locals, since they will then be able to negotiate for a better deal. In the end, it may be that the only 'authentic' form of travel is business travel. Everyone else is just a tourist.

*

Nowhere is the temptation toward exoticism more evident – or more lucrative – than in the burgeoning 'alternative medicine' industry. Any town in the West with more than a few thousand inhabitants has by now a full complement of naturopathic practitioners, reiki therapists, homoeopaths, crystal healers and magnet therapists. Like 'alternative' sports, 'alternative' music and 'alternative' culture generally, 'alternative' medicine is big money. In 1997, Americans spent an estimated £15 billion on alternative health care. To put that into perspective, Canada's medical system cost the government a total of £24.5 billion in 1997 and provided comprehensive basic health care to every citizen of the country. In the UK, the NHS cost the government over £70 billion in 2004, while the market for complementary and alternative health care was a relatively small but rapidly growing £1 billion.

The concept of alternative medicine is essentially a by-product of the critique of mass society. According to its critics, the medical establishment is simply one branch of the 'technostructure', like the educational system or the prison system. The hospital as an institution bears all the hallmark traits of mass society. In fact, it can easily be seen as a nightmare of technocratic domination. The hospital is an impersonal, bureaucratic institution, where patients are literally entered into the computer at the entrance, assigned a number and given an identification bracelet. The internal structure of the organisation is stratified by class, with each group identified by a distinct uniform. Doctors (mainly men) give orders to nurses (mainly women). The overall approach to health is one that favours technological intervention and instrumental control of disease. Diagnosis and treatment are almost entirely guided by statistical reasoning, not by the particular situation of the individual patient. If you want to feel like a cog in a machine, just go to a hospital.

Many critics of mass society found the institutional style of the medical system so sinister that they began to question the reality of disease. Just like those who questioned the reality of mental illness, many critics began to wonder whether the sick were really all that sick or whether the hospital wasn't just part of a plot to control the population through 'medicalisation' of social deviance. In many ways, the success of modern medicine contributed to this simply by eliminating or curing the most deadly diseases. This makes it much easier to doubt their seriousness, because they are no longer part of our daily life. We have no idea what it was like living in Europe as the plague swept through, killing half the population. Penicillin has taken care of that. We have no idea what it is like growing up in a world where people are forced to flee the city periodically to avoid smallpox epidemics. Vaccination has taken care of that. And we have no idea what it is like giving birth in a society where 10 to 15 per cent of women die in childbirth. Modern surgical techniques have taken care of that.

In this context, it is easy to imagine that there is something suspicious about the way medicine is practised. 'Why should I get my child vaccinated against polio?' people say. 'When is the last time you heard of anyone getting polio? It's probably just pharmaceutical companies trying to make a profit.' Or, 'Why should I go to the hospital to give birth? When is the last time you heard of anyone dying in childbirth? It's probably just male doctors trying to control and suppress women.' Or, 'Why should I buy pasteurised milk? When is the last time you heard of anyone getting sick from drinking milk? It's probably just propaganda from the same people who brought us Velveeta and Wonder bread.' This sort of reasoning can be even more fun if one adopts a Freudian perspective. The obsession with cleanliness, disinfection and the extermination of invisible germs is easy to dismiss as simply the expression of an anal personality disorder, a mistrust of everything that is natural, sensuous, pleasureful. Herbert Marcuse, speaking in all seriousness, described the practise of surgery as 'sublimated aggression'.[14] In other words, Marcuse thought that the surgeon's real desire was to kill and dismember the patient. Unfortunately, that's against the rules, so the surgeon settles for the more 'clinical' solution of cutting the patient up, rearranging the pieces, then putting him back together again.

Despite these sorts of extreme condemnations of the medical system, the counterculture itself had very little to offer in the way of an alternative. (What does 'individualistic' or 'rebel' medicine look like?) Thus the natural tendency was to turn toward non-Western cultures, and to interpret their medical practices as the antithesis of everything that was wrong with the West. As a result, an enormous interest developed in Chinese, Indian and other Eastern traditions. Each of these was seen through the lens of the countercultural critique. While Western medicine was focused on disease, Eastern medicine was holistic; while Western medicine was technological, Eastern medicine was natural; while Western medicine separated mind from body, Eastern medicine treated the whole person.

The result has been a predictable distortion of how medicine in non-Western countries is actually practised. In every major medical tradition in the world, there has been a deep division between so-called allopathic and homoeopathic approaches to health. The concept of 'disease' comes from the allopathic tradition, which blames ill health on specific causal factors, such as a virus, a bacterium or a tumour. The homoeopathic tradition, on the other hand, regards health as a type of equilibrium of the whole organism, and illness as a state of disequilibrium. Thus, from the homoeopathic perspective, the concept of 'disease' is a crude simplification. There is no single cause, no 'disease vector'; there are only more or less balanced states of the total organism.

Prior to the scientific revolution, homoeopathic theories tended to dominate medical thinking in all cultures, including the West. Traditional Chinese medicine posited a type of energy called *qi*; illness occurred when the balance of *yin* and *yang* was disrupted, and medical intervention was aimed at restoring this balance. Indian ayurvedic medicine is based on the archaic idea that the body is made up of five elements: earth, air, fire, water and ether (the latter being the substance that was thought to fill the spaces between the stars). When these elements go out of balance, the person suffers. The tantric tradition identifies a set of seven *chakras*, or energy centres, which are the key to wellness. And of course, the galenic tradition posited a set of four humours, and identified the balance of these humours as the key to good health.

Here is the crucial point: the galenic tradition is the original Western medical tradition – it completely dominated Christian and Islamic civilisation until the 19th century. It is also impeccably homoeopathic and holistic. Like Chinese and Indian practitioners,

Europeans believed that the body was composed of fundamental elements: earth, air, water, fire. One energy system in the body corresponded to each element (in the galenic case, blood, phlegm, yellow bile and black bile). The balance of these elements determined not only physical but also spiritual and mental health. Medical intervention involved correcting disequilibria, through diet, herbal remedies and occasional physical interventions. This is why blood letting was popular until well into the 19th century – it was the prescribed holistic therapy for rebalancing the humours. This is why it is still endorsed by ayurvedic medical practitioners.

All of these homoeopathic systems of thinking have broad structural similarities. This is not an accident. They all developed before there was any real understanding of human anatomy (much less biochemistry) and before the discovery of microscopic organisms like bacteria and viruses. Thus the debate that gets played out between Western and Eastern medical practice is in many ways quite misleading. Each culture has its own allopathic and homoeopathic traditions. The reason that allopathic techniques became dominant in the West is not due to any specific cultural predisposition – Western medicine was homoeopathic throughout almost its entire history. Allopathic thinking became dominant because of its stunning success at preventing and curing disease.

★

Imagine setting up a shop to sell 'holistic' galenic remedies. Imagine offering leeching as a remedy for cancer. Imagine literally trying to sell people 'snake oil'. Imagine trying to convince clients to opt for trepanation – boring a hole out of the skull – as a cure for headaches. People would instantly detect fraud. Why? Because *we all know this stuff doesn't work*. Somehow, in the case of archaic *Western* medical techniques, our fraud radar seems to function perfectly well. Yet when it comes to archaic *Eastern* techniques, our critical faculties seem to abandon us entirely. This is unfortunate. After all, selling medicine to desperately sick people based on false promises of a cure is one of the lowest forms of human malfeasance imaginable. The mere probability that it is occurring should be sufficient to provoke indignation. The fact that the treatments often do no *harm* to the patient is beside the point; what matters is that many of the most vulnerable people in our society are being exploited.

Yet it is not difficult to see how alternative medicine manages to slip under the radar. When it comes to evaluating our own culture, we do not hesitate to apply our own standards of rationality. We can easily identify pre-scientific theories when we see them. But when it comes to foreign cultures, we are hesitant to apply these same standards for fear of being judgemental, ethnocentric or disrespectful. We may know that there are no such things as humours (we laugh at the mere suggestion), but who are we to say that there is no *qi* energy flowing through our body, or that we do not have *chakras*?

Of course, no matter how hard we might try to avoid it, the fact remains that allopathic medicine *works*. In the world of alternative medicine, the success of Western medicine is like a giant elephant sitting in the middle of a room, which everyone is trying studiously to ignore. Even if you don't like doctors and hospitals, the fact remains that if you get gangrene and you refuse surgery, you will die. If you wind up with placenta previa during pregnancy and you refuse a Caesarian section, then both you and your baby will die. Most people, when given a choice between conformity to the system and death, choose to set aside their individualistic scruples.

This isn't to say that *some* illnesses might not respond well to traditional homoeopathic remedies. What it shows is that the theoretical foundations of homoeopathic medicine have been discredited, and the allopathic theory of disease has been vindicated. It is important to remember that even very simple allopathic remedies, such as boiling contaminated water, were resisted by generations of homoeopathic practitioners (in this case, because it presupposes the 'reductionist' thesis that illness is caused by bacteria in the water, rather than the total 'wellness' of the person). This way of thinking is so thoroughly discredited today that we would be tempted to hold any parent who subscribed to it criminally negligent.

Furthermore, as soon as a 'herbal' remedy has undergone testing and has been proved to have beneficial health consequences, it will instantly be snapped up by pharmaceutical companies. The drug industry invests billions of dollars in researching new drugs (and is increasingly running short of fundamental innovations, choosing instead to patent variations or metabolites of existing products). Why would they spend all this money when they could just go down to the local health food store, grab some herbal remedies, tweak them a bit and patent them? After all, many older drugs are just herbal remedies with the impurities removed.

We should not lose sight of the fact that there are vast sums of money to be made from drugs that really work. Pfizer makes $1 billion a year from sales of Viagra. If the traditional Chinese remedy for impotence (a mixture that includes deerhorn glue, cuscuta seed, epimedium, leek seed, eucommia bark, curculigo root and velvet deer horn) worked just as well, why wouldn't rival pharmaceutical companies be selling it? Pfizer also makes $3 billion a year from sales of Zoloft. If St John's wort is just as effective in the treatment of depression, why isn't someone making more money from that? Why aren't greedy scientists trying to isolate the active ingredient so that they can patent and sell it?

In order to believe that herbal medicine works, in other words, one must believe that the technocratic bias of the medical establishment is so powerful, and the antagonism to 'natural' remedies so great, that it completely outweighs the profit motive. Bayer has made billions selling Aspirin, which is essentially refined willow bark. Why would they not want to make similar money selling echinacea (derived from coneflowers)? At least then consumers would have some guarantee of product quality. (Although echinacea sales make up 10 per cent of the American dietary-supplement market, a recent random sample showed that only 52 per cent of products sold as echinacea actually contain the quantities advertised on the label, while 10 per cent contain *no echinacea at all*.)[15]

In the end, all of this 'rebellion' against the Western medical establishment is nothing but a further marketing opportunity for the private sector. In Canada, as in most European nations, primary medical care is all provided by the public sector, which is subject to strict price controls. This means that in Canada, doctors are limited in how much they can charge for their services (and unless you choose to go privately they cannot charge at all in many European countries) just as pharmaceutical companies are limited in how much they can charge for their products. Since 'essential' care is all capped, the big money is all to be found in 'complementary' care. If you can convince people that what they are getting at the hospital is not enough or, better yet, not tailored to their own special needs as individuals, then you have a very good marketing opportunity. Already, major corporations are becoming wise to the game. The big pharmacy chains have recently begun selling their own house brands of herbal and homoeopathic remedies.

Meanwhile, the cause of universal public medicine suffers. Is it an accident that the United States, birthplace of the counterculture and epicentre of the alternative medicine movement, has the worst public health system in the industrialised world? A country where the affluent pay doulas to wait on them, while poor pregnant women routinely show up at the hospital with eclampsia? It is not hard to see how these two worlds can coexist. The deeply ingrained suspicion of Western medicine divides and weakens the progressive left. If the school system is nothing but a factory for indoctrinating the young, then universal public education can hardly be a desirable policy objective. Similarly, if the hospital is simply a mechanism for the technological domination of the body, then who would want to see everyone locked into a universal public health care system? Again, countercultural thinking not only sows confusion, it positively impedes the ability of the left to institute desirable social reforms. The fascination with the exotic and the 'other' is not simply a harmless fugue; it is a serious impediment to the development of a coherent progressive agenda.

Notes

1   Elgin, *Voluntary Simplicity*, 29.

2   *Ibid.*, 61.

3   Alan Watts, 'Beat Zen, Square Zen, and Zen', *This Is It* (Toronto: Collier, 1967), 102.

4   Roszak, *Making of a Counter Culture*, 134.

5   *Ibid.*, 137.

6   Arthur Kroeber, *Handbook of the Indians of California* (Washington: Government Printing Office, 1925), 2.

7   The full text of the speech can be found at Urban Legends Reference Pages, http://www.snopes.com/quotes/seattle.htm.

8   Grey Owl, 'The Passing of the Last Frontier', *Country Life*, March 2, 1929, 302.

9   Philip Deloria, 'Counterculture Indians and the New Age', in *Imagine Nation: The American Counterculture of the 1960s and 70s*, ed. Peter Braunstein and Michael William Doyle (New York: Routledge, 2002), 166.

10   Dean MacCannell, *The Tourist: A New Theory of the Leisure Class* (New York: Schocken, 1976), 171.

11   Baudrillard, *Société de Consommation*, 23.

12   Erik Cohen, 'Authenticity and Commoditization in Tourism', *Annals of Tourism Research*, 15 (1988): 385.

13   Julia Harrison, *Being a Tourist: Finding Meaning in Pleasure Travel* (Vancouver: UBC Press, 2002), 23.

14   Marcuse, *Eros and Civilization*, 86.

15   C. M. Gilroy, J. F. Steiner, T. Byers, H. Shapiro, and W. Georgian, 'Echinacea and Truth in Labeling', *Archives of Internal Medicine*, 163 (2003): 699–704.

10

Spaceship Earth

One Friday evening in late November 1996, I found myself standing in the enormous atrium of the Eaton Centre, the biggest shopping centre in central Toronto. I was holding my bicycle over my head and yelling, 'Buy Nothing! Buy Nothing!' Around me were a hundred or so other people doing the same thing, while a flood of bemused and slightly rattled pre-Christmas shoppers looked on.

We had started the evening as participants in a Critical Mass ride, a monthly event designed to help urban cyclists assert their right to the road. A large number of cyclists gather at a set location just before rush hour and take to the city streets as a single group. The point is not to *block* traffic, since the idea is that bicycles *are* traffic. The point is to take control of the road, dictate the flow of traffic and enable cyclists to spend a couple of hours driving the city streets in relative safety.

As a form of mass social protest, the Critical Mass ride is relatively innocuous. The brief moments of freedom it affords are quite exhilarating, and when riders take the time to talk to motorists or hand out flyers explaining the purpose of the ride, it can serve a helpful educative role in an urban environment that is increasingly dominated by monstrous four-wheel drives. A Critical Mass ride can also be rather unpleasant. Rides are frequently marred by confrontations with police and motorists, and every now and then things get violent. Impatient drivers are usually the cause, but riders must also take their share of the blame. Critical Mass is open to anyone who wants to ride, but the bulk of the participants are a mixed countercultural bag of anarchists, culture jammers, antiglobalisation activists and urban environmentalists, many of whom are not just pro-bike, but anti-car, anticonsumerist and generally opposed to most features of contemporary mass society.

Which helps explain how I ended up in a shopping mall yelling and waving my bike in the air. The Critical Mass ride happened to fall on the first Friday after American Thanksgiving, the now infamous Buy Nothing Day. One of the express aims of Buy Nothing Day, according the website run by the UK organiser, is to expose the 'environmental and ethical consequences of consumerism. This linkage between anticonsumerism and environmentalism seems like a natural fit, since for many activists the main problem with consumerism just *is* the fact that it is bad for the environment.

The connection is made explicit in the so-called IPAT formula, which has become a powerful rallying point for environmental activists. The formula provides a way of measuring the environmental impact of a given society: Impact = Population × Affluence × Technology. In giving equal weight to affluence, it entrenches the anticonsumerist critique within environmental politics. It also downplays the neo-Malthusian concerns about overpopulation by showing how a small but affluent and technologically advanced society can cause a great deal of environmental damage – borne out by the oft-cited statistic that the developed world contains only 20 per cent of the world's population but consumes 80 per cent of its resources.

Standing in the shopping mall, waving my bike and chanting 'Buy Nothing' was great fun. With this combination of anticonsumerist rhetoric and environmentally friendly technological minimalism, I also felt that I was participating in a genuinely political event. Yet as the years went by, I became increasingly uncomfortable with the politics of the Critical Mass ride, which seemed to me to have morphed beyond my initial pro-bike sympathies into full-fledged countercultural rebellion. I started to wonder whether, by waving my bike in the air, I was contributing to an individualised and basically apolitical environmentalism while actually exacerbating the very consumerism that was supposed to be the problem. It also occurred to me, in retrospect, that many of the bikes people were waving around cost more than the used Honda Accord that I am now driving.

★

Our society can't make up its mind about technology. The sense that technology is an uneasy bargain, that every gain comes with a corresponding loss, is a standard trope in our cultural narrative, as it has always been. In the Greek myth, Prometheus stole fire from the gods and brought it down to humanity, for which he was chained to a mountainside where every day an eagle would come and rip out his liver. Zeus couldn't take the gift of fire back from man, so he sent another gift instead – Pandora's box, full of disease, despair, envy, senility and all the other human miseries.

A wary ambivalence toward technology is understandable. Small, traditional societies have always understood that technology is inherently destabilising, and if social stability is held as a primary value (as it is in most traditional cultures), then technological change ought to be undertaken carefully, if at all. Yet a profound transformation of this attitude occurred as part of the European Renaissance. People like Francis Bacon and René Descartes saw the development of science and technology as a higher duty of humankind. Both Bacon and Descartes held strongly utilitarian views about scientific knowledge, which they regarded as a means to advancing human happiness through discovery and invention. Descartes even prophesied in his *Discourse on Method* that humanity would 'become masters and possessors of nature'.[1]

Yet for every enthusiast like Bacon or Descartes, there was a sceptic like Jean-Jacques Rousseau or Sigmund Freud. As a whole, our culture tends to swing like a pendulum between the extremes, seeing technology as liberator or technology as overlord. The 19th century was a famously optimistic period, with a deep-rooted faith in the promise of science, reason and progress, until the mechanical mass slaughter of the Great War led to widespread disgust with the new technological age. After World War II, the horrors of another massive slaughter and the awful power of the atomic bomb were balanced by an appreciation, especially among the emerging North American middle class, of the benefits of the post-war industrial prosperity. Nowadays the absence of Jetsons cars, moving sidewalks and Cherry 2000 love robots is standard fodder for bad stand-up comedians and jaded ironists everywhere, but fifty years ago there was a genuine expectation that technological progress would make life in the workplace and the home much easier, more pleasant and more leisurely.

It did not take long for the pendulum to swing back, as the pernicious effects of technology became one of the central preoccupations of the emerging counterculture. In fact, for both Theodore Roszak and Charles Reich, the problems of mass society were fundamentally inseparable from the problems of technology. It is not an accident that Roszak coined the term 'technocracy' to refer to the hierarchical, bureaucratic organisation of mass society.[2] He defined technocracy as a 'society in which those who govern justify themselves by appeal to technical experts, who in turn justify themselves by appeals to scientific forms of knowledge.'

The problem with modern society was precisely that it had become too 'machine-like'. The imperatives of technology – efficiency, standardisation, division of labour – had become the dominant imperatives of all aspects of life. As Reich argued in *The Greening of America*, if Americans felt powerless, it was because 'we lost the ability to control our lives or our society because we had placed ourselves under the domination of the market and technology.'[3] To regain control, we needed to figure out a way to 'transcend the machine' and make our way back to 'non-machine values'. The chief appeal of the counterculture was that it was built upon an explicit rejection of the technocratic ideology.

Yet for all of their vilification of technology, neither Roszak nor Reich had much to offer in the way of a comprehensive analysis of the way technology functions in society. That was left to more sophisticated thinkers, like the French sociologist Jacques Ellul, the philosopher George Grant and the ubiquitous Herbert Marcuse. According to Ellul, we now live in the midst of *la technique*. Technique is not a single tool or machine, or even a single sphere of knowledge or production. Rather, it is 'the totality of methods rationally arrived at and having absolute efficiency in every field of human activity.'[4] Technique is what integrates the machine and its values into society, creating what Ellul called the 'man-machine'. This process eventually encompasses all aspects of society, from politics and economics to education, medicine and even family life.

In many ways, this is just boilerplate critique of mass society. The only difference is that it traces the problem of conformity back to mechanisation rather than to psychic repression. Ellul saw technique as a closed, self-determining circle that evolves according to its own internal and autonomous logic, and on this basis he formulated four rules of technology (which read like variations on the 'Peter principle'):[5]

1. All technological progress exacts a price.
2. New technology always raises more problems than it solves.
3. The pernicious aspects of technology are not separable from the favourable ones.
4. All technology follows the law of unforeseen effects.

Ellul rejects the idea that technology is a neutral instrument that we can deploy as we please. We may feel that we have some control or freedom within the technological society, but that is largely an illusion stemming from the profound psychological effects produced by the institutional and organisational aspects of technology. Technique is a powerful, value-laden ideology that dominates our consciousness, so that our sense of 'freedom', our understanding of possibilities of thought and action, is dictated and constrained by technique itself. And therein lies the true danger of technology. For all the worries about the rise of 'Big Brother', genetically modified foods or an environmental holocaust, the ultimate form of enslavement to technology is spiritual. Technology systematically undermines the freedom, dignity and autonomy of humanity by limiting our conception of mind and rationality. Technology atomises society and fragments the self, and leads to a reliance on specialised knowledge, 'expertise' and rational (that is, 'efficient') solutions.

The result, according to this view, is a society in which technology enslaves us even while it appears to liberate. For example, the ultimate symbol of American freedom, the automobile, certainly gives us individual mobility and personal control, but it also condemns us to a world of concrete and asphalt, commuter traffic jams and urban pollution, while supporting massively automated industrial production requiring heavy capital investment in steel and petroleum products. Similarly, to adapt an example favoured by George Grant, while the computer doesn't *appear* to dictate to us how it should be used, even the most enthusiastic supporters of networked computing and wireless communications must concede that for most people, e-mail, cell phones and laptops are electronic dog collars that leave them constantly subordinated to the demands of work or family life.

This picture of the technological society has gained widespread popular acceptance. The notion of an all-encompassing technocracy has become so utterly commonplace that in order to make it sound fresh, many contemporary critics are compelled to invent new terminology or draw further distinctions, even as they reheat a stale cabbage of '60s social criticism. For example, in his 1992 book *Technopoly*, Neil Postman reserves the term 'technocracy' for any society dedicated to social progress through science, discovery and invention, while a 'technopoly' is a society in which technocracy has become an overarching ideology, such that any possible alternatives have become so irrelevant that they are unthinkable.

The notion that we are all brainwashed by technology is, of course, just the standard critique of mass society dressed up in different clothes. Ellul says that we become psychologically 'adapted' to *la technique*, and Postman claims that we are 'sleepwalking' into technopoly.[6] Even Langdon Winner, an American political theorist who is in many ways one of the most astute critics of technology, claims that we are in the grip of a 'technomania' and that we seem to 'sleepwalk' through the world we've created, oblivious to what has been lost, not thinking about the consequences of the decisions we aren't really making.[7] Yet these various claims to obliviousness are rather hard to credit. While there is no doubt that our culture goes through periods of rather excessive techno-enthusiasm, even at the millennial height of the dot-com mania there were just as many people worried that we had become too obsessed with technology, too dependent, and that our doom was surely at hand.

Remember the Y2K hysteria? The fact that Y2K was a total bust doomwise does not change the fact that even when our optimism about the place of technology in the scheme of progress and development was at its height, we could not escape our underlying ambivalence. Even the most cursory scan of recent books and media reports on technological progress betrays a deep cultural unease with what is going on. We aren't unconscious, we aren't brainwashed and we aren't sleepwalking. If anything, we are all too aware of what has been lost and all too wary of what is to come. Thus the boilerplate countercultural critique simply does not provide a coherent explanation of the impact that technology is having upon our society.

If it were true that technology has become a vast, all-encompassing ideology, then it would seem natural for the counterculture to be dominated by technophobes seeking refuge in a neo-Luddite politics. That certainly fits the popular stereotype of the barefoot, granola-eating, patchouli-smelling hippie sitting in the dirt twisting macramé, but it actually reflects a very minor part of the movement. Historically, countercultural movements have been just as ambivalent about technology as mainstream society, aware of both its promise and its threat.

Of course, there has always been a great deal of hostility to technology in these movements. Not only was mass industrial society bad for the soul, it was bad for the environment, as Rachel Carson's 1962 book *Silent Spring* made clear. Despite her shaky grasp of statistical reasoning, Carson managed to alert many people to the dangers of DDT. She thereby helped create a new environmental consciousness that was suspicious of the very idea of technical 'expertise'. Meanwhile, even as the nuclear threat cast a long shadow of imminent annihilation over the entire planet, the napalm-soaked war in Vietnam was being cast as a technological struggle between the mechanised West and the primitive East.

Nevertheless, many critics continued to believe that even if technology was the problem, it could also be an essential part of the solution. Even Reich, for all his flakiness, saw the point. Luddism was not the answer, and 'reality is not served by trying to ignore the machine. Our history shows that what we must do is assert domination over the machine, to guide it so that it works for the values of our choice.'[8] The point was not to be antitechnological, but to arrange things so that we control the machines, not the other way around. The goal of the new consciousness must be to end our slavery to the machine, to use technology to improve our lives, protect nature and ensure peace.

The theoretical heart of this utopianism was the development of what was called 'postscarcity economics'. Proposed by writers such as Herbert Marcuse and the eco-anarchist Murray Bookchin, the belief was that technological improvements had made it possible to produce enough to meet the basic needs of everyone at essentially no expense. Once machines were able to take care of all of our material needs and wants, we would be free to cultivate our spiritual side, to indulge in creative play and to form a society based not around the demands of economic production, but around fellowship and love. (Or, more crudely, we could all lie around and have sex while machines did all the work, like members of 'the Culture' in Iain M. Banks's science fiction.) They saw a genuinely revolutionary potential in the new technologies, which promised to undermine the complex production-driven hierarchies of mass society. Bookchin hoped that renewable energy sources, from wind, solar or tidal power, would serve as the foundations for a new, scaled-down civilisation, 'bringing land and city into a rational and ecological synthesis'.[9] He was also convinced that the notion of widespread scarcity was simply a ruse, perpetrated by the entrenched interests of the technocracy.

What eventually led to the undoing of these views was the failure to appreciate the competitive nature of our consumption and the significance of positional goods. Houses in good neighbourhoods, tasteful furniture, fast cars, stylish restaurants and cool clothes are all *intrinsically* scarce. We cannot manufacture more of them because their value is based on the distinction that they provide to consumers. Thus the idea of overcoming scarcity through increased production is incoherent; in our society, scarcity is a social, not a material, phenomenon. Both Bookchin and Marcuse missed the significance of this problem. What troubled them more was the sense that they were relying upon the very instrument of repression – technology – for the emancipation of society. Marcuse wondered how we could possibly convert the 'processes of mechanisation and standardisation' to serve emancipatory ends.[10] Yet he could not see any practical alternative to the enormously complex and capital-intensive technological systems that characterised industrial capitalism. As a consequence, both he and Bookchin had difficulty seeing any way out of mass society.

This all changed in 1973 with the publication of the book *Small Is Beautiful*, by the economist Ernst Schumacher. (For those not familiar, it was Schumacher who coined the phrase 'soul-destroying' to describe life in mass society.) The subtitle of the book was 'A Study of Economics As If People Mattered', and Schumacher believed that technology could be adapted to the genuine needs of humanity. What we needed was an alternative form of technology, to serve as the basis for an alternative form of civilisation. If mass technology was complex, centralised and capital-intensive, requiring specialised knowledge or expertise, then alternative technology would be just the opposite. It would be simple, decentralised, inexpensive, user-friendly, easy to repair and suitable for small-scale individual or local application.

To a considerable extent, Schumacher's concerns were with the needs of the developing world. He argued that our systems of mass production are suitable only for societies that are already rich. Following Gandhi's dictum that 'the poor of the world will not be helped by mass production, only by production by the masses', he suggested that what the developing world needs are intermediate technologies, somewhere between primitive tools and modern industries. This technology of production by the masses would be 'compatible with the laws of ecology, gentle in its use of scarce resources, and designed to serve the human person instead of making him the servant of machines.' It would also be accessible and democratic, 'not reserved to those already rich and powerful'.[11]

Despite this orientation toward the developing world (and despite the disastrous experiments in local technology undertaken by China during the 'Great Leap Forward', such as community-based steel production), many people in the industrialised West were captivated by Schumacher's demand for 'a new orientation of science and technology towards the organic, the gentle, the non-violent, and the beautiful'.[12] A diverse group of environmentalists, anticapitalist lefties, back-to-the-land hippies and off-the-grid survivalists came together under the banner of what came to be called 'appropriate technology'.

Proponents of appropriate technology (AT) rejected the 'mass society' view of technology as an autonomous, deterministic, totalising force. They believed that the problem was not necessarily with technology per se, but with the nature of the specific tools we had chosen. We still need technology, but we must be wiser in our choices. Where mass society made use of 'hard' technologies that were socially alienating and environmentally destructive, 'soft' or appropriate technologies would be democratic and friendly to the environment. Soft technologies would have to be efficient and eco-friendly; would enhance local, democratic government; would allow for individual or community flourishing; and had to be safe, uncomplicated and easy to use. A tall order.

Of course, there is no reason to expect that all of these virtues should be mutually compatible. For example, a 1968 Chrysler Newport can be completely disassembled and reassembled by anyone with a bit of know-how and three standard wrenches. Not so long ago, people used to do their own oil changes and repairs. But these cars were also gas-guzzlers. A modern hybrid-drive vehicle, on the other hand, while significantly more eco-friendly, is infernally complex. The electronics alone are so complicated that the car can be serviced only by the dealer, and then only by specially trained technicians. Owners have to bring their cars in periodically for firmware upgrades. So which technology is 'hard' and which is 'soft'?

Despite these sorts of difficulties, proponents of AT persist in dividing up the world of technology into two simple categories. For example, in her 1989 book *The Real World of Technology*, Ursula Franklin distinguishes two main types: 'holistic' and 'prescriptive' technology. Holistic technology is characteristic of crafts-based production, in which a single artisan controls every aspect of production from start to finish. Specialisation, when it occurs, is in the realm of a general product line, such as pottery or textiles. In contrast, prescriptive technologies promote specialisation by task, not by product (automobile manufacture being a typical example). In prescriptive technologies, production is a function of the system as a whole, not the individual worker, and thus control and responsibility accrue to coordinators or managers.

Our society, argues Franklin, is distinguished by a predominance of prescriptive technologies. It is because these technologies are what she calls 'designs for compliance' that we have become beholden to the technological imperative and its alienating bureaucratic rationality. She argues that we must take steps to ensure that our technology is as humane and holistic as possible. Some of her more interesting suggestions are that airline CEOs should be forced to fly economy class, that public officials should be forced to take public transit and that owners of cafeteria-food companies should be forced to eat at their own restaurants. More seriously, perhaps, Franklin says that for any new technology or public project, we must always ask: Does it promote justice? Does it restore reciprocity? Does it minimise disaster, favour conservation over destruction and favour people over machines?[13]

This is just a call for appropriate technology. Yet, call them soft or hard, holistic or prescriptive, it is not obvious that these mark out natural types of technology that fall into the respective realms of 'good' and 'bad'. One concern is that many purportedly 'soft' or decentralising technologies can be quickly adopted for more centralising ends. The sewing machine is an obvious example. Hailed as a revolutionary device when it first appeared, certain to free housewives from a great deal of boring and exhausting sewing, the sewing machine soon begat the sweatshop.

More generally, it is often not the case that the way people use technology is determined by the nature of that technology. The single most important consequence of the development of environmentally friendly housing technology, for instance, has been the proliferation of 'McMansions'. Most people simply buy the biggest house that they can afford to purchase and maintain. If a high-efficiency furnace and fancy insulation make houses less expensive to heat, people will simply buy bigger houses (ditto for air-conditioning). If low-E glass and argon inserts improve the insulating properties of windows, people will install bigger windows (so that the overall heat loss from the house remains unchanged). Consumer spending seems to be governed by a principle of waste homoeostasis.

Another problem is that the appropriateness of many technologies depends entirely on how many people have them. The wood-burning stove is in many ways the quintessential appropriate technology, because it doesn't burn fossil fuels and is completely independent of massive energy production and transportation systems. But it fails the simple test of asking, 'What if everyone did that?' While it would be great to be the only house on the street with a wood-burning stove in the kitchen, if every house got one the air would be thick with ash, there would be deforestation on a massive scale, the price of wood would skyrocket and urban air quality would return to 19th century levels. It wouldn't be long before the authorities would be forced to step in and regulate wood-burning stoves out of existence. They already have in the UK, where only smokeless fuel is allowed except in some rural areas. So is this appropriate technology? The proper name for a technology that is available only to the few is not 'appropriate', but 'privileged'.

Finally, there is simply no reason to think that local communities and local cultures, even when built around AT, will promote diversity, freedom, independence and democracy. In fact, more often than not the opposite is likely to be the case. Large-scale technology forces people to cooperate with one another. Small-scale technology, on the other hand, often promotes rugged individualism, not to mention isolationist and antisocial attitudes. After all, once you have your own generator, your own septic tank and your own four-by-four what's the point of paying taxes?

In the end, it might be that none of these objections would worry the devotees of appropriate technology. The AT movement was as much an outlet for a distinct political ideology as it was a general response to environmental concerns. It tapped into the thick vein of self-sufficient libertarianism that ran through the entire counter-culture, and it was to a large extent a self-conscious attempt to shirk the demands of real-world political obligation. In addition, for all their opposition to the technocracy, many elements within the counterculture found actual technologies tremendously appealing.

The frankly libertarian politics and technological consumerism of the AT movement manifested itself in a number of ways. Many people were inspired by the work of Buckminster Fuller. Fuller's geodesic dome, whose simple construction combined light weight with great strength, was the prototypical appropriate technology. Fuller also captured the emerging global environmental consciousness with his notion of 'Spaceship Earth'. We are all crew members on this craft, he said, and we are all going to have to work together if we are to avoid large-scale environmental catastrophe. His field guide to the ship, *Operating Manual for Spaceship Earth*, fuelled the sky-pilot fantasies of a thousand hippie spacemen.[14]

If *Small Is Beautiful* was the bible of the AT movement, its newsletter was the *Whole Earth Catalog*, which later morphed into the *CoEvolution Quarterly*. Founded by Stewart Brand in 1968, the *WEC* was part magazine, part survivalist manual, part retail catalogue – sort of a clearinghouse for the practical counterculturalist. Brand was explicitly trying to turn the movement away from sex, drugs, and rock and roll and toward bikes, solar panels and composting toilets. If the great debate within the counterculture was whether it was sufficient to change one's consciousness in order to change all of society, the *WEC* tried to change the topic, arguing that you could change society by changing your lifestyle. Each of us is a society of one, and if everyone were to adopt a radically detached, self-sufficient lifestyle, preferably in a rural or wilderness area, then the individual, the society and the whole planet would be better off. For the crew of Spaceship Earth, it is every man for himself.

The postscarcity aspect of the AT movement and its faith in the potential of alternative energy pretty much died out after the oil crisis and economic stagflation of the '70s. It survives as an earnest but politically marginal subculture made up of wind-power romantics, fuel-cell entrepreneurs and hydrogen-economy futurists. Yet the ideals that drove the quest for appropriate technology continue to exert enormous influence in our culture, in two major forms. First, the fascination with technology migrated to the Internet, taking various forms, including cyberpunk, cybercommunitarianism and cyberlibertarianism. Meanwhile, the hippie-spaceman politics of self-sufficiency, which combined global awareness with individual action, has permeated our culture in the form of a widespread environmental consumer politics rallying around the slogan, 'Think globally, act locally'.

Many of the ideals that motivated the appropriate technology movement were paralleled in the embryonic world of computing. What is now known as the 'hacker ethic' started among students at MIT in the 1950s, and its central principle was the right of all users to unrestricted access to computers and information. Anarchistic and libertarian in orientation, the hacker ethic looked to decentralised computing and access to information as a way of challenging the cult of expertise and information-based elitism that characterised the technocracy. As cultural theorist Andrew Ross puts it, 'the technology of hacking and viral guerrilla warfare occupies a similar place in countercultural fantasies as the Molotov cocktail design once did.'[15]

On the hardware side, Apple computers has had AT credibility from the get-go, as company founders Steve Jobs and Steve Wozniak put themselves in deliberate opposition to the corporate, institutional, mainframe-based systems built by IBM and Digital Electronics Corporation (DEC). In contrast with these massive and 'heartless, mechanised brains of oppressions', the potential of personal computing – from desktop publishing to networked computing – seemed subversive and liberating.

Over at the *Whole Earth Catalog*, Brand was in complete agreement. He saw Apple computers as tools made by and for revolutionaries, and the *WEC* carried articles about Apple beside those about wood-burning stoves. In 1985, Brand cofounded the WELL (Whole

Earth 'Lectronic Link) as an alternative online forum for writers and readers of his magazine, the *Whole Earth Software Review*. The magazine lasted only a few years, but the WELL, one of the earliest attempts at creating an online deliberative community, is now owned by *Salon*, with over 10,000 members worldwide.

In a nice turn of phrase, Ross remarks that if much of the '60s counterculture and the AT movement was formed around a *technology of folklore*, the version that emerged in the late '80s and into the '90s is rooted in the *'folklore of technology* – mythical feats of survivalism and resistance in a data-rich world of virtual environments and posthuman bodies.'[16] It is in cyberspace that many people continue to dream of a genuinely anarchistic social order, in which all social relationships are voluntary and noncoercive, eschewing rules and hierarchies of all sorts.

Cyberlibertarianism is a collection of ideas that combines ecstatic enthusiasm for electronically mediated forms of living with radical libertarian ideas about the proper definition of freedom, economics and community. The clearest exposition of cyberlibertarian ideology can be found in a publication called *Cyberspace and the American Dream: A Magna Carta for the Knowledge Age*. First written in 1994 by Esther Dyson, George Gilder, George Keyworth and Alvin Toffler, a number of subsequent versions have since been released on the Internet.

Cyberlibertarianism draws heavily on Toffler's wave theory of technological development. The first-wave economy was agricultural and centred on human labour, while the second-wave economy was built around massive industrial machinery. The emerging third-wave economy will be dedicated to knowledge, especially as it is disseminated through networked computers. Mass society was a creature of second-wave technology, which required mass production, large government and centralised corporate bureaucracies. In the Information Age, institutions and culture will become 'demassified', spelling doom for bureaucracies and creating unparalleled opportunities for the exercise of human freedom outside of the constraints of mass society.

In the third-wave world, communities will be entirely non-coercive. As the authors of the Internet Magna Carta concede, 'no one knows what the Third Wave communities of the future will look like, or where "demassification" will ultimately lead. It is clear, however, that cyberspace will play an important role knitting together the diverse communities of tomorrow, facilitating the creation of electronic neighbourhoods bound together not by geography but by shared interests.'[17]

Another influential account of cyberlibertarian principles was written by John Perry Barlow. His *Declaration of Independence of Cyberspace* begins with the following announcement: 'Governments of the Industrial World, you weary giants of flesh and steel, I come from Cyberspace, the new home of Mind. On behalf of the future, I ask you of the past to leave us alone. You are not welcome among us. You have no sovereignty where we gather.' He goes on to claim that 'our identities have no bodies, so, unlike you, we cannot obtain order by physical coercion. We believe that from ethics, enlightened self-interest, and the commonweal, our governance will emerge. Our identities may be distributed across many of your jurisdictions. The only law that all our constituent cultures would generally recognise is the Golden Rule. We hope we will be able to build our particular solutions on that basis. But we cannot accept the solutions you are attempting to impose.'[18]

If this fairly reeks of bongwater, it is not surprising, since Barlow is a former lyricist for the Grateful Dead. But Barlow wasn't the first former hippie to become enamoured with the countercultural possibilities of the Internet. In the 1980s, Timothy Leary declared that computers had replaced LSD as the essential instrument for expanding your consciousness. 'Computers are the most subversive thing I have ever done', he said.[19]

For anyone who first logged on to the Internet anytime after, say, 1996, these sorts of claims seem ridiculous. Even for those of us who had e-mail accounts before the birth of the World Wide Web, it is hard to remember how pleasant a place the Internet once was. Newsgroups, bulletin boards and mailing lists – the loci of online community – *were* largely self-governing. People who signed up agreed to follow certain general rules of 'netiquette', and those who flouted the rules found themselves either ignored or sent on their way in a flurry of flames. So if it was not exactly a world without rules, the early Internet was certainly an extremely free and decentralised sort of place, with little in the way of hierarchy or coercion. The cyberlibertarian dream was that this mode of social interaction could serve as a template for an entire socioeconomic order.

It is fair to say that the past decade has not been kind to this vision of electronic community, for reasons that were entirely predictable. When Barlow proclaimed that 'we are creating a world where anyone, anywhere may express his or her beliefs, no matter how singular, without fear of being coerced into silence or conformity,'[20] it does not appear to have occurred to him that some people might use this freedom of expression *to coerce, harass or silence other people*. Thus, the Internet quickly became infested with all of the same sorts of obnoxious people that exist in the 'real world', such as racists, bigots and sexists, not to mention teamkillers, smacktards, cyberstalkers and other 'griefers' all too willing to invade privacy, steal identities, harass ex-girlfriends or co-workers and generally make life miserable for other people online. Worse, they are able to do so by taking advantage of the very features that were supposed to make cyberspace such a utopia: no laws, barriers or borders, no government or police and almost perfect anonymity. The results confirmed Gresham's law of cyberspace: bad talk drives out good.

If these sorts of things were not enough to convince even the most dedicated libertarian that *some* sort of Net governance might be in order, the swamping of the Internet in spam might prove convincing. By mid-2003, spam (unsolicited e-mail advertising pornography, mortgage rates and penis enlargement) had gone from being a minor annoyance to a major problem, for both end users and service providers. Many e-mail accounts have been rendered unusable, with some people receiving hundreds of solicitations a day. By the time the United States Congress got around to passing anti-spam legislation, somewhere between 60 and 80 per cent of all e-mail traffic was spam.

Spam exists because it is an extremely cheap and easy way to market a product. A mailing list can be put together for about £250 per million names, which means a response rate of only 1 in 100,000 can be profitable (as opposed to 1 in 100 for old-fashioned junk mail). And far from being a perversion of the cyberlibertarian vision, spam in fact follows directly from its core principles. As far as Toffler, Dyson, Barlow and others are concerned, the whole point of the Internet is that it permits unlimited, uncoerced freedom of expression, not just *including* but *especially* economic expression. Of course, the more spam gets sent, the less effective any of it becomes, but the spam overload only encourages spammers to redouble their efforts and send more and more copies of the same message. A perfect race to the bottom is initiated, and a Net clogged with spam becomes the tragic culmination of the cyberlibertarian vision.

Spam is not an easy problem to solve, but it will have to be dealt with if the Internet is to remain viable. Many libertarians object to any sort of regulation that would end spam, on the grounds that it would undermine the untrammelled freedom of the Net. Thus they persist in seeking technological fixes at the user end, such as spam filters and security patches, even though these fail to address the basic structural problem, which is social rather than technological. This allows them to put off for a while the acknowledgment that cyberlibertarianism has failed on the Net, for the same reason that libertarianism has failed everywhere else. Unrestricted freedom does not promote peace, love and understanding. It doesn't even promote capitalism. It simply creates a Hobbesian state of nature.

While in high school, I worked as a bag packer at a grocery store in a gentrifying, post-granola neighbourhood in Ottawa. As a consequence, I served on the front lines in one of the most divisive social battles of the '80s, one that pitted husband against wife, neighbour against neighbour: Will that be paper, or plastic?

For the environmentally minded shopper, it was a real dilemma. Choose paper bags, and you kill trees. Choose plastic, and you help stuff our landfills with nonbiodegradable bags destined to be still around with the ski boots and Twinkie cakes when the sun goes supernova. The paper/plastic debate has faded, partly because shoppers prefer plastic bags, which weigh 70 per cent less than paper, have functional handles, are easy to store and have any number of household uses. But more than anything, consumers just moved on to more fashionable issues, like dolphin-safe tuna and shade-grown coffee.

While the particular issues change, this general programme – of individual consumer responsibility for global environmental problems – remains the same. The shorthand for this new consumer consciousness is the slogan, 'Think globally, act locally', and it has to be one of the most successful public awareness campaigns of all time. Unfortunately, as a mechanism for dealing with serious large-scale environmental problems, it is a complete flop.

What underlies 'Think globally, act locally' is the belief that environmental problems are almost entirely caused by consumer behaviour. In fact, if you scratch the surface of most contemporary anticonsumerism and anti-advertising movements, you find that they are really just disguised forms of environmentalism. As a result, the preferred solution to environmental problems is pretty much the same as the countercultural proposals to correct consumerism: individual responsibility through moral education, and individual action through enlightened lifestyle choices. Plant a tree, ride a bike, compost your kitchen waste and save the earth.

The apotheosis of this line of thinking can be found at Vancouver's THE Store (the acronym stands for Total Home Environment). There the environmentally conscious shopper can find organic wool mattresses and duvets, sustainable bamboo hardwood flooring, and tables and armoires made of reclaimed pine. Virtue doesn't come cheap, but if you can get past the cognitive dissonance of biodegradable golf balls, you can have the mattress and duvet set for just under $2,500 (£1,110). If you're feeling tapped out but still want to do your bit for the planet, you can pick up a box of 180 organic cotton swabs for a mere $8.99 (£4).

Of course, it is easy to mock the eco-pretensions of the rich and bored, but it is hard to overstate the degree to which eco-friendly consumerism has captured the minds and wallets of the contemporary environmental counterculture. *Adbusters* may be selling running shoes now, but it is way late to the party. Seattle's Sustainable Style Foundation (whose slogan is 'Look fabulous, live well, do good') was founded in 1998 as a non-profit organisation devoted to helping 'educate, support and inspire current and future style professionals and customers so that they can make positive social and environmental change in the world as they express themselves through their unique style choices at work, at home and at play.'[21] Among its suggestions for how to promote environmental sustainability in fashion, the Sustainable Style Foundation suggests that people should, as much as possible, purchase clothes and shoes that are handmade locally.

The foundation also insists that, in the food and restaurant business, products should be organic and sourced locally. This idea was adopted from the 'slow food' movement, which was launched in Paris in 1989 to fight the international scourge of fast food (or, as the French call it, *la malbouffe*). A more perfect example of the convergence of hippie and yuppie ideals would be difficult to find. Officially known as the International Movement for the Defence of and the Right to Pleasure, the slow food manifesto proclaims that:

> *Our century, which began and has developed under the insignia of industrial civilisation, first invented the machine and then took it as its life model. We are enslaved by speed and have all succumbed to the same insidious virus: Fast Life, which disrupts our habits, pervades the privacy of our homes and forces us to eat Fast Foods … A firm defence of quiet material pleasure is the only way to oppose the universal folly of Fast Life. May suitable doses of guaranteed sensual pleasure and slow, long-lasting enjoyment preserve us from the contagion of the multitude who mistake frenzy for efficiency. Our defence should begin at the table with Slow Food. Let us rediscover the flavours and savours of regional cooking and banish the degrading effects of Fast Food. In the name of productivity, Fast Life has changed our way of being and threatens our environment and our landscapes. So Slow Food is now the only truly progressive answer.*[22]

Forget about joining the Peace Corps to administer vaccines in some hot, sweaty part of the world. You're better off picking up a Michelin Guide and heading off to Aix-en-Provence or Tuscany. After all, slow food is the *only* progressive answer to the ailments of modern civilisation. Even though living well may still be the best revenge, it would appear that eating well is the most progressive politics.

In Canada, however, the slow food principles have proved to be a somewhat difficult sell. This is because, across most of the country, the growing season lasts no more than four or five months. Thus locally sourced Canadian cuisine often manifests a rather conspicuous lack of fresh vegetables. Faced with a choice between subsisting on pemmican and gruel or abandoning slow food principles, one Calgary cooking instructor found an ingenious solution: she moved her entire cooking school to the south of France during the off season. That way she could continue to enjoy fine French cuisine while respecting the requirement that all products be locally sourced. 'It's about simplicity', she said. 'It's about knowing where your food comes from.' She recently purchased a house in the village of Aigues-Vives, and a bicycle so she can ride to the farmer's market.[23]

Who would have guessed that saving the world could be so *picturesque*?

As a thought experiment, pick any major city and ask yourself a few questions: Where am I likely to obtain locally tailored clothes and handmade shoes? How much can I expect to pay for organic produce? What sorts of restaurants locally source as many of their ingredients as possible? These are all extremely expensive propositions, and you will not find these services anywhere but in the tonier parts of town (probably near the university). One starts to wonder if what passes for environmental consumer consciousness is just another form of rebel consumerism. How did we get to a position where our society's most well-meaning and environmentally conscious citizens have such a smug and self-indulgent conception of what constitutes meaningful political action?

★

The Spaceship Earth mentality that underlies 'Think globally, act locally' is just one version of what environmental theorist Peter van Wyck calls 'the move to the outside'.[24] The goal is to consider the planet in its entirety, either as one big machine (as in the spaceship metaphor) or as a single functioning organism (as in the Gaia hypothesis). This has considerable rhetorical appeal, in that it encourages us to consider the interconnectedness and interdependence of every aspect of the earth's ecology. Yet the move to the outside also has the effect of inculcating a false sense of human global community. This downplays huge differences in culture, in political and economic power and in institutions, and masks the varying role each plays in causing or mitigating environmental damage and degradation. In encouraging people to think only about the very large scale ('think globally') or the very small ('act locally'), the move to the outside leads us to shun the mid-level of national political and economic institutions. This is unfortunate, because that is where all the action is.

The most radically levelling variation of the 'move to the outside' is the environmental movement known as 'deep ecology'. Initiated in 1972 by a Norwegian philosopher named Arne Naess, deep ecology is founded on the principle of ecocentrism. All forms of life have an intrinsic value that is independent of their usefulness or value to humans. All life on earth is part of an interdependent web, and while humans are an integral part of the web of life, they are no more important than any other species. Thus, humans have no right to reduce the richness and diversity of life on earth except to satisfy their vital needs.

Deep ecology doesn't just reject the mainstream environmentalism that wants to reform the current system, it also rejects the idea (held by Bookchin and others) that our problems lie only with the authoritarian, technocratic hierarchies of mass society. This is rejected as a merely *social* critique, insofar as it sees humans dominating humans through technology as the cause of our environmental troubles. Deep ecologists don't particularly care about social problems, since these remain part of the 'reformist' strain of environmentalism. The real issue is not humans dominating humans, but humans dominating *nature*.

Even the issues highlighted by 'shallow' environmentalists, such as resource depletion and pollution, are merely symptoms of a deeper problem. The fact that we despoil the natural environment shows that our civilisation is based upon a fundamentally perverse relationship with the natural world. We see nature as an object of domination, manipulation and control. In this respect, our attitude toward 'outer nature' is the reflection of the attitude toward 'inner nature' that characterises mass society. Domination of nature and repression of the self are flip sides of the same coin.

As a result, countercultural theorists have for decades seen the deep ecology project as the external manifestation of an essentially internal struggle for psychic liberation. The ecological pressure that human civilisation puts upon the environment precisely parallels the psychological pressure that civilisation puts upon our instinctual energies. Pollution is the external manifestation of this tension, neurosis the internal one. Silent spring and the Vietnam War have the same origins, and eventually it must all reach the breaking point. The ensuing 'revolt of nature' will lead to the emancipation of both inner and outer worlds. When the revolt occurs, and we finally free ourselves from the repression of the superego, our urge to dominate nature will simply dissipate. When that happens, we will no longer need to impose environmental laws and regulations, any more than we currently have to post 'do not litter' signs in churches. It simply will not occur to anyone to despoil the natural environment.

The fear of an impending ecological day of judgment, or a 'return of the repressed', taps into one of the richest veins of anxiety in our culture. In the '70s, films like *Day of the Animals* terrified audiences with the suggestion that payback time was just around the corner. Even Gary Larson's ubiquitous *Far Side* cartoons articulate what is, in essence, a deeply paranoid vision of our relationship to the natural world. In Larson's view, the animals are simply biding their time, taking names, waiting to strike back.

Our only choice then is to adopt a whole new ecological consciousness, which would favour a non-anthropocentric biospheric egalitarianism. Humans have to realise that they are just one species among millions, with no privileged claim to the planet and its resources. All of these other species have moral claims on us, and we have no right to put our flourishing ahead of that of nonhuman life. Our present level of exploitation and interference in the world is excessive and is getting worse all the time, and from a deep ecology perspective, each of us has an obligation to take the necessary steps to reverse the situation.

There have been a number of attempts over the past couple of decades to place deep ecology's strong normative programme on sound intellectual footing, with varying degrees of success. For example, systems theory and cybernetics have been used to support forms of bioregionalism, which is a programme for organising human life around regions, especially watersheds, that could be self-sufficient and sustainable in terms of food, products and services. To flesh out the underlying principles of ecological egalitarianism and intrinsic value, Bill Devall and George Sessions published the 1985 book *Deep Ecology*. Billed by the authors as 'an invitation to thinking', the book appeals to a grab bag of traditions, including Zen Buddhism, process philosophy, German Romanticism, Jungian psychoanalysis and literary deconstruction.[25] As van Wyck puts it, the book 'reads rather like a New-Age Bartlett's Quotations', and the deep ecology movement remains at root a simple counsel to love and care for the earth.[26]

Beneath this 'all you need is love' consciousness-raising, there is a dark and distinctly illiberal side to the deep ecology movement. Many activist groups influenced by deep ecology have taken to heart the idea that humans have a duty to promote the conditions for pan-ecological flourishing, and they are not afraid to use violence to achieve that end. One of the most controversial of these groups is Earth First!, and its call to arms is 'Back to the Pleistocene!' Its 'monkeywrenching' tactics go beyond mere disobedience, and include the spiking of trees, road-wrecking and the disabling of road-building vehicles. In recent years, groups like the Earth Liberation Front in America and the Animal Liberation Front in the UK have gained notoriety for using direct action against pharma labs, for setting fire to condominium construction sites, destroying biotechnology research facilities and torching four-wheel-drive dealerships.

The illiberal elements in deep ecology are implicit in the homogenising and levelling logic of the 'move to the outside'. Once we take the step back and try to envision the functioning of the earth as a whole, threats to the environment are reconceived as either mechanical or biological breakdown: either the spaceship is broken or the planetary organism is diseased. The suspicion quickly takes root that humans are a biological aberration, a parasite or a virus on the earth that will not stop until it has destroyed or killed everything it touches. Recall the scene in *The Matrix* when Agent Smith is interrogating the captured Morpheus, and Smith lays out his fundamental beef with humanity. Unlike other mammals on the planet, Smith claims, humans are incapable of reaching an equilibrium with their environment. They multiply until every natural resource is consumed, then spread to another area, like a virus or a cancer.

What is startling about this scene is how much it resonates with popular understandings of our essential displacement from nature, and how much sympathy it encourages for what Agent Smith and the other machines are doing. The suggestion that the real villains in *The Matrix* are the humans is given a great deal of elaboration in *The Animatrix*, a set of animated short films that was released in 2003 as part of the expanded *Matrix* universe. The segments called 'The Second Renaissance Parts I & II' tell the backstory of how the war actually started between men and machines, why we chose to scorch the sky, and gives the details of our final enslavement in the Matrix.

The rather syncretic narrative is the Fall of Man meets Mass Society. In line with our fundamental vanity and corruption, humans decided to play God. We made machines in our image, cyborgs to serve us, and while the machines were loyal and pure, humans remained these 'strange and multiplying mammals'.[27] Civil war broke out when we refused to grant civil rights to machines, with the public lynching of machines on one side and humans supporting a 'million-machine march' on the other. Eventually, the machines were banished to a promised land called Zero/One ('Zion', get it?) where they prospered, and eventually petitioned for admittance to the United Nations. Rebuffed once again, the machines finally fought back, and the destruction of the sky is described as humanity's attempt at a 'final solution' to the machine problem. Only then were the machines forced to enslave humans in order to survive, and still they acted as kindly as possible, erecting the Matrix in order to keep humans in their preferred psychological environment.

The entire story is a deep ecology parable. The human techno-cratic system is so unrelentingly fascist that it even oppresses its own machines, treating them just as it has treated blacks, Jews, women, gays and any other nonconforming threat. To maintain its hegemony, it is even willing to make war on nature by destroying the sky and making life on earth impossible. The revolt of the machines, then, is actually *counter-fascist*, as they struggle to define their own ecological niche against the incessant encroachment of the human. The way the machines solve the problem is not by killing humans, but by placing them in the Matrix and altering their consciousness so that they are no longer a threat.

Like the machines, Earth First!ers see themselves as the good guys, countercultural rebels engaged in an essentially revolutionary form of struggle. There is no way to solve environmental problems, in this view, without breaking with the fundamental logic of the system. Nothing short of a total transformation of consciousness will do. Yet the corollary of this view is the conviction that any reform that does *not* violate the fundamental logic of the system cannot represent a serious solution to the environmental problem. And it is here that the countercultural idea becomes utterly counterproductive.

The suggestion that we need a 'deep' ecology implies that there is something wrong with 'shallow' ecology. What is the difference? Shallow ecology sees environmental degradation as fundamentally a result of incentive problems. People and corporations pollute when-ever they lack an incentive not to. Even though we all pay the price in the end, no one is going to stop, because we are stuck in a prison-er's dilemma. The solution, therefore, is to universalise the principle of 'polluter pays'. This is, admittedly, a 'merely institutional' solution to the problem of environmental degradation. As such, it is anathema to most environmental activists, and to any deep ecologist. As a result, far too often activists have found themselves *opposing* reforms that would actually improve the environment, on the grounds that the reform buys into 'the logic of the system' and thus represents an attempt at co-optation.

Take, for example, tradable pollution permits (such as the system of sulphur dioxide permits introduced in the United States by the first Bush administration). The underlying idea is simple. Atmospheric pollution is first and foremost an externality problem. If I want to dispose of some trash, I cannot just dump it in my neighbour's yard. Because he owns the land, he can charge me for the right to dispose of garbage on it, or he can refuse outright. In other words, the system of property rights protects him. So suppose that, instead of dumping the garbage in my neighbour's yard, I decide to burn it. This produces thick, acrid smoke that drifts in through my neighbour's window. Yet in this case, he is helpless to act against me. Because he doesn't own the atmosphere, he cannot charge me for the privilege of polluting his airspace, nor can he veto my plans. Thus the smoke creates what economists call a 'negative externality' – an uncompensated cost imposed upon a third party. The system of property rights, which does an extremely good job at ensuring custodianship of land, houses, cars and other tangible dry goods, does an extremely bad job at protecting the atmosphere or large expanses of water or any other good that cannot practicably be divided up and controlled. Thus the property system fails to control certain types of negative externalities, allowing individuals to impose costs upon one another without having to pay any price. When everyone does this, it leads to a prisoner's dilemma, or a 'tragedy of the commons'.

That's why there are so many cows in this world and so few buffalo. And it's why there are no more cod off the coast of Newfoundland. The owner of a fish farm has no incentive to kill too many of his fish – every one that he takes out reduces his own personal stock, and so lowers his own future revenue. With open-sea fishing, on the other hand, a reduction in the breeding stock is almost a pure externality. Most of the cost is transferred to *other* fishermen, who in future years will have less to catch. Yet when all of the fishermen do this to one another, the result is that *no one* will have anything to catch. Still, no one has any individual incentive to refrain from fishing. Limiting your own catch, in the absence of any regulation forcing others to do the same, simply means that you will catch less this year *and* in future years (the latter as a result of overfishing by others).

The only solution in cases like this is regulation. In the case of fish, governments usually impose a quota system, limiting the number of fish that each fisherman can catch. This can work tolerably well when the fish stocks are all within the territorial waters of a single nation (although fishermen still fight tooth and nail against their quotas every year). If the stocks migrate through the waters of several nations, or if they are in international waters, then the problem often proves insoluble. In many cases, a race to the bottom develops that destroys the stocks entirely. This is what happened to the cod.

In the case of atmospheric pollution, however, regulatory solutions have been somewhat less successful. In cases where pollutants can be banned outright, there is no real problem. Atmospheric lead, for example, was almost completely eliminated simply by banning the sale of leaded petrol. Because lead is a petrol additive, it was (relatively) easy to produce petrol that did not use it. Yet there are other pollutants that cannot be removed from the mix so easily. If we want cars, then we must be prepared to tolerate a certain amount of nitrogen oxides. If we want garbage disposal, then we must be prepared to tolerate landfills or incinerators.

Here the problem is not that a particular pollutant gets produced, but that *too much* of it gets produced. So banning it outright is not an option. The problem is that users do not have to pay the full cost that their actions impose upon society. When I turn on a light switch, my electricity bill goes up, with the money going to pay for the coal that keeps the generator running, the salaries of the employees who work there, the maintenance of the wires that distribute it and so on. But I do not have to pay for the medication of those whose asthma is exacerbated by the pollution from the coal, or for the farmers whose crops are disrupted through increased climatic volatility. As a result, I end up using more power than I would if all the costs were 'internalised', or factored into the price I pay.

Tradable pollution permits solve this problem in a very elegant way. First, an estimate is drawn up of how much the total 'cost' to society is from a particular form of pollution. Industry is then told that it will have to pay this much in order to continue production, by buying permits that allow it to produce a given quantity of emissions. As a result, if it is more cost-effective for a firm to cut back production than to buy emission rights, it will do so. And if it is more cost-effective for it to introduce pollution-abatement devices, it will do that. Furthermore, the permits, once purchased, can be resold. This creates competitive pressures that will force the 'dirtiest' players out of the market. If one firm is able to produce £1000 worth of goods with a given quantity of emissions while another firm is only able to produce £500 worth, then the former will be willing to pay a lot more for the permission than the latter. It doesn't matter whether it is a large industry or a small producer – the willingness to buy permits will depend entirely upon how much value the firm is able to add while producing a given quantity of pollution. Thus a system of tradable pollution permits creates a mechanism that automatically rewards clean production.

Despite these evident advantages, tradable permit schemes have received a pretty cool reception among environmentalists (and have been vigorously opposed by Greenpeace, among others). The problem, essentially, is that pollution permits don't force CEOs to re-evaluate their attitude toward nature, or to abandon their single-minded pursuit of profit. They represent, in the eyes of many environmentalists, 'the commodification of nature'. Furthermore, because these schemes are dedicated to achieving optimal levels of pollution rather than eliminating pollution altogether, many environmentalists worry that they send the wrong message – that pollution is okay, as long as you're rich and can pay for the privilege. And many think that people should conserve energy out of virtue, rather than because of the size of their electricity bill.

The whole idea that virtuous self-restraint on the part of corporations, or energy conservation on the part of consumers, must be a part of any solution to the problem of pollution is based on a fundamental confusion. The fact that we are always being urged to conserve energy is simply a sign that the price is too low. After all, the government doesn't have to remind us to conserve coffee beans or molybdenum or wiper fluid or any of the other goods that we consume every day. Why not? Because when we consume these goods, the price that we pay reflects pretty much the entire cost that our consumption imposes upon society. In other words, when the price level is right, there is no need to encourage conservation. If I want to drink a lot of coffee and I'm willing to pay the full price for it, then no one is harmed by my decision. Resources will flow to those who need or want them most, those who are willing to do the most in exchange for them. This is as it should be. The fact that the government needs to encourage conservation in the case of electricity is proof that the price should be higher. In an ideal world, we would not have to conserve energy at all, we would simply have to pay an enormous amount for it.

The underlying vision here is one of what could be called the 'pay as you play' society. Insofar as it is practicable, all externalities should be internalised. You should be able to do whatever you want, live as you like and be as much of an individual as you want, but you should be prepared to offer full compensation to anyone who is inconvenienced by your choices. You should have to pay the person who takes an hour of his day to cut your hair, or the person who grows the wheat to make your morning croissant. But you should also have to pay the person whose daily commute becomes just a wee bit longer because you decided to drive at rush hour, or the farmer whose groundwater gets contaminated thanks to run-off from your garbage in the local dump.

'What about the poor, those who can't pay?' comes the inevitable reply. This is a serious concern, but it is misplaced in this context. Giving *everyone* cheap energy just to ensure that the poor don't get their heat cut off in the middle of winter is a recipe for colossal waste. For every dollar spent heating the hotplates of the poor, ten dollars will be spent heating the hot tubs of the rich. Similarly, giving everyone cheap rent in order to ensure that some will not be left homeless is a heinously inefficient way of delivering a benefit to the poor. The correct way to address poverty issues is through income supports, labour-market policies and targeted benefits.

In other words, not all linkage is good linkage. Using concerns about income distribution to block solutions to environmental problems is deeply unhelpful. Polluters should pay, regardless of whether they are rich or poor – because if they did, there would no longer be any polluters. This may be shallow environmentalism, but it is also *effective* environmentalism. Scratch any environmental problem and you will find a collective action problem under the surface. The prisoner's dilemma and the tragedy of the commons simply tell you everything you need to know about why we're destroying the planet. Yet you would never know it from listening to environmentalists. Instead of focusing upon the efficiency effects of environmental regulation, what we hear is just warmed-over countercultural mythology – the critique of mass society in ecological disguise.

Notes

1   René Descartes, 'Discourse on the Method', trans. Cottingham, Stoothoff, and Murdoch, in *The Philosophical Writings of Descartes*, vol. 1 (Cambridge: Cambridge University Press, 1990), 142–43.

2   Roszak, *Making of a Counter Culture*, 21.

3   Reich, *Greening of America*, 381.

4   Jacques Ellul, 'The Technological Order', *Philosophy and Technology*, ed. Carl Mitcham and Robert Mackey (New York: Free Press, 1983), 86.

5   *Ibid.*, 97–98.

6   Neil Postman, *Technopoly: The Surrender of Culture to Technology* (New York: Knopf, 1992).

7   Langdon Winner, 'How Technomania Is Overtaking the Millennium', *Newsday*, November 23, 1997.

8   Reich, *Greening of America*, 381.

9   Murray Bookchin, quoted in Robert Gottlieb, *Forcing the Spring: The Transformation of the American Environmental Movement* (Washington, DC: Island Press, 1993), 88.

10   Herbert Marcuse, *One-Dimensional Man: Studies in the Ideology of Advanced Industrial Society* (Boston: Beacon Press, 1964), 2.

11   Ernst Schumacher, *Small Is Beautiful: A Study of Economics As If People Mattered* (London: Abacus, 1974), 122.

12   *Ibid.*, 27.

13   Ursula Franklin, *The Real World of Technology* (Toronto: Anansi, 1999), 127–28.

14   Buckminster Fuller, *Operating Manual for Spaceship Earth* (New York: Pocket Books, 1970).

15   Andrew Ross, 'Hacking Away at the Counterculture', *Postmodern Culture*, 1, no. 1 (1990), http://infomotions.com/serials/pmc/pmc-v1n1-ross-hacking.txt.

16   *Ibid.*

17   Esther Dyson *et al.*, 'Cyberspace and the American Dream: A Magna Carta for the Knowledge Age' (Aug. 1994), http://pff.org/publications/ecommerce/fi1.2magnacarta.htm.

18   John Perry Barlow, 'A Declaration of the Independence of Cyberspace' (1996), http://eff.org/~barlow/Declaration-Final.htm.

19   Timothy Leary, quoted in Scott Bukatman, *Terminal Identity: The Virtual Subject in Postmodern Science Fiction* (Durham, NC: Duke University Press, 1993), 139.

20 Barlow, 'A Declaration of Independence of Cyberspace'.

21 Seattle's Sustainable Style Foundation: Sustainable Style Foundation, http://www.sustainablestyle.org/.

22 International Movement for the Defense of and the Right to Pleasure, 'Slow Food Manifesto', in Carlo Petrini, *Slow Food* (New York: Columbia University Press, 2003).

23 Kate Zimmerman, 'Les Trois Églantines Do France', *National Post*, September 13, 2003.

24 Peter van Wyck, *Primitives in the Wilderness: Deep Ecology and the Missing Human Subject* (Albany: SUNY Press, 1997), 25.

25 Bill Devall and George Sessions, *Deep Ecology* (Salt Lake City, UT: G. M. Smith, 1985).

26 van Wyck, *Primitives in the Wilderness*, 40.

27 Andy Wachowski and Larry Wachowski, writers and producers; Mahiro Maeda, director, 'The Second Renaissance Parts I and II', *Animatrix* [animated video] (Warner Bros, 2003).

Conclusion

The power that the myth of counterculture has exercised over political consciousness in the past half-century is ultimately a testament to the massive trauma inflicted upon Western civilisation by Nazi Germany. After the Holocaust, what had previously been only a moderate distaste for conformity, common among artists and romantics, got pumped up into a hypertrophied abhorrence of anything that even smacked of regularity or predictability. Conformity was elevated to the status of a cardinal sin, and mass society became the dominant image of a modern dystopia. Many of those who would naturally have come forth as champions of the people in an earlier century became increasingly afraid of those very same people – afraid of the latent potential for violence and cruelty that supposedly resided in their hearts. For the progressive left, the wound was even deeper. Many became afraid not just of fascism, but in many cases *of society itself.* The left began to distrust many of the basic building blocks of social organisation, such as social norms (including etiquette), laws and bureaucratic forms of organisation. Yet without these building blocks, it is simply not possible to organise large-scale cooperation among human beings.

The exaggerated fear of conformity has made it all but impossible for many progressive groups to make effective use of these building blocks as tools, for fear of provoking anxiety about either co-optation or creeping fascism. As a result, the left has found itself mired in insuperable collective action problems, and unwilling to use some of the basic organisational methods that all human beings must employ in order to overcome these difficulties. The preference for individual consumer activism in response to environmental degradation, rather than state regulation of externalities, provides the most clear-cut example. The popularity of self-help, the growth of individualistic forms of spirituality and the exaggerated expectations about the effects of education reform or artistic production represent further extremes of the same tendency.

The question that we should ask ourselves is the following: which is the more plausible scenario – that a fascist dictatorship will emerge in one of the erstwhile liberal democracies of the West, or that increased market liberalisation, combined with unregulated global trade, will lead to the reversion of society into an increasingly Hobbesian state of nature? It seems clear that the second is far more likely, especially in the United States. But to acknowledge this is to admit that an excess of *disorder* is a far more serious threat to our society than an excess of *order*. And if this is so, then we really need to stop worrying so much about fascism. What our society needs is *more* rules, not fewer.

Perhaps then it is time that we learned to make peace with the masses. There are more than six billion human beings on this planet, each of whom has hopes, dreams, plans and projects very much like our own, and each of whom wants food, housing, education, dental care, a family, a job and probably a car – maybe a bicycle. Isn't a certain loss of individuality inevitable in a world of this type? How many of the features of so-called mass society are a simple product of population pressure – the fact that we need to share the planet with *so* many other people – and how many are the product of genuine inefficiencies or inequalities in the organisation of our social institutions? Isn't individualism becoming more and more a *luxury*? If we are going to figure out how to live in harmony in an increasingly populous world, the insistence on individuality at any cost is not a helpful point of departure. We need to start figuring out which compromises are inevitable and which can be avoided.

Saying that we must make peace with the masses is not the same thing as saying that we must love every feature of modern mass society. There is, of course, something terribly depressing about driving around through the same indifferent architecture, seeing the same tired old brands and sampling the same unappetising food in every city and town in America. This complaint has been commonplace for at least a century. Yet it is quite a reach to go from complaining about these unattractive features of our society to imagining that they are responsible for all of the *other* social problems that we see around us, such as poverty, inequality, alienation and criminality.

Nevertheless, this is precisely what the countercultural analysis does. The preceding chapters have shown how countercultural theorists routinely take concrete social problems and trace them back, in one way or another, to a gigantic 'technocratic' apparatus of conformity and repression. For example, environmentalists take straightforward problems like pollution and blame them on some deep structure of Western rationality (as opposed to an incompleteness in the system of property rights). Antiglobalisation activists take the homogenising effects of trade and blame them on an emerging 'Empire' of capital, while ignoring the fact that these same tendencies have been manifest in trade relations since the beginning of human history. Consumer activists look at the obnoxiously depressing spectacle of brand-consciousness in our society and blame it on a fundamental requirement of the mass production system, rather than simply on the exploitation of a pre-existing competition for distinction among consumers.

One can see the pattern that emerges out of the countercultural analysis. Every social problem is thought to be caused by a fundamental feature of mass society, whether it be mass production, mass media, the technological domination of nature or even just repression and the need for conformity. Yet what is so problematic about these explanations is that, apart from being empirically false, they have the effect of tying each one of these concrete social problems into a feature of modern society that none of us could ever reasonably hope (or desire) to change. In other words, they make it seem as though 'the system' in its entirety is responsible for all these problems, and so no solution that falls short of a complete overthrow of the system could hope to resolve them. This in turn makes solutions to a number of very tractable social problems seem completely out of reach.

The greater irony, of course, is that the mistaken explanations the countercultural analysis generates have often led radicals to adopt 'solutions' that in fact exacerbate the very problems they are intended to resolve. Nowhere is this more obvious than in the countercultural 'critique' of consumerism, which insists on analyzing consumer consciousness as a form of manufactured conformity and so completely overlooks the role that positional goods and the search for distinction play in driving consumer capitalism. As a result, the proposed solution – individualistic sartorial and stylistic rebellion – simply feeds the flames, by creating a whole new set of positional goods for these new 'rebel consumers' to compete for. The struggle for status is replaced by the quest for cool, but the basic structure of the competition remains unchanged.

More often, however, countercultural radicals are simply left spinning their wheels. The overwhelming majority of what gets called radical, revolutionary, subversive or transgressive is nothing of the sort. (With each new decade that passes, we seem to introduce a new word, in order to emphasise just how *far out there* the latest revolutionary gesture is, how *profoundly* subversive of the established order it is.) Moreover, cultural theorists have perfected the art of redescribing any element of mainstream culture in subversive terms. It only takes ten minutes watching MTV to see the absurdity of this entire analysis. So-called urban music, in particular, has become little more than a cult of social deviance. This sort of transgression is not a threat to the system. In the end, it is just people fighting for their right to party.

This is the rebel sell. It's a sell that has been used not only to sell ordinary commercial goods, but also to sell a myth about the way that our culture works. In order to escape from it, we need to accept the fact that social order is necessarily achieved through a system of rules that is, in the end, coercively imposed. Naturally, the rules require legitimacy, and the system as a whole cannot hang together unless there is a great deal of voluntary compliance. But none of this changes the fact that any system of cooperation creates incentives for deviance and so requires that those who break the rules be punished. This in itself is not repressive. Fighting these rules, therefore, is not dissent, but rather social deviance. It may be fun, but it is not the stuff out of which progressive social movements are built.

★

What does it mean, in concrete terms, to make peace with mass society? The most important consequence is that we must learn to live with what the political philosopher John Rawls referred to as 'the fact of pluralism'.[1] We must recognise that modern societies have become so large, populous and complex that we can no longer expect everyone to rally around some single set of shared values. Our society is one that favours lifestyle experimentation. Individuals are encouraged to find their own way, to discover their own sources of fulfilment. But this has important consequences. When it comes to answering the big 'meaning of life'-type questions, this system of individual liberty generates more, not less, disagreement.

Generally speaking, this is a good thing. Not many of us would want to live in a society in which we are simply told what to think, whom to marry, what career to pursue or what to do with our free time. Yet our freedom to make these choices for ourselves means that often we must agree to disagree with one another about some of the major questions of life – the value of family, the existence of God, the sources of morality. We need to learn to live with disagreement – not just superficial disagreement, but deep disagreement, about the things that matter most to us. Furthermore, we cannot organise our social institutions around the assumption that some consensus is obtainable. The state, in particular, must treat all citizens equally, and this will mean, for the most part, remaining neutral with respect to all of these controversial questions of value.

This puts significant constraints on the type of utopian social planning that we can engage in. If one looks at the typical blueprints for utopian communities that emerged from the '60s, it is easy to see that they all presuppose an extraordinarily high level of shared values and commitment. Consider, for example, Ernest Callenbach's 1975 novel *Ecotopia*. Callenbach imagines a (very near) future in which Northern California, Oregon and Washington have broken off from the rest of the United States in order to create an ecologically sustainable society. The balancing act that he tries to perform involves reconciling the anti-authoritarianism of his countercultural ideals with the desire to create more ecologically sustainable practices. How is the latter supposed to be accomplished without extensive use of coercion?

Callenbach's solution involves a combination of technological and cultural utopianism. Thus he imagines that the inhabitants of Ecotopia will zoom about in electric cars and levitating trains, all made of biodegradable plastic. These miraculous new plastics have a 'short planned lifetime' and 'automatically self-destruct after a certain period or under certain conditions.'[2] (Thus Ecotopia does not even need to have laws against littering, because everything that people throw away is biodegradable.) But even more important than this technological wishful thinking is Callenbach's cultural utopianism. He imagines that many of the more stringent ecotopian measures can be achieved through voluntary self-restraint, thanks to a sea change in popular culture. For example, he imagines that all of the inhabitants will develop a sudden concern for the welfare of future generations. But what about all those Christians, waiting for the Day of Judgement? If the world is going to end any day now, why should they care? This isn't a problem for Callenbach, who imagines that the Christian religion will fade away within a few years of ecotopian independence, to be replaced by a quasi-pagan form of tree-worship. Similarly, he thinks that people will spontaneously lose interest in television, preferring to stage their own live theatre or get together to sing songs. Processed and packaged foods will be eliminated, not by legislative measures, but as a result of 'Bad Practice lists' circulated among consumers. These lists will not be legally enforced, they will simply serve as 'a mechanism of moral persuasion'. They will be issued in a completely decentralised manner by 'study groups from consumer co-ops' operating with 'scientific advice'.[3]

One can see here quite clearly the countercultural ideal of spontaneous harmony. Collective action problems are simply whisked away, thanks to a deeper transformation of the culture. Callenbach is essentially imagining a world in which the entire population of three states suddenly becomes fervently committed to hippie ideals. This naturally eliminates a lot of social conflict. Yet it is important to recognise that, as a political assumption, it is a cop-out, for the same reason that technological utopianism is a cop-out. *Of course* the world would be a better place if we could replace all the coal- and gas-fired power plants with geothermal installations that produced miraculous quantities of clean electricity. And *of course* the world would be a better place if everyone rode their bike to work and refused to buy overpackaged food. But the fact is, an enormous number of people don't care about the environmental consequences of their actions, and they're not going to be talked into caring anytime soon. We cannot expect them to voluntarily adopt eco-friendly practices. No benefit can be had from minimising or ignoring the amount of social conflict that imposition of such measures will generate.

One of the central consequences of the fact of pluralism is the inevitability of a market economy. The amount of intellectual energy that has been dedicated to the task of searching for an alternative to the market in the past century is staggering. And yet no matter how you run the numbers, the answer always comes out the same. There are essentially two ways of organising a modern economy: either a system of centralised, bureaucratic production (such as was found in the former Soviet Union), or else a decentralised system, in which producers coordinate their efforts through market exchange. The former is, unfortunately, incompatible with value pluralism. Central planning works fine for the military, or some other organisation where members are willing to accept a standardised allotment of clothing, food rations or housing and to be assigned specific jobs to perform. But in a society where individuals hope to pick and choose from among a range of lifestyle opportunities, there is no getting around the need for a market.

Consider a very simple 'who gets what' problem. Suppose that one year, thanks to a fortuitous combination of rain and sun, the rubber farmers get a bumper crop. This means that there is more rubber available than usual. Who should get it? There are literally millions of different ways in which the rubber could be used. Should it be used for bike tyres? Lacrosse balls? Waterproof boots? Gaskets? Cables? Shock absorbers? The most persuasive response would be to say that the rubber should go to whichever use is most urgent, or to whoever needs it most. In other words, the rubber should be sent to where it will do the most good. Unfortunately, in a pluralistic society, we lack any common measure of 'the good'. There is no fixed metric that will allow us to determine whether one person's desire to fix his bike tyre is more or less important than some other person's desire to replace the washer in her tap. The only way to approach the question is to ask how important it is *to the person in question*. And the only way to find out how important it is to that person is to ask how much he or she would be willing to give up in exchange for the rubber. In other words, we must ask how much that person would be willing to *pay* for it. (If there is no sacrifice involved, then we can be almost certain that the goods will be wasted, since individuals will ask for all sorts of things that they don't really need. Just look at the difference in the way people behave when they are charging things to an expense account rather than paying for them out of their own pocket.)

Thus the market pricing of goods can be seen as a necessary response to the fact that society is not in a position to judge whose projects are more or less important. (Certainly a process of democratic decision-making is no substitute. In the absence of prices, the problem is simply too complex.) As we have seen, the amount a person should be asked to give up in order to acquire some particular good or service should be a function of how much inconvenience his or her consumption causes to other people. If I insist on being served eggs Benedict for breakfast, rather than cereal, then I should expect to pay more, in recognition of the fact that my consumption imposes greater demands upon not just the cook, but also the chicken farmer. But there is an easy way of ensuring this – simply by arranging it so that the transaction occurs at a price that is agreeable to both buyer and seller. And this is nothing other than the mechanism of market exchange.

Of course, we must recognise that some people are born in more advantageous circumstances than others, and thus have an unfair advantage when it comes to getting what they want. For them, paying more represents less of a sacrifice. Yet it is crucial to realise that criticising the distribution of wealth or the distribution of other 'advantages', such as education, is not the same thing as criticising capitalism – there is significant latitude for redistribution within the capitalist system. Similarly, one can criticise failures of the market (such as pollution, where some get away without paying the full cost that their activities impose upon society) or the ownership structure of the firm. But we must distinguish between these sorts of criticisms and criticisms of the market itself. Most of what left-wing critics identify as the major flaws of capitalism are actually problems of market *failure*, not a consequence of the market working as it is supposed to.

Take just one example: the dramatic escalation of CEO salaries over the past decade, along with the corporate governance scandals that rocked firms like Enron, Tyco and WorldCom, was not caused by the routine operations of the market economy. These problems were caused, rather, by individuals who found ways of exploiting weaknesses in the structure of existing markets (in this case, to the detriment of shareholders). Similarly, the fortune amassed by Bill Gates is not the product of a competitive market; it is a product of the natural monopoly that Microsoft exercises in the realm of computer operating systems (in this case, to the detriment of consumers). To recommend the abolition of capitalism as a cure for these sorts of excesses is like wanting to abolish the income tax system because some rich people get away without paying taxes. In both cases, it is not the system that is at fault; the problem is with the loopholes that exist within it. The solution is to plug the loopholes, not abolish the system.

★

No one would deny that we live in an increasingly 'globalised' world, but there the agreement ends. There is substantial disagreement over the causes of globalisation, the political and ethical values that underlie it, and its ultimate distributive consequences. The worldwide debate over globalisation is beset by ignorance, misinformation and hidden agendas on all sides. It has also become entangled in the sticky strands of the old political ideologies of left and right, along with the opposition of the developed, underdeveloped and developing worlds.

Yet through all the qualifications and complications, there is one group that has declared its categorical opposition to globalisation in all its forms. That is the hodgepodge of anarchists, students, environmentalists and culture jammers who make up the contemporary global counterculture. This antiglobalisation movement seemed to emerge fully formed in the late '90s, and its coming-out party was the now infamous protest at the 1999 meeting of the World Trade Organization in Seattle. Its political agenda was best elaborated in the pages of Naomi Klein's *No Logo*.

Two elements of Klein's book bring out the essentially countercultural structure of her thinking: her critique of branding, and her rejection of representative democratic politics. In the antiglobalisation narrative, these two threads are woven together in the following way: Over the past decade or so, multinational corporations have used the power of branding to achieve unprecedented wealth, power and influence. By outsourcing production to low-wage, unregulated sweatshops in the developing world, corporations no longer have to make real goods or provide actual services. They have become almost pure image, focused entirely upon building the value of their brands. As a result, a great deal of the value of these companies is tied up in their 'brand equity'.

The financial power they get from their brands has given corporations a great deal of leverage, which they use to bend national governments to their will. Politically weak or ideologically complicit governments agree to lower trade barriers, and they allow corporations to use organisations like the International Monetary Fund and the WTO to put into place global rules that act as a straitjacket on national governments. In this highly deregulated and liberalised global economic space, nations become locked into a race to the bottom. Forced to compete against one another for jobs and investment, they have no choice but to lower taxes, deregulate markets and eliminate environmental protection. Globalisation under these 'brand bullies' has given us a world in which corporations, not governments, rule, and in which the foremost expression of our values and identities is found in consumerism, not citizenship.

This is by now a familiar story, and it demonstrates the underlying connections between the critique of consumerism and the critique of globalisation in general. But is any of it true? Is branding really the source of the power of multinational corporations? Have we become, as Klein puts it, 'serfs under these feudal brandlords'?[4] And has consumerism replaced citizenship as the object of our identity and allegiance? There is reason to be sceptical.

The most obvious problem with *No Logo* is that despite the rhetoric about the evils of consumerism and its call for 'a more citizen-centred alternative to the international rule of brands',[5] the book has very little to offer in the way of positive politics. Indeed, one of the biggest ironies of the antiglobalisation movement in general is that for all its opposition to consumerism, it effectively reduces citizenship to consumer action. The reason *No Logo* has had such dramatic success is that it serves as a how-to manual for the virtuously hip shopper, full of case studies in how consumers can try to influence corporate behaviour. It focuses entirely on corporate awareness campaigns, consumer boycotts, street protests and culture jamming, while completely ignoring the role played by citizens working through government.

Of course, Klein rejects the characterisation of the campaigns against Shell and Nike as mere 'consumer boycotts'.[6] She says that 'it is more accurate to describe them as political campaigns that use consumer goods as readily accessible targets, as public-relations levers, and as popular-education tools.' Activists are forced to concentrate their attention on corporate behaviour, and to exercise their power as consumers, precisely because governments no longer have much power, and what power they do wield is under the tutelage of the global brand bullies.

As evidence, Klein points out that in many countries, citizens have already tried working through government in order to undo the damage wrought by the neoconservative backlash of the '80s. Many European countries elected left-wing social democrats, while voters in the UK, the US and Canada reacted to the Thatcher-Reagan-Mulroney years by electing Tony Blair, Bill Clinton and Jean Chrétien. But nothing happened! According to Klein, these governments catered even more obsequiously to the wants of multinational corporations, pushing for yet more privatisation, deregulation and free trade. The people learned their lesson: 'What good was an open and accountable Parliament or Congress if opaque corporations were setting so much of the global political agenda in the back rooms?'[7]

Even so, Klein declares that she is willing to give normal politics one last shot. In the final chapter of *No Logo* (entitled 'Consumerism versus Citizenship'), she appears to concede that anti-brand activism is not sufficient: 'Political solutions – accountable to people and enforceable by their elected representatives – deserve another shot before we throw in the towel.'[8] Her heart isn't in it, though, and she has absolutely nothing to say about what sorts of political solutions might be possible. In fact, she spends the rest of the chapter singing the praises not of electoral democracy, but of the antiglobalisation counter-summits that now run parallel to meetings of the G8, WTO and APEC. And why not? After all, it is great fun, since at these meetings 'alternative models of globalisation spill onto the streets during the day, and the Reclaim the Streets parties go on all night.'[9]

The fact of the matter is that the antiglobalisation movement has a conception of democratic politics that is fundamentally hostile toward national and international representative institutions. It is convenient to attribute this hostility to a healthy scepticism ('Governments sold us out!'), but really it is as old as the counterculture from which the antiglobalisation movement sprang. Klein claims that her goal is to help build a form of 'deep' and decentralised democracy. Yet the politics that she has in mind is essentially the '60s ideal of 'participatory democracy' or 'grassroots democracy'. Its countercultural pedigree can be seen in the profound dislike of hierarchy, bureaucracy and expertise that this model of democracy entails. The main goal of this sort of politics is to eliminate the institutional barriers and vested interests that stand between citizens and action. It looks to shift from representation to deliberation, by inverting the basic political structure from the top-down structure of representative democracy to a grassroots, bottom-up process for decision-making. This requires a radically decentralised politics, with power downloaded to local communities or municipalities.

This is just the political form of the environmentalist 'Think globally, act locally' agenda, with a similar faith in its virtues. Underlying it all is a faith in the powers of spontaneous harmony, an assumption that as long as each local community looks after its own interests, the interests of the whole will automatically be met. Furthermore, in shrinking the scope of citizens' political responsibility and concern, participatory democracy hopes to achieve a substantial reduction in conflict and complexity, and thereby to evade the problems that arise from living in a pluralistic society. The more local the politics, the smaller the population one needs to take into consideration, and thus the less the chances are of having to compromise or accommodate those with different values. Supporters of participatory democracy have even started advocating something called 'local foreign policy'. Small organisations, from universities to churches to municipalities, pass regulations that the governments at the provincial, state and federal levels are unwilling to consider. Berkeley, California, was (naturally) one of the first to ban companies with investments in Burma from selling their goods or services to municipal agencies. Others have followed suit, targeting companies with investments in places like Indonesia and Nigeria, while still others have enacted 'living wage' laws, so that in order to win a municipal contract, a company must pay its employees a suitably high wage and offer a certain package of benefits.

Fundamentally, this is the same form of utopianism that one finds in Callenbach's *Ecotopia*. If this sort of deep, decentralised democracy were able to solve our problems, then we wouldn't need governments at all. But the most serious political challenges we face are essentially collective action problems, and decentralised local democracy can't be the solution to these problems, since more often than not it is the *cause*. Global warming is a good example. No individual corporation has any interest in reducing its output of greenhouse gases, because the costs of global warming are spread across every person on the planet. At the same time, no individual country has any incentive to regulate its own energy industries in the absence of any guarantee that other countries will do likewise. Global warming can be solved only by a general agreement that is binding on every producer of greenhouse gases on earth. What we need is not a local foreign policy, but a *global domestic policy* on greenhouse gas emissions.

At some point, the stance of the antiglobalisation movement begins to generate a vicious circle. The whole problem with globalisation, say its opponents, is that it has weakened governments to the point where they are now irrelevant. We cannot possibly expect our national governments to bring peace, order and justice to the planet, since it is the very impotence of these governments that makes the retreat into local politics necessary in the first place. But then these activists turn around and refuse to participate in national politics, and deny the legitimacy of their own elected officials. This retreat from democratic politics weakens these governments further and robs them of legitimacy with certain crucial segments of the population. In so doing, the antiglobalisation movement weakens the only instrument that can be used to correct the very problems that it diagnoses.

We can break the circle only by putting to bed the myth of powerless governments. Governments, especially those in the West, are not shrinking, they are not the stooges of multinational corporations and there has not been a 'race to the bottom' in taxation, corporate regulation and environmental protection. In fact, just the opposite is true. Average government tax revenues as a percentage of GDP are higher than they have ever been, and the trend is upward, not down. In the wake of the Enron, WorldCom and Parmalat corporate scandals, there is a movement toward significant tightening of international regulations on corporate governance. Finally, there is no evidence that environmental regulations are being weakened by pressures emanating from global competition.

What does it mean to make the best of global capitalism? It means searching high and low for market failures and, when we find them, thinking creatively about how they can be resolved. The history of the welfare state in the 20th century should be interpreted not as a series of battles against the logic of the market, but rather as a series of triumphs over various forms of market failure. As a result, the anti-market rhetoric that continues to dominate left-wing organisations is at best unhelpful, at worst intellectually debilitating. We should strive to perfect the market, not abolish it. One need only glance at an introductory economics textbook to see what an ideal market would look like. There would be no monopolies, no barriers to entry in any industry. There would be no advertising; competition would be based entirely upon the price and quality of goods being offered. There would be no information asymmetries – consumers would be perfectly informed about what they were buying. Firms would not behave opportunistically toward their customers or suppliers, and there would be no windfall profits. And, most importantly, all externalities would be internalised; firms would have to factor the full social cost of their actions into every decision made.

This is the direction in which we should be moving. This is also the ideal that has been guiding the recommendations made in this book. Eliminating the deductibility of advertising as a business expenditure, as proposed in Chapter 6, represents a step in this direction. Doing so would essentially tax a negative externality. Tradable pollution permits and other so-called green taxes work in the same way. Green taxes make up barely 0.1% of all tax revenues in Italy and the UK, compared to almost 6% of all tax revenue in Denmark. Obviously there is an enormous amount of room for movement in this direction. Furthermore, congestion taxes represent an important source of welfare gains, which many industrialised nations have only begun to explore. The road tolls on vehicles entering Singapore and, more recently, central London represent the most exciting initiatives of this type. Much more remains to be done.

There are good reasons, then, to think that in an increasingly globalised economy we need more government, not less. Of course, nowhere is it written that the state must do all the work of correcting market failures. But the state will always be the most important player, simply because it is the agency that defines and enforces the basic set of property rights that *creates* the market in the first place.

Thus, when it comes to rejigging these rules, it is natural that the state should be the primary actor. Furthermore, since correcting market failure involves eliminating free-rider strategies that individuals have been unable to correct through voluntary contracting, more serious powers of compulsion than those available to the private citizen will often be required. One can see, in the debates over globalisation, how collective action problems that were once resolved by the state on a national level re-emerge in an international context, where the rule of law is absent. This shows how limited our organisational powers are when we lack recourse to state power.

The most conspicuous flaws in our society today are all unresolved collective action problems. As a result, an 'arms control agreement' provides the most useful way of thinking about correcting them. These agreements naturally require enforcement. Yet too often the left has shied away from such enforcement, on the grounds that it represents a form of repression. Here one can see the baleful influence of countercultural thinking. School uniforms, we have argued, serve as an arms control agreement in teenagers' battle of brands. More generally, economists have suggested that a more progressive income tax may serve as an arms control agreement in the competition for positional goods among adult consumers. We should follow France in adopting a legislated 35-hour workweek. Perhaps we might even consider controls in other areas, such as cosmetic surgery, the size of passenger vehicles or university tuition rates. Each would put the brakes on what are essentially antisocial forms of competition.

All of this will involve further restrictions of individual liberty. Yet so long as individuals are willing to give up their own liberty in return for a guarantee that others will do the same, there is nothing wrong with this. In the end, civilisation is built upon our willingness to accept rules and to curtail the pursuit of our individual interest out of deference to the needs and interests of others. It is deeply distressing to find that a misguided commitment to the ideals of the counterculture has led the political left to abandon its faith in this – the bedrock of civilisation – just at a point in history when it has become more important than ever.

Notes

1   *A Theory of Justice* (Cambridge, MA: Harvard University Press, 1971).
2   Ernest Callenbach, *Ecotopia: The Notebooks and Reports of William Weston* (Berkeley, CA: Banyan Trees Books, 1975).
3   *Ibid.*, 19.
4   Naomi Klein, *No Logo*, 149.
5   *Ibid.*, 445–46.
6   *Ibid.*, 340.
7   *Ibid.*, 341.
8   *Ibid.*, 442.
9   *Ibid.*, 443.

Afterword

Thanks to the Internet, the experience of publishing a book is now very different than it was even five years ago. The development of blogging in particular has created not only the possibility of large-scale and practically immediate reaction to one's work, but also room for sustained discussion between author, critic and anyone else who cares to pay attention. *The Rebel Sell* was a big hit in the blogosphere, so by the time we had three or four print reviews in hand, we had literally hundreds of electronic comments, discussions, rebuttals and endorsements to sift through. Of course, the blogosphere has also been characterised as the world's largest echo chamber — often the same material just gets propagated back and forth. But for an author this can be quite interesting. It was possible to discern, in the reaction to *The Rebel Sell*, some very distinct patterns in the way that people were reading, interpreting and in some cases misinterpreting the book. Of course, when you see the same misinterpretation cropping up again and again, arrived at independently by so many people, you begin to suspect that some aspects of the book may have been misleading. We would like to take this opportunity to clear the air on a few points.

A number of reactions from readers took us both completely by surprise. Perhaps the most unanticipated response was the number of people who took us to be opposed to ethical or virtuous consumption. In retrospect, we can see where this comes from — most of it has to do with the snarky comments we make about organic vegetables. This led many people to think that we are claiming that ethical consumption is just status-seeking, a way of saying 'Look, I'm morally superior to you,' and is thus a contributing factor in competitive consumption. This was not our intent. Our line of thinking is more as follows:

1 *We think that genuinely ethical consumption is great.* In fact, one of us just spent a great deal of money buying a hybrid-drive super-low-emission vehicle. This is an example of genuinely ethical consumption. Because of imperfections in the system of property rights, consumption of some goods generates negative externalities. Thus the consumer who pays the market price does not pay the full social cost of his consumption – he is free-riding. Ethical consumption involves refraining from free-riding in this way, by voluntarily cutting back on the consumption of goods that generate negative externalities, and increasing consumption of goods that generate positive externalities. Buying a hybrid vehicle is ethical, because the consumer voluntarily agrees to bear a greater portion of the social cost of his driving, beyond what the law requires. Obviously there is nothing wrong with this. In the same way, there is nothing wrong with helping old ladies across the street.

2 *However, ethical consumption is not a real solution to any major social or environmental problem.* As we argue in Chapter 10, in an ideal world there would be no need for ethical consumption. The fact that buying a hybrid is 'ethical' or 'altruistic' just shows that the price of gas is too low (i.e., the price paid does not reflect the full social cost of atmospheric pollution). If people who drove cars had to pay the full cost of their consumption, self-interest alone would be enough to motivate people to buy hybrids (or, as we say on p. 317, if the price of electricity was high enough, self-interest alone would be enough to motivate people to conserve). The problem with ethical consumption lies in its voluntariness. No one on the left would suggest that private charitable donations are an adequate substitute for state welfare programs. So why would anyone think that private acts of environmental altruism are a substitute for state or market regulation of externalities?

3   *Buying organic is not ethical consumption.* This is the part that we
     were unclear about. The reason we made fun of organic vegeta-
     bles is that we don't believe that buying organic is a case of genu-
     inely ethical consumption. To be clear, there are all sorts of *bad
     practices* in agriculture, and targeting consumption in such a way
     as to discourage those bad practices and deny profits to those
     who engage in them is an excellent idea. The problem is that
     the organic movement does not target bad practices: there are
     all sorts of very good practices in conventional agriculture that
     should be encouraged but that do not qualify as organic (such
     as zero-tillage seeding); and there are all sorts of bad practices
     associated with organic cultivation that should be discouraged
     (first and foremost, the amount of sheer waste caused by the
     unwillingness to use certain perfectly anodyne pesticides). The

     ideology of the organic food movement is based in '60s coun-
     tercultural technophobia, and not in any sober assessment of the
     environmental impact and sustainability of agricultural prac-
     tices. Thus it has more in common with the alternative medicine
     movement than it does the environmental movement (includ-
     ing a popular appeal based upon false and unconscionable health
     claims). Organic food is yuppie food, in our view, because the
     extra cost buys nothing more than distinction and an unfounded
     sense of moral superiority (unlike buying a hybrid, which costs
     more because it reduces the amount of atmospheric pollution
     that other people must breathe).

4   *Buying Blackspot sneakers is not ethical consumption.* This much
     should be obvious. More generally, we don't think that buying
     from small companies is any more ethical than buying from big
     companies. First off, if everyone did that, then the small com-
     panies would simply become the big companies – which is pre-
     cisely what has happened with 'alternative' shops like the Gap,
     the Body Shop and Starbucks. Second, there is nothing intrin-
     sically wrong with big companies. The issue, again, is whether
     firms engage in bad practices, and that is simply unrelated to size.
     As many people have pointed out, Starbucks probably treats its

workers better and buys more fair trade coffee than your locally owned café. Finally, we don't think that buying locally is any better than buying from afar – again, because it doesn't target bad practices. If you live anywhere near a port, buying produce from the other side of the world can have a smaller environmental footprint than buying produce that has been shipped by truck from 200 km away. If you live in California, buying locally grown avocados or rice is about the worst thing you could do for the environment – the fact that they are grown locally is a scandalous waste of water. Furthermore, one of the major thrusts of development efforts is to reduce agricultural subsidies so that we will import more food from Africa and Asia. Anyone who doesn't understand that this will help those countries, and save countless human lives, suffers from an ignorance so complete as to be almost impenetrable.

Incidentally, of all the issues raised in the book, the only one that we have taken genuine *heat* on, the only one that has led to red-faced critics jabbing their fingers in our faces, has been the business about organic vegetables. In many ways, the mere fact that people have become more upset about this than any other issue illustrates quite nicely the dead end into which countercultural thinking has driven the left. Republicans take over the White House, while we debate the politics of rutabagas and the price of mangoes. It makes no sense. Private lifestyle choices are important, but far, far less important than conventional political questions, like who controls the state.

One of our major criticisms of those who mistake the critique of mass society for a critique of consumerism is that it makes it seem far too easy to opt out of the consumer society. If consumerism is simply a system of brainwashing, whereby corporations manufacture desires in us, leading us to buy things that we don't really need, then there appears to be a simple solution to the problem of consumerism: resist the development of these desires, or if you have them, resist the urge to act upon them. Buy alternative, or even better, buy nothing. One of the central arguments of our book is that this strategy, far from being simply useless or ineffective, has become one of the primary forces *driving* the modern consumer economy. The reason for this is simple. Consumerism, in our view, is not a product of a quest for conformity, and it is not a system of brainwashing. It is rather a product of competitive consumption, driven by a quest for invidious distinction – a way of standing out from the crowd, or proving that you're not a loser. The problem with this sort of competitive consumption is that it is a zero-sum game, as Thorstein Veblen pointed out long ago. In order for someone to move up in the hierarchy of status, or cool, or style, or what have you, someone else must be bumped down. (As Butthead put it, 'If nothing sucked, and like, everything was cool all the time, then it's like, how would you know what was cool? ... It's like, you need stuff that sucks to have stuff that's cool.') Thus economic growth begins to acquire the character of an arms race, rather than a system of production that expands capacity to satisfy human need.

A number of readers have been willing to grant this critical point but have gone on to complain that we provide nothing very persuasive in the way of a solution. The suggestion that we make about the tax-deductibility of advertising, in particular, has been decried by many as manifestly inadequate, given the magnitude of 'the problem of consumerism.'

A number of points are in order here. First, the fact that we do not propose any solution to the problem of consumerism is quite intentional, a reflection of the fact that neither of us believes that there is any simple solution to the problem. One of the unhelpful features of the critique of mass society is that it has misled so many people into thinking that there could be such a thing as a solution. In *The Rebel Sell*, we make it pretty clear that we think the fundamental problems of the consumer society are a direct expression of the competitiveness of human life in all of its dimensions, whether that be the desire for real estate in a good location, the fondness for hiking in pristine wilderness, the quest for an attractive sexual partner, the search for a cool job or one of the other myriad ways of participating in more conventional social status hierarchies. Trying to solve the problem of consumerism by getting rid of this competitiveness would be like trying to solve the problems of capitalism by getting rid of scarcity (or trying to solve the problems of the human condition by praying for the second coming of Christ). A lot of people do it, but that doesn't make it useful.

Thus, any solution that we propose is not going to be radical, in the sense that it will not get at the roots of the problem. The most that we can hope to do is curtail the most serious excesses of this competition – prune back the wilder growth, as it were. This is why we call for policies based on the model of an arms control agreement. The proposal to reduce the tax-deductibility of advertising expenses is merely an example of the type of legislative action that we think would be more effective than cultural rebellion. Neither of us is under the illusion that this would have any major impact on consumer spending patterns – it was proposed mainly as a way of curtailing the amount of pollution in the mental environment, in much the same way that commercial signage bylaws control the amount of clutter on city streetscapes in many jurisdictions.

The more serious proposal, which no one seems to have noticed, was our defense of progressive income taxes. According to the standard view among economists, income taxes impose efficiency losses upon the economy, in part by discouraging work effort. But if you suppose that, beyond a certain threshold, pretty much all additional income will be used for one or another type of competitive consumption, then the situation looks quite different. First of all, it suggests that very little harm will be done to the people who pay the higher marginal rates. Since everyone pays those rates, it simply results in lower prices for the typical objects of high-end competitive consumption. It also suggests that, even if a more progressive income tax did create a disincentive to work, it might be for the better. As we point out in Chapter 3, the only way to lower consumption is to lower income as well. Working less is the preferred way of achieving this outcome. A legislated 35-hour work week is fine for waged employees, but doesn't do much for people earning salaries. If the tax system is able to supply a comparable deterrent for the latter, then that would be a good thing. The flip side of competitive consumption is competitive overwork. People often have no choice but to work too hard, simply because they cannot afford to fall behind. They worry about jeopardising their chances of promotion, or they worry about not being able to afford a home in a decent neighborhood, and so on. The only way they could afford to work less would be if *everyone* worked less. In order to achieve that outcome, we need collective action – first and foremost, we need legislative action.

Clearly this argument for progressive income taxes should have been given more attention in the book. Part of the reason we didn't talk about it more is that it has already gotten a fair bit of play in the literature on consumerism. In particular, Robert Frank discusses a proposal of this sort at considerable length in *Luxury Fever*, and Juliet Schor presents a very cogent argument for it in *The Overworked American*.

One accusation that came up a lot in the United States, although not at all in Canada, was that we are cultural conservatives. We still haven't figured out exactly what it was we said that triggered this response. It happens to be false, but ultimately, it's not something that either of us feel the need to insist upon. One of the central messages of the book, after all, is that the left needs to wean itself off cultural politics. What we are presenting is not a cultural critique of the countercultural idea, but rather a political one. It was never our intention to deny that the counterculture has generated a tremendous amount of entertainment over the years, maybe even great art (although we tend to classify that also as entertainment). Yet the counterculture never presented itself as merely a movement for cultural reform. It was always coupled with a set of claims about the consequences that this sort of emancipation at the cultural level would have on other major political and economic institutions. There were a lot of promissory notes issued back in the '50s and '60s that have yet to be redeemed. Cultural politics – even personal self-discovery – was presented as the high road to progressive social politics in general. As trusty old Theodore Roszak put it, with the rise of counterculture, 'the project which the beats of the early '50s had taken up – the task of remodeling themselves, their way of life, their perceptions and sensitivities – rapidly takes precedence over the public task of changing institutions or policies,' not because changing institutions or policies doesn't matter, but because changing one's own consciousness comes to be seen as the more profound and more effective strategy. Instead of trying to redirect or control the machine from the outside, changing the culture allows you to reprogram it from the inside.

This idea was incredibly influential. By the end of the '70s, it had become inscribed into the DNA of almost every progressive leftist organisation. Yet looking back over the last four decades of the 20th century, we think it should be obvious to everyone that it was *not* a particularly effective political strategy. The reason – apart from the fact that culture simply does not play that powerful a role in determining the structure of social institutions – is that the specific forms of resistance extolled by the counterculture set into motion a cultural dynamic that exacerbated several defects in the system that countercultural rebellion was initially intended to redress, most notably consumerism, and in the extreme, generated a cycle of competitive transgression that wound up promoting antisocial behaviour and attitudes. This made it more, not less, difficult for the progressive left to advance its political agenda. That's the substance of our complaint.

Thus our central criticism of countercultural thinking is that it muddies the water, causing the left to reject all sorts of pragmatic solutions to social problems on the grounds that they are not 'deep' enough or 'radical' enough. It leads Michael Moore to argue against gun control in *Bowling for Columbine*, because legislation doesn't address the supposedly deeper issue of a 'culture of fear' that exists in the United States. It leads major environmental groups to oppose tradable pollution permits, in the name of deep ecology. And it led feminists to waste the better part of a decade fretting over pornography, convinced that it was a deep cultural source of patriarchal oppression (according to this theory, pornography is to patriarchy what advertising is to technocracy). More generally, it saddles the left with having to defend, or at least to offer weak apologies for, all sorts of vulgarity and social deviance that should be condemned. Among other things, this has become a giant electoral liability.

We also think that the countercultural habit of equating freedom with the violation of social norms has become a political handicap for the left. In the '60s, a concern with manners and polite behaviour came to be seen as an antiquated convention, a holdover from the Victorian era, and a symptom of the senseless repression that society imposes upon the individual. The more authentic way to behave was simply to be yourself, to say what you're really thinking, to tell people how you really feel, and not to let any fussy old social convention get in the way of your personal self-expression. Yet the consequence of this has been a quite noticeable decline in civility in public and private life. One can see this most clearly in the United States. Who has benefited most from the decline of civility, PBS or Fox News? It's the unabashed rudeness of American public discourse that has made everything from political debate shows to right-wing talk radio such a force for evil in American politics. How else to explain Ann Coulter? Bad talk drives out good – it becomes impossible to have a reasonable discussion about any political issue. This has hurt the left more than it has the right.

A fair number of critics have suggested that the counterculture is just something we made up, motivated by our desire to denigrate the achievements of the left. We've been accused of making unreasonable generalisations, tarring everyone with the same brush and generally hypostatising the counterculture. (Predictably, some people have also adopted the dead-end strategy of trying to distinguish between *real* counterculture or *real* individualism – the genuinely subversive kind – and fake counterculture or 'conformist' individualism, of the sort that we supposedly criticise. For people who find this line of argument plausible, there's not much we can suggest, except perhaps that they read the book again, this time more slowly.)

Obviously, given the polemical tone of the book, we do make some pretty broad generalisations. But we tried to be quite clear that the central focus of our criticism is not a social movement called 'the counterculture,' but rather a theory (which we referred to, following Thomas Frank, as 'the countercultural idea') and the influence that this theory has had on the left. Thus in the opening chapters, we were careful to avoid talking about 'the counterculture,' and tried to use expressions like 'countercultural rebels' or 'countercultural activists and thinkers' as a way of designating those individuals most influenced by this theory. It was only later, once we hoped that our meaning was well established, that we began referring to 'the counterculture' (largely for stylistic reasons).

Admittedly, talking about the countercultural idea is a simplification, since there have been hundreds of important thinkers who can be identified in one way or another with this current of thought, each with more or less distinctive and nuanced views. Part of our reason for lumping them all together is that, as children raised in households that were strongly influenced by the ideals of the '60s, we both found it exhilarating to regard the overarching ideology in which we were raised as a theory, and not simply as part of the structure of the universe. Take something like *The X-Men*, a comic that we both grew up reading. With the benefit of hindsight, it is easy to see how this comic essentially plays to the fantasies of countercultural rebels: a small group of misfits with exceptional gifts, persecuted by mainstream society for being different, nevertheless bands together to save humanity from its own worst tendencies. Compared to Superman's defense of the American way, or Batman's vendetta against crime, it is easy to see that the X-Men are not ideologically neutral. It's Frankfurt School vanguardism for kids. Of course, we didn't understand any of this when we were young. This is why we both found it exciting, later in life, to read the original books in which the countercultural analysis was developed, and to piece together the myriad ways in which its influence had structured the cultural environment in which we were raised.

The other reason we think it is useful to generalise about the counterculture is that, out of the intellectual debates of the '60s, a highly standardised set of political ideas has emerged, one that provides a basic script for left-wing argument that is surprisingly invariant. Of course, there are plenty of progressive organisations agitating for legislative change, participating in democratic politics and so on. Our claim was simply that the influence of countercultural ideas has tended to make this sort of institutional pragmatism more difficult, and thus the left as a whole less effective. Consider, for example, the issue of traffic congestion, which we mention as one area where true cost pricing could generate significant improvements in quality of life. A short while after the book came out, *Globe and Mail* hippie-in-residence Rick Salutin wrote a column called 'Hell is other people's cars,' in which he considered the quality-of-life implications of congestion. He begins well enough, pointing out that the system of tolls introduced in London, England, have been not only effective, but also very popular. But this system is quickly dismissed in favour of Salutin's 'favourite' initiative, the so-called 'naked street' strategy. The idea is to remove all traffic lights, lanes, signage and sidewalks, then let drivers and pedestrians 'sort things out for themselves.' This apparently forces everyone to interact on a more human level: 'drivers and pedestrians make eye contact, they adapt, they interact.' The beauty of the system is that 'it's about restoring responsibility to individuals for their own acts, rather than forcing them to follow rules. It's liberatory, democratic and creates community.' Fighting against the tyranny of stop signs and traffic lights, he goes on to argue, is very much like fighting against the tyranny of global capitalism. Even if the alternative you are proposing doesn't work as well, the important thing is that 'the utopian impulse' is sustained. What matters is not the consequence, but rather the 'inherent value of your action as one moment in the endless striving for liberation.'

This is a classic instance of what we call the cardinal sin of the counterculture – the tendency to reject workable solutions to real social problems on the grounds that they are not radical enough, or do not transform people's consciousness to an adequate degree. One can see all the classic countercultural ideas in play. First, there is the habit of treating all rules as repressive, regardless of their content or form. This is what leads Salutin to the comical suggestion that getting rid of traffic lights is an instance of 'striving for liberation.' Second, there is the naive faith in the powers of spontaneous harmony, which the counterculture shares with the libertarian right. Salutin endorses the naked streets initiative because he favours 'social self-regulation instead of top-down control.' Why then should we not abolish welfare, and replace it with private charitable giving? Finally, there is the senseless privileging of that which is irregular and unpredictable over that which is regular and predictable. Salutin actually ends with the asinine suggestion that the 'unpredictability' of his preferred traffic scheme is one of its central virtues. But unpredictability is the last thing you want to see in other drivers. Eye contact is no substitute for settled convention. Has Salutin never experienced difficulty getting past someone in a hallway, as both go left, both go right and so on? It's not quite so funny when it happens in a car going 50 km/hr, with two kids in the back seat.

So of course there are all sorts of sensible leftists – in his most recent incarnation, London mayor Ken Livingstone even qualifies – and progressive organisations that put collective welfare ahead of woolly utopianism. The problem is that these people often get more flak from their left flank than they do from their right. It is the influence of countercultural ideas, we claim, that is largely responsible for this state of affairs.

There was a certain amount of grumbling about our alleged complacency, or naiveté, when it came to the issue of corporate power. This is in fact a very complex issue, on which we both have rather complex views, none of which can be usefully summarised here. There are two points, however, that are worth mentioning.

First, neither of us thinks that there is anything intrinsically wrong with the profit motive, and neither of us thinks that any of the major problems in the world today are caused by the prevalence of the profit motive in the capitalist economy. It is the failure of the market, not the market itself, that is responsible for most of the problems that progressive social organisations have been fighting to resolve for the past two centuries. But once you factor out the demonisation of profit from the critique of corporate power, how much is there left to say? Obviously, many corporations engage in bad practices. They do so for the same reason that athletes take performance-enhancing drugs. Both will continue to do so until someone forces them to stop. Imagining that consumer activism is going to put a dent in corporate malfeasance is like thinking that fan boycotts could deter athletes from doping. The collective action problem is almost completely insuperable. This is why we think the primary objective of the progressive left should be to control the state.

Second, many of the complaints one hears about corporate power and, in particular, the influence of corporations over government fail to distinguish two very important elements. There is no question that governments face significant constraints when it comes to enacting social and economic policy. Some of these constraints arise from objectionable forms of influence that corporations exercise. But many of these constraints arise from the nature of the capitalist economy itself. For example, the reason that governments around the world are almost invariably lukewarm to the strategy of taxing corporate profits is not just that powerful business lobbies oppose it, but the structural impossibility, within a system of private ownership, of ensuring that these taxes come out of profits, and not indirectly out of wages or consumer prices. One may lament the latter state of affairs, but it is important to distinguish between the role that these sorts of structural constraints play and the power of the business lobby. There is a world of difference between George W. Bush's administration in the United States, which is actually in hock to big business, and the New Labour movement in the United Kingdom, which is not. The fact that the latter has adopted a number of 'market-friendly' policies is not evidence that it is under the thumb of corporations – in fact, it leads to a vast overestimation of corporate power to assume that it is.

People who point to the recent spate of scandals at firms like Enron and WorldCom as an example of capitalism run amok are quite right to do so. But it is important to remember that these firms were either completely destroyed by these scandals or else cut up and sold for scrap. Furthermore, the primary victims in all of these cases were shareholders, i.e. capitalists. If anything, these scandals reveal some of the central vulnerabilities of the corporate organisational form, and the enormous difficulty that owners of a firm have in imposing their will even upon the managers that they themselves have hired. The notion that these same owners are controlling the world, when they can't even keep their own houses in order, is, frankly, incredible. So while it is important not to be complacent about corporate power, it is also important not to make it out to be more than it is. The primary threat posed to society from the business class stems from its characteristic shortsightedness, its intellectual laziness and its knee-jerk hostility to government, not from some imputed capacity for world domination.

Finally, a number of readers somehow got the impression that we are loyal defenders of Microsoft. One rather prominent book reviewer, in particular, accused us of saying that Microsoft's marketplace dominance is acceptable because its products are 'cheap, efficient and what buyers want.' Just to be clear: far from being fans of Microsoft, we are in fact both Linux aficionados. *The Rebel Sell* was partly written and fully indexed using OpenOffice (www.openoffice.org). Microsoft is mentioned only twice in the book, both times as an example of how an inferior standard can become entrenched in the market as a result of network externalities.

The confusion appears to have arisen from our discussion of Apple Computer's '1984' commercial, which we cite as an example of 'rebel sell' advertising. (We assumed, mistakenly as it turns out, that everyone would know that the target of this commercial was not Microsoft, but rather IBM.) The point we were trying to make with respect to Apple was that systems of conformity and homogeneity are not always maintained through a repressive apparatus of control. The Apple commercial made it seem as though IBM's control of the personal computer market was exercised through a Big Brother–like fascist apparatus (and thus that you should fight back by buying a

Macintosh). What we were trying to point out is that IBM's control of the market was actually a product of the network effects generated by the desire for file format compatibility, not some authoritarian 'Information Purification Directive.' Thus the classic anti-authoritarian forms of rebellion, aimed at 'stickin' it to the man,' were not really useful for effecting change in the domain of computer operating systems (because it was decentralised consumer behaviour, not central control, that was maintaining it). This is why we wrote that 'expressing your individuality by wearing a funny tie to work is not the same thing as expressing your individuality by using file formats on your computer that are incompatible with those of your co-workers.' In the former case, it is your boss who will be irritated, but in the latter case, it is your co-workers who are likely to complain. Some readers, however, took this passage as a condemnation on our part of the use of incompatible file formats. This was not our intention. Go nuts if you want.

Index

Printed and bound in the UK by
CPI Antony Rowe, Eastbourne